All About
Global Investing

M

N

The All About Series

All About Fond Funds
Werner Renberg

All About Global Investing
Thomas D. Saler

All About Annuities
Gordon K. Williamson

All About
Global Investing

Thomas D. Saler

John Wiley & Sons, Inc.

New York · Chichester · Brisbane · Toronto · Singapore

To the memory of Margaret Hawkins

Library of Congress Cataloging-in-Publication Data:

Saler, Thomas D.
        All about global investing / by Thomas D. Saler.
        p.   cm.
        Includes index.
        ISBN 0-471-12188-6 (alk. paper)
        1. Investments, Foreign.   2. Portfolio management.   I. Title.
        HG4538.S24   1995
        332.6'73—dc20   95-37788

Printed in the United States of America

10 9 8 7 6 5 4 3 2 1

Preface

When the idea for a book on the subject of global investing first grabbed for a share of my attention some time ago, I decided to do some market research. No need to rush into things, I thought, since such a vital and seemingly popular topic would certainly have already been adequately covered by any number of authors. Upon checking the usual sources, however, I was surprised to find quite the opposite. Not only were there only a handful of books addressing the issue, but those that were available seemed mostly to contain information so arcane or dated as to be virtually useless for most individual investors. Thumbing through a typical volume, I would find myself thinking, "This is nice, but what do I *do* with it?"

And so I decided to write a book on global investing that was both authoritative *and* practical. But shortly after getting started, it became painfully clear to me why so little has been written on foreign markets. Having authored two previous books, both on the subject of U.S. securities, I thought I was prepared for the task of accumulating, digesting, and reformulating the mountains of information necessary to do justice to the subject. What I found, however, was that acquiring the kind of data necessary to uncover relevant information about overseas economies and markets is not only difficult and time consuming, but, in many cases, virtually impossible. Researchers and writers delving into things American are often spoiled by the magnitude and breadth of historical information available on all aspects of U.S. life, including its economy and financial markets. The American government may have many flaws, but data accumulation is not one of them. Keeping accurate records—or any records at all for that matter—is a problem for many foreign countries, particularly those only recently harboring aspirations of joining the First World of developed economies. Some nations, for example, do not have price histories on their primary equity-market index going back even a few years.

Fortunately, organizations such as the International Monetary Fund and World Bank have been taking copious notes for decades on hundreds of economies.

v

Together with equity-market data supplied by Wilshire Associates and the International Federation of Stock Exchanges, it is possible to piece together a picture of a country's economic and financial-market history that is fundamental to investors making informed choices. The fact that the Wilshire country indexes are each compiled under the same format makes comparisons of the various stock markets more useful. A comprehensive listing of all the data sources is given in Chapter 6, Understanding the Data.

A word about the selection of the data itself: This book has attempted to take a historical approach to the subject of global investing and the foreign economies that underpin the various financial markets. This is done for several reasons. First, books that address only the present circumstances in a given market run the risk of being both wrong and late. Not only are near-term predictions notoriously unreliable, but the lag time between when a book is written and when it is published would render such prognostications useless anyway. Second, attempting to make money in foreign markets by divining the short-term outlook is just plain bad policy. Timing any market—even the developed bourses of the United States and Europe—is virtually impossible, but basing investment decisions on short-term guesses of emerging markets is especially dangerous and counterproductive. Finally, when it comes to a nation's handling of its economy, past truly is prologue. To understand where a country is, it is absolutely vital to understand where it has been. And while it is certainly possible for a nation to change its ways (both for the better and for the worse), a study of history will always give an investor a better feel for the underlying conditions that an economy and its financial markets face.

Despite the advantages of taking a long-term, historical approach to evaluating foreign economies and markets, it is also necessary to recognize the limitations of such an outlook.

Data on the 21 stock markets contained in this book dates to January 1988, thus encompassing virtually the entire relevant history of many emerging markets. Before the late 1980s, for example, most emerging markets were simply too small (in terms of capitalization or number of listed securities) to generate useful data. But although the entire relevant existence of a number of markets may well be adequately referenced from the 1988 to 1994 period covered in this book, it is also important to realize that seven years is a mere blink of an eye in the context of what is to come. It is dangerous to assume that the intramarket relationships, correlations, and patterns formed over the past 7 years will necessarily remain unchanged over the next 7, or 17, or 27 years. Even the 30 years of history that form the basis of the economic sections of this book might best be viewed as only a recent chunk of information.

It should be pointed out that this book covers mostly the countries' stock markets and their underlying economies and politics, touching only indirectly on the bond exchanges of the various countries. This is done for both practical and theoretical reasons. Opportunities for regional or country involvement in credit markets are virtually nonexistent, making any examination of the issue moot. Also, the primary reason behind global diversification of an investment portfolio is to participate in the underlying growth of the world economy. This objective is best accomplished by being an owner, not a lender. As is the case with stocks and bonds in the United States, foreign stocks tend to outperform foreign bonds by a wide margin over the long term.

Despite my attempt to keep this book as user-friendly as possible, I'm certain that the sheer quantity of information contained herein will at times stupefy the reader or even induce a kind of paralysis by analysis. Overwhelming quantities of information are unfortunately a fact of investment life. And when it comes to putting one's hard-earned money at risk in a market—much less a market half a world away—it is not possible to know too much. But it *is* possible to understand too little, and such a deficiency can be a by-product of being bombarded with minutia. And so, what follows is my attempt to distill the essence of the story down to its bare essentials, to put the whole idea in a form that will have you thinking not only "This is nice," but also "And here is what I'll do with it."

At its heart, it is a simple story. We are fortunate to live at a historically opportune moment, a time when a number of factors have combined to make investment in foreign countries both possible and highly worthwhile. In a more idealistic vein, it might be argued that, quite apart from investor profits, the most substantive benefits flowing from this rare alignment of the economic and political constellations will accrue to the people of the developing economies themselves, as living standards increase and at least some measure of discretionary income is created. The factors fueling this trend are not complicated; the discrediting and collapse of socialist economies in a kind of reverse domino effect have put governments in a race to privatize and grow their national wealth more quickly. Stock markets are the most efficient method for raising the kind of private capital needed to accomplish economic decentralization. As statism has collapsed, equity markets have emerged and companies have been born, all aided by a new information technology that allows for the transfer of trillions of dollars of wealth around the globe in mere seconds. Just as transportation systems began to link far-flung agrarian communities in the United States some 150 years earlier, information systems are now bridging the last earthly barriers of time and space. Sellers have met buyers as never before.

What you should do with this information is actually quite simple: *just be there*. Do not expect—and do not even try—to always be in the right place at the right time. Know that markets go up and markets go down. Accept that you'll never be able to tell exactly when they'll do either. Accept that progress in many foreign countries will ebb and flow and will ultimately be measured in decades, not in years. Accept that the same kinds of global liquidity gushers that push U.S. stocks to occasional extremes will do the same abroad, only with more startling effect. And accept that interest in global investing will come and go as money is made and lost. But also know that the current cycle of economic privatization and political liberalization is likely to last well into the twenty-first century. If you do not try to outsmart yourself, if you invest only for the long term, and if you place your money with qualified managers who have a history of success, the odds are good that you also will benefit along with the people in the countries where your investments ultimately are placed.

It is my hope that the information in this book inspires you to be present at the economic re-creation of our world.

Thomas D. Saler

Milwaukee, Wisconsin
November 1995

Acknowledgments

Heartfelt appreciation is extended to the many people and institutions that have provided the material and emotional support needed to complete this book. Among them are Wilshire Associates of Santa Monica, California, which generously donated data from its proprietary country indexes to foster a more thorough understanding of the world's financial markets—without the lode of historical data from Wilshire, or the International Monetary Fund, or the Federation Internationale des Bourses de Valeurs in Paris (FIBV), this book would not have been possible. Thanks also go to Morningstar, Inc., the Chicago-based provider of high quality information on mutual funds and ADRs (American depositary receipts); to Jane Jordan Browne, my agent, who placed the project; and to Jacqueline Urinyi, the capable and always-encouraging editor at John Wiley & Sons, who believed in the idea. Special thanks to Mary Dykstra for her love, support, wisdom, and humor during the typically arduous creative process. Apologies are also in order to Ms. Dykstra for my inability to include sections on the barely emerging markets of Belize and Costa Rica, countries in which she has a special interest and to whose rain forests she has journeyed often. As always, the deepest thanks are for my parents, Bernard and Clara Saler, whose unfailing love is still the best example of what our world has to offer.

T. D. S.

Contents

Introduction

Five centuries after history's most stunning accident, Christopher Columbus's original voyage of discovery is finally arriving at its intended destination. Land ho!

Underwritten by Old World money, the mission Columbus undertook five centuries ago was to gain access to the markets, products, and riches of Asia. As everyone knows, of course, what actually happened was the greatest example of economic serendipity in recorded history, the entirely unintended discovery of a nearly virgin continent so abundant in its own untapped wealth that full development would absorb much of the world's finances for the next half millennia. Five hundred years later, however, a new set of equally return-driven investors are finally overseeing the completion of the mission originally discharged to Columbus, setting a course to the Orient not on three creaky marine vessels but via electrons bouncing off orbiting spacecraft at virtually the speed of light.

Taken as a whole, the so-called Pacific Rim and Asiatic regions—loosely defined as the vast area from the Philippines in the east to Turkey in the west, from Australia and New Zealand in the south to Japan in the north—probably represent the most exciting, volatile, dynamic, and potentially explosive investment opportunity of our time. If the nineteenth century belonged to the United Kingdom and the twentieth century to the United States, it might be argued that to Asia belongs the twenty-first century—a time when, after 6,000 years of rich cultural history, conditions were at last ripe for a thorough economic blossoming of one of mankind's cradles of civilization. A primary reason behind the final realization of Asia's economic potential has to do with a fundamental tenet of capitalism: Sellers need buyers and buyers need sellers—and Asia has plenty of both. Simply put, Asia is where the people are and have been for most of recorded history. As early as 1650, more than half of the world's population lived in Asia; as of 1995, that number had grown to 60 percent. Already 9 of the world's 20 most populous nations are in the Asian/Pacific region, as are fully half of the

1

world's 40 largest cities. At a combined 3.3 billion people, Asia's population is more than triple that of the United States and Europe combined. The hub of the Asian economic wheel, of course, is China, with its 1.2 billion people representing one-fifth of the world's population. But even without China, Asia is a behemoth; by 2020, non-Chinese Asian nations will be home to more than one out of every three people on earth.

For most of its history, Asia has remained a mostly backward region economically. As recently as the 1960s, the label "Made in China" was a metaphor for cheap and generally unattractive goods. Hobbled by a widespread and endemic cultural resistance to outside influence, along with chronic political instability, the region's economies grew relatively slowly through much of the first half of the twentieth century, especially considering the small base from which they were expanding. Over the past 30 years, however, as Japan has recovered from the devastation of World War II and the older industrialized economies of the United States and Europe have reached maturity, the Asian economic giant has begun to stir. Between 1964 and 1993, Asian economies grew by an average of 484 percent, compared with 157 percent for the world's so-called industrialized nations and just 130 percent for the United States. Asian economic outperformance has accelerated sharply since a serious recession shook most Western economies in the mid-1970s; since 1973, average Asian real gross domestic product has grown by 6.7 percent per year, nearly triple the rate for the United States and other industrialized nations. The changing of the economic guard has become still more evident in the past decade; between 1984 and 1993, China, South Korea, Thailand, Taiwan, Singapore, Malaysia, Hong Kong, Indonesia, Pakistan, India, Sri Lanka, Australia, and Japan have each outgrown traditional economic superpowers Germany, the United Kingdom, and the United States by a wide margin.

That Asia should lead the world in economic growth heading into the twenty-first century is the result of a number of factors. By the mid-1970s, many Western economies had already become so large that their growth rates would have had to decline, if only because their large bases made rapid percentage gains all but impossible without intolerable inflation. And as real growth slowed in the mature economies, return on investment fell, sending capital elsewhere in search of new investment and new markets. Around this time, Japan began to compile enormous merchandise-trade surpluses with the United States, resulting in an ever-growing number of Japanese banks stuffed to their high-rise ceilings with yen. Discouraged from putting all their chips on the American market because of the weak dollar, Japanese investors looked in at least equal measure to the nearby Asian economies, many of which represented better values than those found in the United States and with less currency risk. Japanese banks, flush with the trophies of their merchandise-trade surplus, began to expand into such Asian cities as Hong Kong, Seoul, Manila, Bangkok, Taipei, and Kuala Lumpur. Deals cut by Japanese financial institutions soon powered impressive economic growth, which, in turn, led to the creation of large financial-services and high-tech industries in other Asian nations. Heading into the twenty-first century, some of the non-Japanese Asian economies are themselves beginning to export capital and investment. Asia's four so-called "Little Tigers"—Taiwan, Hong Kong, South Korea, and Singapore—are each now considered "developed" economies, meaning that per capita gross domestic product is above the $8,626 annual figure that the World Bank has established as the minimum criteria for inclusion as a First World economy.

Another factor in the relative rise of Asian economic power is the region's above-average ratio of investment to consumption. By its very nature, consumption is short-term and fleeting; aside from the immediate benefits of additional liquidity coursing through an economy, simply consuming a product does nothing to increase a nation's pool of capital, capital that in turn can be used to invest in new plants and equipment, thus raising productivity. And because improved productivity is the only true way to increase national wealth, countries that save and invest will usually outgrow those that borrow and consume. By that measure, Asia is the unqualified champion of the past three decades. Over the 30 years 1964 to 1993, the Asian nations profiled in this book (excluding Hong Kong and Taiwan, for whom comparable data is not available) have invested an average of 37 cents for every dollar consumed, compared to 29 cents on the dollar for the world as a whole and just 23 cents for the United States. And the 30-year averages actually understate the magnitude of the present disparity in savings and investment. As of the mid-1990s, Asia's investment-to-consumption ratio had reached nearly two and one-half times that of the United States and roughly double the world average. The clear leader in fostering savings and investment is Singapore, which as of 1993 had invested 84 cents for every dollar consumed, as compared to the U.S. ratio of a mere 20 cents for every dollar.

But while Asia may be the Main Street of the New Global Village, it is hardly the only street. In fact, three of the top four stock markets since 1988 are located not in the high-powered economies of Asia but in our own backyard, in the developing nations of Latin America. As is common after a period of intense and prolonged economic pain—a condition that characterized many Latin American economies in the late 1980s and early 1990s—fiscal responsibility is breaking out at long last in the lands south of the Rio Grande. First in Chile, then in Mexico, then in Argentina, and finally in Brazil, governments have adopted a "Hold the presses!" economic strategy, reversing the time-honored tradition of printing money to finance budgetary and trade deficiencies. But as the December 1994 financial meltdown in Mexico demonstrated, the transition to free and open markets will not be easy, smooth, or even guaranteed to succeed. Latin American economies are something akin to teenagers: volatile, changeable, excitable, unpredictable, yet often highly rewarding. The vastly different social ethos in many Latin American countries also comes into play, with its alternate vulnerability to authoritarian rule and periodic uprising in the name of political freedom.

If Latin American economies are the rowdy teenagers of the new world order and Asian countries its young adults, European states are the global senior citizens. Mature, stable, wise, dependable, and even fabled, the Old World economies of Germany, Switzerland, France, and Great Britain can still offer investors advantages not found in the younger hot spots of the global market place. The old playgrounds of Europe still have the fire to produce spectacular cyclical bursts, but mostly their appeal is in the high-quality products of their economy and the general predictability of their markets. The dogged insistence of many European nations to defend their currencies even at the expense of overall growth is a common characteristic of economic "haves"—those countries whose citizens already hold considerable wealth and whose main objective is simply to keep its value. The currencies of the five European nations profiled in this book gained an average of 60 percent against the U.S. dollar since 1964, and their average per capita gross domestic product of $22,000 is roughly equivalent to that of the United States. Reflecting the wealth and stability of their economies, European stock markets have by far the lowest downside volatility of the three global economic regions.

In any given year, the stock market of virtually any country could top the global honor roll as fickle liquidity flows quickly pass through one bourse on its way to another in a restless quest for relative value. But this year's beneficiary of mass euphoria could just as likely be next year's victim of collective panic. Over the long term, the performance of a country's stock market will tend to reflect the general health of its economy. And although it may not be possible to name with specificity which economies will lead the globe into the twenty-first century, it is possible to list several criteria that are likely to characterize those top performers. Keep in mind that economics is somewhat of a zero-sum game, that one nation tends to gain advantage at the expense of another in much the same way that one company gains market share over a competitor within an economy. While the aggregate output of the global economy will increase steadily over time, the distribution of real gains in global wealth is almost always nonuniform and related to factors that can be understood in advance. Those factors include financial strength (as measured by balances in budget and trade accounts), economic diversity, an educated workforce, a strong work ethic, a high investment-to-consumption ratio, a large middle class, political pluralism, moderate birth-rates, and the governmental and private managerial ability to adapt to changing world economic conditions, especially as they relate to one's own position in the global economic food chain. Those countries that best achieve all or most of these criteria will be your economic winners and will usually have the best-performing stock markets over the long haul.

In this book, you'll find information to help you make those kinds of determinations for yourself or to help you hire people who have compiled long-term track records of success in making exactly those types of calls. Chapters 1 through 5 give you the background on the foreign stock markets and information and guidelines for wisely and profitably investing your money in those markets. Chapter 6 explains the data presented in Chapters 7 through 27—the "country" chapters—each of which deals with the political and economic picture of one country. The 21 countries treated in Chapters 7 through 27 have a combined market capitalization of $8.87 trillion, or 99.3 percent of the value of all non-U.S. equity markets as of year-end 1994. From those nearly $9 trillion worth of companies are surely some of the best-managed, fastest-growing enterprises available on the global marketplace. As you consider the occasionally mind-numbing quantity of choices available, always keep in mind the single most important message of this book: *Just be there.*

CHAPTER 1

There's Always a Bull Market Somewhere

Imagine that you've compiled a list of prime investment opportunities. You've checked them all out, jotted them down, and are ready to start buying the most promising among them. But before you buy, you complete one final step: You pull out a pencil, grab a ruler, and proceed to draw a line through 58 percent of the list. You indiscriminately cross out more than half of the businesses for no investment-related reason.

If such a selection process seems counterproductive, it is, nonetheless, no different than the approach that the overwhelming majority of Americans take to building their stock portfolios. Despite a strong but uneven surge in enthusiasm for investing overseas in the first half of the 1990s, most U.S. investors continue to exclude almost 6 out of every 10 investment opportunities simply because they are not U.S. investments. While there are signs that investors are beginning to think at least somewhat more globally—Americans added approximately $1 billion a week to their foreign holdings throughout 1993—most portfolios remain significantly underweighted in foreign stocks. As of year-end 1994, Americans held $331 billion of foreign equities. Given that U.S. investors owned $5.89 trillion of the $6.23 trillion value of the the U.S. stock market at year-end 1994, best estimates would put the total amount of American overseas portfolio investment at just 5.3 percent of total assets.

Three decades or more ago, such an oversight would not have meant much. In 1960, U.S. stocks represented roughly 78 percent of the aggregate market value of the world's corporations. In other words, more than three-quarters of the world's investment opportunities at that time were in the United States. Buying only U.S. stocks meant excluding just a small minority of investment opportunities. Over the past 35 years, however, the value of U.S. stocks relative to the rest of the world has fallen steadily; by 1995, the American equity market represented just 42 percent of the $14.89 trillion aggregate value of the world's stock markets. Reflecting the strong relative growth of non-U.S. commerce, 61 of the world's 100 largest corporations are foreign-based, including 91 of the 100 largest banks and 30 of the 50 largest insurers. American investors without at least some degree of foreign-stock ownership are effectively placing off-limits between one-half and two-thirds of all publicly traded corporations.

Arbitrarily excluding 58 percent of the world's businesses from your stock holdings is only part of the story. *Where* those businesses are located is equally important. Many of the investment companies necessarily excluded from U.S.-only equity portfolios happen to be operating from the fastest growing economies in the world—economies that have growth rates that dwarf that of the United States and that have the potential to continue to outgrow the United States well into the twenty-first century; economies that now are being deregulated and are opening their doors to foreign capital and goods for the first time; economies that are developing stock-and-bond exchanges and that are geopolitically positioned to be prime beneficiaries of the enormous economic stimulus resulting from the opening of the vast Chinese market. Over the past three decades, the annual inflation-adjusted rate of economic growth in the United States not only has lagged that of other industrialized nations, but has been barely half of the growth rate for the economies of developing nations. In particular, many Asian countries represent especially attractive investment opportunities, with long-term gross domestic product (GDP) growth rates nearly triple that of the United States. The relatively pedestrian growth in the U.S. economy is directly translated into a substantial loss of economic market share: Over the past 30 years, the American share of the global economic pie has shrunk by *42 percent* relative to developing nations and by 20 percent compared to the world as a whole.

Given the slower rate of economic growth in the United States, it should come as no surprise that the performance of U.S. stocks has lagged as well. In 1993, for example, U.S. equities came in *last* compared to the 21 developed stock markets that comprise Morgan Stanley Capital International's Europe, Australia, Far East (EAFE) index. In 1994, U.S. stocks did only marginally better, placing 15th after returns were converted into dollars. Over the more than 25 years since Morgan Stanley Capital International (MSCI) has kept proprietary indexes on the world's developed stock markets, the United States has underperformed 13 of the 21 markets in U.S. dollar terms. Relative to world bourses as a whole, Morgan Stanley's U.S. index stood at 488 (Base: January 1, 1970 = 100) as of mid-1995, as compared to a dollar-based reading of 1061 for the EAFE, indicating that U.S. stocks have underperformed a capitalization-weighted basket of non-U.S. stocks by more than half since 1970. Over the seven-year period from 1988 to 1994, U.S. equities have performed somewhat better relative to non-U.S. markets, lagging 9 of the 21 stock markets profiled in this book, based on proprietary indexes prepared by Wilshire Associates Incorporated of Santa Monica, California (see Table 1.1).

Table 1.1.   Stock Market Performance, 1988–1994

(Return in U.S. dollars)

Chile	+1,317%
Philippines	+1,265%
Brazil	+986%
Mexico	+708%
Thailand	+379%
Malaysia	+284%
Hong Kong	+268%
Singapore	+242%
Taiwan	+137%
United States	**+134%**[1]
Australia	+106%
Canada	+101%
Korea	+100%
Switzerland	+87%
Germany	+85%
New Zealand	+81%
France	+63%
United Kingdom	+58%
Japan	+14%
Sweden	+5%
Indonesia	–12%[2]
Argentina	–72%

[1]Standard & Poor's 500.
[2]1990–1994.
Source: Wilshire Associates Incorporated.

The Global Cushion

Besides providing the potential for superior long-term performance, diversifying your investment portfolio to include a significant amount of foreign equities also can provide a degree of protection against the inevitable downdrafts that periodically afflict the U.S. stock market. The world's economies—and, therefore, the world's stock markets—are not perfectly synchronized. While one country or region is experiencing an economic slowdown, another area of the globe will often be in the midst of a healthy economic expansion. And even when expansionary phases overlap, the conditions driving the markets may vary, creating opportunities in vastly disparate sectors. For example, the early portion of an economic recovery is generally a *disintermediation* phase, or one in which equity prices are driven higher by monetary easing that results in large sums of capital exiting banks or savings vehicles in favor of stocks. During this phase, interest-rate-sensitive equities, such as financial services and banks, often lead. The second, or final, stage of an expansion is usually characterized by an earnings-driven bull market in which stocks remain aloft because of growth in their bottom lines. During this final stage, shares of economically sensitive or so-called cyclical shares often lead the market higher. Astute money managers can play these varying cycles, positioning assets within a mutual fund, for example, to get the best that each market has to offer.

The fact that many of the world's major stock exchanges often march to the beat of their own economic drummer can be good news for the global investor. Markets moving in different directions—or at least by varying amounts if in the same direction—could have the effect of cushioning potential losses in a portfolio for any given year. The calculation that best measures the relationship of price movements between various markets is known as *correlation*. When two markets move in the same direction in exactly the same amount at exactly the same time, the correlation between those markets is said to be 1.00. Conversely, if markets move in opposite directions but by the same amount at the same time, the correlation is −1.00. And if there is no relationship whatever between direction, timing, or magnitude of movement, the correlation is said to be 0.00.

Using monthly data, U.S. stocks have averaged a correlation of just 0.28 with the 21 markets covered in this book, indicating that what is happening in the United States is usually not occurring to the same degree in the remainder of the world. While it is true that very often when the U.S. stock market catches a cold the rest of the world sneezes, it is also true that diversifying a portfolio to include a substantial amount of foreign equities will tend to relieve some of the effects of the illness. In each of the seven declines in the U.S. stock market of 10 percent or more (as measured by Standard & Poor's Composite Index of 500 Stocks) over the past 25 years, returns from the rest of the world's developed markets (as measured by EAFE) would have had the effect of mitigating the size of the loss in the U.S. portion of a portfolio in each case. Based on monthly total returns from the Wilshire Associates indexes for the 1988 to 1994 period, Figure 1.1 shows correlations between American stocks and the 21 equity markets covered in Chapters 7 through 27 of this book. Each "country" chapter will also list the correlation between stocks from that nation and those of the 20 other equity markets.

How Much Is Too Much?

Because many foreign stocks outperform their U.S. counterparts over the long term and because markets are usually at somewhat different points in their bull/bear cycles (thus minimizing potential declines), it may seem only logical to wonder why you shouldn't just load your portfolio with overseas investments and forget about the American market altogether. It turns out, however, that there is a strong argument against totally abandoning U.S. equities: Whereas your total return would likely turn out to be greater by owning only foreign stocks (at least

Figure 1.1.   U.S. Correlation to World Markets
Correlations between S&P 500 and various non-U.S. equity markets
(monthly data).

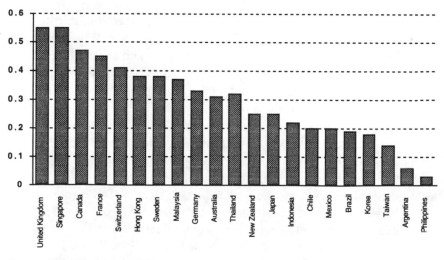

Source: Wilshire Associates Incorporated.

as indicated by EAFE returns over the past 25 years), evidence suggests that, by excluding all U.S. equities from your portfolio, you would be taking on a significantly greater degree of risk. The best strategy is to find the point at which adding foreign stocks to your portfolio increases the return without unduly adding to potential losses. Determining the precise percentage of your assets that should be invested in foreign stocks—the level at which risk and reward are optimized—requires some explanation.

The task of measuring risk can be slippery and potentially misleading. Even agreeing on a precise definition of *risk* can be difficult or impossible because of the widely varying values that each investor may place on the differing components of what may be defined as risk and because investors may hold vastly different portfolios of foreign stocks. For example, many investors view volatility itself as a type of risk. But while there may be a relationship between volatility and risk, choppiness does not always equate to riskiness. Some money managers and academics use a calculation known as *standard deviation* to measure the volatility of markets. Standard deviation captures volatility by determining the degree to which an investment's return varies from month to month or from year to year. A higher number indicates a greater level of variation in return and, by extension, a greater degree of volatility. But does greater volatility actually mean greater risk? Not really; in fact, overall volatility—and, therefore, standard deviation—can be a woefully inadequate and quite misleading yardstick of risk.

A simple examination of two sample portfolios clearly shows that volatility and risk are completely different animals: Portfolio 1 alternately earned between 20 percent and 50 percent per year; Portfolio 2 alternately lost between 40 percent and 50 percent each year. At the end of six years, Portfolio 1 had returned 483 percent on the original investment, while Portfolio 2 had lost 98 percent. Now ask yourself: Which of the two portfolios would you rather own? Which would you consider safer? Obviously, Portfolio 1, which never had a down year and whose worst year was a plus 20 percent return, was not only the better investment but the safer investment as well. An analysis of the two portfolios' relative volatility, however, might have led you to a vastly different conclusion. Portfolio 1, despite its superior return and lower risk, would nonetheless have been deemed *three times* more volatile than Portfolio 2, because its average annual standard deviation of 15 was triple that of Portfolio 2. And because Portfolio 1 was more volatile, it would, therefore, have been considered riskier. When trying to evaluate an investment opportunity, never make the mistake of assuming that risk and volatility are necessarily the same things.

A better way to measure risk than relying entirely on standard deviation is to start with a simple premise: *Investors don't mind upside volatility.* In other words, a portfolio of stocks that produces widely varying degrees of positive returns is not likely to evoke your wrath. The only volatility you and most investors care about is the volatility that costs you money, that is, *downside* volatility. In determining the risk-related (read: downside) volatility of the 21 foreign stock markets in this book (see Table 1.2), five measurements of volatility have been used: total of monthly losses, in percent; number of monthly losses; average monthly loss, in percent; number of monthly losses greater than 5 percent; and standard deviation. Four of these five volatility readings, then, correspond only to downside volatility and, thus, could be considered to have increased an investor's risk. Each of the five volatility readings is weighted equally, added together, and compared with a similarly constructed index for the U.S. market over the same time period. The result is a relative risk index that examines the downside volatility of a given foreign market against that of the United States. Using such a methodology, the median volatility of the 21 markets examined in this book is 2.57 times greater than that of the American market, indicating that your downside risk is slightly more than 2.5 times more in the average foreign stock than it is in domestic equities. Of the three major geographic regions, the Americas contain by far the riskiest markets, with an average relative volatility ratio of 3.93, compared to 3.24 for Asia/Oceania and 1.92 for Europe.

The reasons behind the greatly enhanced downside volatility of foreign equities are numerous. Many countries with highly profitable capital markets nonetheless have unstable governments. Even in Japan, a nation not usually associated with political turmoil and with an economy nearly as large as the United States, governments can come and go at the rate of one or more per year. Economies that are not as diversified as the United States are also more vulnerable to downturns, requiring their fiscal and monetary authorities to guide the economy through a relatively narrow window of opportunity. Countries that may have been badly mismanaged in the past often have heavy debt burdens that can exacerbate the negative effects of cyclical contractions. And some stock exchanges, particularly those in developing countries, may not always be sufficiently liquid to allow for heavy simultaneous selling of shares without substantially upsetting prices. Difficulties relating to foreign exchange (see Chapter 2) only compound existing problems. For all these reasons, it is not unusual to see stocks move 2 percent or more in a single day on many foreign markets.

Given that foreign stocks are generally more profitable over the long term but riskier over the short term, how should you, an investor with literally a world of opportunities to choose among, divide your assets? Should you own only foreign securities, damn the torpedoes? Should you head for safe harbor and buy only American? Or is there some happy balance, a point at which modern capitalization ratios are blended with the reality of risk to produce an allocation that com-

Table 1.2.   Stock Market Volatility[1] Relative to U.S. Stocks

(Monthly data, in U.S. dollars, 1988–1994)

Argentina	8.31
Brazil	5.59
Taiwan	5.08
Philippines	5.00
Indonesia	4.79[2]
Japan	3.13
Korea	3.13
Thailand	3.05
Sweden	2.61
New Zealand	2.53
Hong Kong	2.45
Mexico	2.31
Malaysia	2.27
Chile	2.26
Australia	2.00
Germany	1.96
United Kingdom	1.81
France	1.80
Singapore	1.63
Switzerland	1.40
Canada	1.19

[1]Derived by averaging standard deviation; total monthly losses, in percent; average monthly loss, in percent; number of monthly losses; and number of monthly losses greater than 5 percent; relative to U.S. S&P Composite Index of 500 Stocks.
[2] 1990–1994.
Source: Wilshire Associates Incorporated.

bines potential reward with minimal downside volatility? Because of differences in what specific securities and markets a given investor may be in, there can be no single answer to fit all circumstances. But since foreign stocks represent 58 percent of the world's equity-market capitalization while being an average of 2.57 times as risky, one approach to achieving an appropriate balance between risk and reward would be to divide the theoretically desirable 58 percent (0.58) foreign-capitalization weighting by the 2.57 relative downside volatility. Such a calculation would suggest that something on the order of a 25 percent exposure to foreign equities would reflect a reasonable risk-adjusted weighting. In other words, given $10,000 to invest, $7,500 should remain in the United States, and $2,500 should be placed abroad. And even though a 25 percent foreign share of your portfolio is still a significant underweighting of the non-U.S. portion of the world's equity markets, it nonetheless would represent a fivefold increase from the mere 5.3 percent of assets the average U.S. investor now maintains in foreign stocks. For more information on how to deploy that 25 percent, consult Chapter 6, Principles of Sound Foreign Investing.

The Best May Be Yet to Come

Increasing the percentage of foreign stocks in your portfolio to at least 25 percent may become even more profitable as time goes on. That's because, as well as foreign stocks have performed over the past quarter century, there is strong evidence to suggest that the magnitude of outperformance relative to the United States could increase in the years ahead.

Global Economic Trends

As the twenty-first century dawns, four major global economic trends are unfolding, each of which carries significant positive implications for the long-term health of foreign equity markets: These trends are liberalized trade, increased flow of capital, privatization of business, and increased trade with China.

• **Liberalized trade.**   The passage of regional and multilateral trade pacts, such as the North American Free Trade Agreement (NAFTA) and the General Agreement on Tariffs and Trade (GATT), augurs well for the long-term health of the global economy. The GATT accord, which was signed by 117 nations, calls for a roughly one-third reduction in tariffs across a wide array of products, including, for the first time, some agricultural goods. History is unambiguous in its lesson that freer access to foreign markets is good for the world economy over both the short and long term. And anything that stimulates economic growth is also good for corporate profits, which in turn help to provide a strong underpinning to world stock prices.

Just as important as the boost to overall global output and profitability, however, is the positive effect that increased foreign trade has on keeping a lid on global inflation. Since the early 1980s, the world economy has been in an ex-

tended period of disinflation, or relatively mild price increases. Because inflation is the mortal enemy of financial assets, any development that keeps prices
under control is good for stocks and bonds. The trend toward greater access to
foreign markets will exert continued downward pressure on global prices by
encouraging the most efficient possible use of each country's assets, whether it
be labor, capital, raw materials, productive capacity, technology, or ideas. To be
sure, there will be pockets of losers within each country; less efficient producers
will be forced out of business by the harsh demands of global economic competition. But overall, the continuing and accelerating trend in the reduction of trade
barriers will have the effect of stimulating global economic growth by expanding consumer purchasing power, and its reinforcing effect on global disinflation
is extremely positive for equity markets worldwide.

- **Flow of capital.**   As individual and institutional investors throughout the
world become more knowledgeable about and comfortable with the idea of buying overseas stocks, non-American markets should receive increasing flows of
portfolio investment. As noted earlier, despite a spectacular burst of interest in
owning foreign equities during 1993, the average individual investor in the United
States remains significantly underweighted in foreign stocks. Even more importantly, however, institutional money managers in the United States are beginning
to look seriously at diversifying their equity holdings into overseas markets, and
this mother lode of potential liquidity could be a large factor in helping push
foreign stock prices substantially higher in the coming decades. As foreign equity markets become progressively more open and developed, it is inevitable that
more funds will flow toward these countries, making the emerging markets of
Asia and Latin America the primary beneficiaries of the move toward global
portfolio diversification.

- **Privatization.**   Throughout much of the globe, governments are decentral-
izing control over their economies and liberalizing their financial markets, thereby
creating thousands of new businesses and investment opportunities for the global investor. While reform in the former Soviet Union grabs most of the head-
lines, similar (and far more successful) measures are also underway in Mexico,
Argentina, Brazil, Poland, South Korea, Indonesia, and, of course, China.

- **China.**   If you owned a business and just learned that the market for your
product had increased by 20 percent, you'd be ecstatic, right? The opening of the
Chinese economy—despite the paradox of continued authoritarian political control—has done just that, effectively adding 1.2 *billion* potential customers for the
world's businesses. It also vastly expands global productive capacity, thereby

adding to the disinflationary pressures that are so helpful to the world's financial markets. China has been growing at an inflation-adjusted rate of over 10 percent a year since the mid-1980s, and the greatest beneficiaries are again those markets located in the so-called Pacific Rim, including Malaysia, Singapore, Taiwan, Hong Kong, Indonesia, South Korea, and the Philippines.

Global Investment Opportunities

If you're sold on the idea that adding more foreign stocks to your portfolio makes good investment sense, you might be pleased to learn that opportunities to buy into global markets have become more numerous and carefully targeted in recent years. Mutual funds that invest exclusively in foreign stocks have proliferated since the late 1980s. A growing number of funds invest only in the securities of certain regions, such as Latin America or Asia, whereas other funds precisely target their investments to the securities of a single nation. Americans preferring to buy individual foreign equities can also do so easily, primarily through what are known as American depositary receipts (ADRs), which trade on U.S. securities markets such as the New York Stock Exchange (NYSE) and the National Association of Securities Dealers Automated Quotation system (NASDAQ). As of 1995, more than 700 ADRs were available on these exchanges, including those of some of the world's largest and most profitable corporations, such as Sony and Honda (Japan), Daimler-Benz (Germany), Royal Caribbean Cruises (Liberia), Seagram (Canada), Telefonos de Mexico (Mexico), Royal Dutch Petroleum (Netherlands), and Glaxo Holdings (United Kingdom). For most investors, mutual funds and ADRs are the best ways to increase non-U.S. equity exposure. (Mutual funds and ADRs will be examined at length in Chapters 3 and 4; a subcomponent of mutual funds, the private or separate account, will also be covered in Chapter 3.) Both mutual funds and ADRs, however, will expose your portfolio to foreign exchange fluctuation, which will affect the value of your holdings. (The causes and potential consequences of those currency-related changes will be discussed in Chapter 2.)

Keeping a Safe Distance

The only way for American investors to achieve a measure of foreign diversification without direct currency risk is to buy the stocks of U.S. multinational corporations, that is, those companies that do a large portion of their business overseas. Such a strategy would allow investors to capitalize on at least a portion of the growth in overseas economies without subjecting their investment to the

Table 1.3.   U.S. Multinational Corporations

Company	Exports in Billions of Dollars	Exports as Percent of Sales
General Motors	$14.9	11.16%
Boeing	14.6	58.42
Ford Motor	9.4	8.74
General Electric	8.4	13.97
Chrysler	8.3	19.26
IBM	7.2	11.63
Motorola	4.9	29.42
Hewlett-Packard	4.7	23.32
Philip Morris	4.1	8.11
Caterpillar	3.7	32.23
E. I. du Pont	3.5	1.73
United Technologies	3.5	16.89
Intel	3.4	38.78
McDonnell Douglas	3.4	23.50
Archer Daniels Midland	2.9	29.56
Eastman Kodak	2.2	11.18
Raytheon	2.1	22.42
Compaq Computer	1.9	26.73
Digital Equipment	1.8	12.53
Allied Signal	1.7	14.37
Lockheed	1.7	13.33
Textron	1.6	18.33
Minnesota Mining & Mfg.	1.5	10.63
Dow Chemical	1.4	7.98
IBP	1.4	11.93
Weyerhauser	1.4	15.14
Sun Microsystems	1.3	29.48
Unisys	1.3	17.24
Westinghouse Electric	1.3	11.57

(continued)

Table 1.3.   (Continued)

Company	Exports in Billions of Dollars	Exports as Percent of Sales
Hoechst Celanese	1.1	15.12
International Paper	1.1	8.04
Miles	1.1	16.05
Union Carbide	1.1	24.87
Xerox	1.1	7.37
Abbott Laboratories	1.0	11.99
Deere	1.0	12.49
Merck	1.0	9.55
Bristol-Myers Squibb	0.9	8.04
Cummings Engine	0.9	21.33
Monsanto	0.9	11.79

Sources: Fortune; Hoover's Handbook of American Business 1995.

vagaries of foreign exchange. The following 40 companies, for example, export an average of $3.2 billion of U.S. goods annually, with foreign sales representing nearly 18 percent of revenue (see Table 1.3).

While simply buying a diversified portfolio of American companies that do large amounts of overseas business is certainly a legitimate way of your getting foreign-market exposure, it nonetheless does have its limitations and disadvantages. Owning the stocks of U.S. multinationals would still put you at indirect foreign-exchange risk: If the dollar rises against overseas currencies, profitability of the multinationals will likely be impaired, both because higher foreign prices for American goods cut into sales or profit margins and because earnings are diluted when foreign sales are repatriated into appreciated dollars. Also, buying a basket of large U.S. multinationals on an American exchange only makes you a participant in the growth of foreign consumer markets; it does not make you the partial owner of a foreign-based business that might also stand to gain from increasing global liquidity flows. And finally, along with the foreign-sales component of U.S. multinationals could come domestic headaches. The same com-

pany that racks up impressive export numbers might also have significant problems with the domestic side of its business. In buying the stock of a U.S. multinational corporation, keep in mind that you can't separate one segment of a
company's business from another and that exposure to a growing flow of still
somewhat enfeebled discretionary spending in developing countries is not necessarily as profitable as exposure to cash-heavy global investors bidding to own
a piece of your business.

Innocents Abroad

If you like the idea of investing overseas but are not sure that mutual funds, ADRs,
or U.S. multinationals are the best way to go, you might be tempted to purchase
stock in a foreign corporation by going directly to its home exchange; for example, rather than buying an ADR for Telefonos de Mexico (the giant Mexican
phone company) on the NYSE, you could buy Telmex shares directly on the
Mexico City bourse. But while this type of direct purchase of an individual foreign-based security is often possible, it is usually not desirable. (Taiwan, the third-
largest Asian equity market, flatly prohibits foreign individuals from investing in
the Taipei exchange.) Following are some reasons why most investors would be
wise to avoid buying their foreign stocks directly on overseas markets, even when
they might have the ability to do so:

• **No Securities Investor Protection Corporation (SIPC) insurance from
foreign brokers.**   Most U.S. brokerage firms do not execute orders on foreign
exchanges. If you use a foreign firm to buy and sell shares, the overseas brokerage will not be covered by the SIPC, which insures the accounts held through
most American-based brokers for up to $500,000 per account in the event the
brokerage goes bust. If you bought shares of Sony directly on the Tokyo market
through a Japanese securities firm and if that brokerage proceeded to collapse,
your money would go along with it, regardless of how well Sony stock was doing.

• **High minimums, commissions, and other fees.**   Business conducted on foreign bourses will subject you to a host of fees not encountered on any American
exchange. The brokerage commissions to buy and sell your stock will also be
significantly higher on foreign markets than in the United States. And even if
you are able to find an American broker willing to take your overseas trade (most
don't do foreign business), be prepared for a minimum investment in the range
of $25,000 per transaction.

- **No three-day settlement.** If you sold stock on an American securities exchange, you would receive the proceeds of your trade in three business days. Overseas markets are not so accommodating; payment could take from two to five weeks, even in such established bourses as London or Paris.

- **Different accounting principles.** Calculating earnings and other balance-sheet minutia crucial to making informed investment decisions will be more difficult unless you are thoroughly familiar with the accounting principles utilized in the country in which you are investing. However, for a foreign-based company to be granted a direct listing on the NYSE or to be allowed to trade as an ADR, the firm must conform to most of the same accounting principles that apply to U.S. corporations.

Doing your foreign investing through ADRs or mutual funds can minimize or avert entirely most of the problems just noted. Institutional investors such as mutual funds receive significant commission-discounts because of the size of their purchases, and the managers running the portfolios are usually experienced in the accounting principles used in each foreign country. Institutional investors are also large enough to profitably hedge their currency bets if they deem such a strategy to be necessary, thereby minimizing the effects of any fluctuation in the U.S. dollar. And institutional investors are knowledgeable enough about each of the individual foreign markets to know which stocks are too thinly traded to be bought and sold without upsetting the balance of orders. Unless you are an extremely experienced investor with large sums of money on the table, doing your international investing through the methods described in Chapters 3 and 4 will give you the best chance of capitalizing on the extraordinary long-term growth potential of many foreign businesses and markets.

Regardless of how much foreign stock you presently own or exactly how you go about owning it, you are already a global consumer. By the time you arrive at work each day, you may have had a cup of coffee from South America, watched a television from Asia, and driven an automobile from Europe. And the commerce goes both ways: In the increasingly interconnected world of the late-twentieth century, Asians buy planes built in Seattle (Boeing), Washingtonians buy perfume made in Paris (L'Oreal), and Parisians build TVs and VCRs sold throughout the world under the logos of American corporations (GE and RCA). By adding a significant degree of foreign stocks to your investment portfolio not only will you likely increase your long-term return, you will be making yourself a part owner of the very same companies whose products you already consume.

CHAPTER 2

Dealing with Currency Fluctuation

You've seen the ads touting this or that car, the ones bragging about the model's fuel efficiency. After highlighting the projected mileage a consumer is expected to receive in city or highway driving, the commercials quickly (and sometimes quietly) amend the projections with the caveat, *Individual results may vary*.

When it comes to investing in foreign stocks, it helps to keep the automobile commercials in mind. Because even if you are able to match or exceed the return of the benchmark index for the country in which you are investing, *your results may vary*. The reason: currency fluctuation. With the exception of the American depositary receipts (ADRs) and direct listings discussed in Chapter 4, in order to buy foreign stocks, either you, your mutual fund, or your investment advisor will need to take your dollars and convert them into the local currency, be it yen, deutsche marks, francs, pesos, ringgits, rupiahs, dongs, or whatever. Then, in order to make use of your funds, you will need to repatriate your investments from the local currency back into dollars. Unless the dollar and the local currency have moved in absolute lock step—a highly unlikely occurrence, unless the local currency is that of Hong Kong, which presently pegs its currency to the U.S. dollar—your dollar-denominated return will be at least somewhat different from the return your investments generated in the local currency. And even if your investment is hedged (the practice of offsetting potential currency fluctuations through the use of options and futures contracts), the movements of a nation's currency relative to the U.S. dollar usually have significant repercussions for the economies of both countries.

The rule of thumb for Americans in understanding the effects of currency translation is simple: If the dollar falls relative to the currency of the nation in which you are investing, you win. If the dollar rises relative to the local currency, you lose. Changes in the value of the dollar relative to the currency of your chosen foreign market will usually impact the value of your investments on something approximating a one-to-one basis—a 10 percent decline in the dollar will add roughly 10 percent to your return; a 10 percent appreciation of the dollar will reduce your return by about 10 percent. Americans investing overseas naturally want a weak or at least stable dollar, and, as you will discover later in this chapter, their wishes have frequently been granted, at least against the world's largest economies.

In an ideal world—one in which the citizens of each nation were equally educated and productive; natural resources equally dispersed; markets equally open and deregulated; businesses equally adept at survival; politicians equally free from popular pressure to seek short-term solutions; and the goods and services of each nation equally attractive, desirable, and necessary—currency exchange rates would show little fluctuation except to reflect the relative location of each country within its business cycle. In such an environment, the maximum efficient use of natural and human resources would be allowed to flourish. The economic realities of this or any previous era, however, fall far short of any resembling a perfect world—people are not equally educated or productive, nations have widely disparate access to natural resources, countries produce goods and services of greatly varying attractiveness, financial markets are not equally free or deregulated, import markets are far from equally open, and citizens from different countries have widely varying tolerances to policies that maximize short-term economic gain at the expense of long-term consequences. Given that this unpleasant collection of circumstances is unlikely to change in the near future—or probably ever—Americans looking to invest overseas should accept the reality of currency fluctuation and learn how best to deal with its consequences.

Those consequences can often be significant. In 1994, a broad-based decline in the dollar turned what would have been losses for American investors in many foreign bourses into gains. Only 7 of the 21 mature markets measured in the Morgan Stanley Capital International Europe, Australia, Far East (EAFE) index showed positive returns in 1994 when calculated in the local currency; when translated into dollars, however, 14 of the 21 markets showed gains, with the average dollar-conversion benefit of 9.75 percent nearly matching the 8.18 percent fall in the dollar relative to the unweighted currencies of the 21 nations. Stocks in Switzerland, for example, declined nearly 10 percent in Swiss francs; when converted into dollars, however, the loss was turned into a slight gain. Since the dollar in 1994 rose against only one of the currencies (Canada), an American investor buying stocks in each of the bourses included in the EAFE index would have seen total return enhanced after currency repatriation in 20 of the 21 foreign markets.

Several of the improvements in dollar-denominated returns would have been dramatic. The weak dollar relative to Finland's markka would have added 27 percent to the already hefty 23.8 percent return of the Finnish market in 1994, as measured by a Morgan Stanley Capital International proprietary country index. American investors in Japan would have gained an additional 12.8 percent because of the dollar's decline against the yen. Investments in more than half the markets included in the EAFE would have benefited by at least an additional 10 percent when converted into American dollars. When viewed on a non-trade-weighted basis, however, the performance of the dollar becomes considerably less dismal. Over the past three decades, the dollar has actually gained ground on most currencies (with the notable exceptions of Japan, Switzerland, Germany, and Singapore) and traded on a roughly equal basis with a handful of others.

The Dollar Also Rises

Despite the publicity that the dollar's woes relative to the yen and mark often receive, the data in Table 2.1 suggests that U.S. investors should be under no illusion that a weak dollar will always be around to mitigate or cancel altogether the consequences of otherwise unprofitable excursions abroad. The collapse of the Mexican peso in late 1994, for example, turned an otherwise serious drubbing for Americans investing in the Mexican Bolsa into a rout. When measured in pesos, Mexican stocks fell by nearly 9 percent in December 1994; after converting the investment back into U.S. dollars, however, the loss climbed to over 36 percent. Investors looking to diversify abroad can take some comfort in the fact that when measured against a trade-weighted basket of currencies, the long-term trend of the American dollar does have a mild downward bias. Within that secular bear market, however, there have been the usual ebb and flow of cyclical bear and bull phases, during which an American investor with foreign exposure would have been alternately helped and hurt by the dollar's fluctuations. As of early 1995, an index created by the U.S. Federal Reserve to measure the performance of the dollar relative to a trade-weighted basket of currencies from nine of the world's largest industrialized democracies showed that the dollar had declined by a little over 33 percent since 1971 (see Figure 2.1).

The loss of roughly one-third of the U.S. dollar's value over the past 25 years means that American investors buying stocks abroad have generally been aided by the market movements of their home currency. In the absence of long-term policies to reverse this trend, it is a reasonably safe bet that the slow, secular, downward drift of the dollar will continue, with the net effect of making investing overseas still more attractive for Americans. But the dollar's performance

Table 2.1. Currency Performance Relative to U.S. Dollar (1964–1994)

Japan (yen)	+298%
Switzerland (franc)	+231%
Germany (mark)	+154%
Singapore (dollar)	+114%
Malaysia (ringgit)	+20%
France (franc)	–9%
New Zealand (dollar)	–12%
Australia (dollar)	–15%
Thailand (baht)	–17%
Canada (dollar)	–23%
Sweden (krona)	–31%
United Kingdom (pound)	–45%
South Korea (won)	–67%
Philippines (peso)	–84%
Indonesia (rupiah)	–89%
Mexico (peso)	–99%
Chile (peso)	–99%
Brazil (real)	–99%
Argentina (peso)	–99%

Sources: International Monetary Fund; International Financial Statistics Yearbook.

has not always resulted in easy money for globe-trotting U.S. investors. There have been times over the past quarter-century when rallies in the dollar would have severely diluted the return on foreign holdings, and those cyclical uptrends can be expected to continue, even if they occur within a long-term bear market.

From 1971 through mid-1995, there have been 13 distinct cycles in which the dollar moved at least 10 percent in one direction or the other. Six of those cycles have been bull markets, or periods in which the dollar rose, cutting into the returns of Americans investing overseas. The average bull market in the U.S. dollar took the currency up by an average of nearly 31 percent over 20 months, with the greatest bull move the 92 percent climb in the dollar between July 1980 and February 1985. It was during that period that Federal Reserve Board Chairman Paul Volcker pursued a dedicated tight-money policy aimed at ridding the U.S.

Figure 2.1.   Value of U.S. Dollar
Trade-weighted exchange value of U.S. dollar (monthly data).

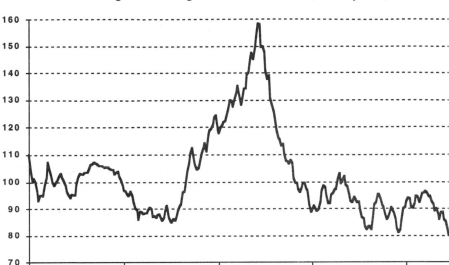

Source: Federal Reserve.

economy of the inflation that had been a problem for over a decade. The monetary medicine used to treat the economic patient   extraordinarily high real interest rates—sucked in huge amounts of foreign capital, exerting upward pressure on the dollar. The seven intervening bear markets in the dollar pushed it lower by an average of 22.7 percent over slightly more than two years. The most severe cyclical bear market in the U.S. currency began in earnest in late 1985 after monetary authorities from the United States, Japan, Germany, France, Italy, Canada, and the United Kingdom agreed to work in concert to drive the dollar lower. In one of the few examples of effective and sustained cooperation between the monetary authorities of competing economies in manipulating the movement of a currency, the U.S. dollar fell by nearly 50 percent over the ensuing two years.

Table 2.2 shows all changes of at least 10 percent in the trade-weighted value of the U.S. dollar relative to the currencies of nine large industrialized democracies between January 1971 and May 1995.

It is axiomatic that the value of a nation's currency is a report card on its overall economic health. But while evidence does confirm a general relationship between economic well-being and strength in a currency, a precise definition of *economic*

Table 2.2. Dollar Cycles

Phase	Beginning	Ending	Price Change
Bear	January 1971	July 1973	−23%
Bull	August 1973	January 1974	+17%
Bear	February 1974	May 1975	−13%
Bull	June 1975	June 1976	+14%
Bear	July 1976	July 1980	−21%
Bull	August 1980	February 1985	+92%
Bear	March 1985	December 1987	−46%
Bull	January 1988	June 1989	+20%
Bear	July 1989	February 1991	−23%
Bull	March 1991	July 1991	+19%
Bear	August 1991	September 1992	−18%
Bull	October 1992	January 1994	+23%
Bear	February 1994	May 1995	−15%

health is required. History shows clearly that simple economic growth, as measured by inflation-adjusted gross domestic product (GDP), cannot be the sole yardstick for determining economic health. Some of the fastest growing economies in the world—including some of the Latin American nations whose equity markets posted impressive returns over the past several years—have spectacularly weak currencies. And investors need only look to the U.S. dollar for evidence that a strong and diversified economy by itself is not enough to rescue a currency. The American economic machine remains the largest and most diversified in the world. Its immunity to catastrophic events is unmatched, witness the predictable run to the dollar and U.S. government securities in the wake of most global economic, political, or social disasters. In 1994, the U.S. economy grew by 4 percent, well above its historic trendline and the strongest growth of any mature industrial economy, including Germany and Japan, which were still throwing off the lingering effects of recession. Yet in 1994, as noted earlier, the U.S. dollar was in a bear market, falling by roughly 10 percent against both the Japanese yen and German mark. Clearly, the level of diversification within an economy or its relative rate of real growth is not the sole determinant of a currency's fate. It is also useful to keep in mind that the world's economies are far from synchronous. Some economies will inevitably be expanding while others are contracting; some governments will be easing monetary policy while others are tightening. As each nation passes through its version of a business cycle, market dynamics create conditions that temporarily reward or punish a currency.

Factors Affecting Currency Value

The relationship between a nation's economic health and its currency, then, can only be understood if the definition of *economic health* is broadened to include a variety of factors in addition to growth and if the performance of a currency is measured over the long term, thereby removing temporary cyclical influences. In addition to inflation-adjusted growth, there are several specific factors that affect the value of a nation's currency. Often, however, these factors are at somewhat cross purposes—one policy may be working to push a given currency higher while at the same time interacting with other policies having the opposite effect. These factors may include the following:

• **Quantity of money.**   When a nation's central bank decides to stimulate its economy, printing money (or simply increasing the assets on its balance sheet) is the easiest way to do it. Increasing the supply of money will almost always perk up an economy over the near term, especially if government authorities are unconcerned about treating potential inflationary consequences. Many political leaders, especially those from countries with low per capita incomes, are under enormous popular pressure to foster policies that encourage economic growth first and worry about price stability later, if at all. Regardless of national boundaries, people view the problem of inflation as irrelevant if they do not have a secure job. The short-term political rewards for promoting economic growth (or maintaining budget deficits) by goosing the money supply are often irresistible for many leaders. Consequently, money is often created faster than it can be used to enhance productivity or production, leading to a de facto devaluation of the currency. This is an especially acute problem for many poor nations, but, paradoxically, it is also one of the reasons that, over the long term, such countries tend to remain impoverished. Countries that lack a stable currency—an inevitable by-product of an overly accommodative monetary policy—will fail to attract the kind of foreign investment necessary to finance productivity improvements, the only true means of developing national wealth over time.

• **Trade deficits**.   The value of one nation's currency relative to that of another nation swings heavily on the balance of trade between those two nations; for example, a major reason for the long-term downtrend of the U.S. dollar against the Japanese yen has been the chronic U.S. merchandise-trade deficit with Japan, which currently runs roughly $50 billion per year. When American consumers buy Japanese products, the dollars they use to make their purchases are eventually sold by American retailers, and the proceeds are used to buy yen in order to pay off their Japanese suppliers. All other factors being equal, if the number of dollars sold by American businesses exceeds those bought by Japanese companies to finance their U.S. imports, the result will be a lower American currency against the yen. Nations with chronically weak trade positions will often have a weak currency, unless other measures are taken to offset the resulting flow-of-funds imbalance.

• **Discrepancy in interest rates**.   One of the ways that governments can offset a weak trade position and stabilize their currencies is to hike domestic interest rates. If the higher rates are a better deal than investors can find elsewhere (taking into account risk to principal), money will usually flow toward that nation's paper, creating a demand for its currency and, therefore, upward pressure on the currency's value. One of the reasons for the appreciation of the German mark against the U.S. dollar in recent years has been the German central bank's determination to fight with higher interest rates the possible inflationary effects of reunification, at the same time the U.S. Federal Reserve (the Fed) was pushing American rates sharply lower to counter the lingering economic malaise of the early 1990s. As the Fed pushed short-term rates lower, yields on the long end of the curve fell as well, making them less attractive on a current-return basis than those found in Germany. International investors, in turn, either sold or avoided U.S. bonds, while pushing up the mark through their purchase of mark-denominated financial assets.

• **Attractiveness of financial assets**.   In the new world order of global investing, a large and ever-growing pool of money sits at the ready to flow toward whichever country's stock and/or bond market offers the best return per unit of risk. Net inflows of foreign capital, of course, will push a currency higher because of the overall positive demand. Because equities tend to perform best when a nation's economy is growing steadily (therefore producing higher corporate profits), a strong currency tends to accompany economic strength. But here is where the equation becomes somewhat muddled—if the economic strength is deemed excessive, unsustainable, inflationary, or fueled primarily by earnings derived from a devalued currency, bond prices in that nation will be pushed lower, discouraging foreign investment and forcing the currency lower. (This scenario occurred in the U.S. financial markets through most of 1994, when the American dollar declined, despite above-trend economic growth, because inflationary fears gripped the credit markets and led to net selling by foreign investors. As foreigners cashed in their U.S. chips and new buyers failed to show up, the dollar fell despite the robust pace of economic growth.) At this point in the cycle, a lower currency and higher interest rates begin to feed off each other: The reality or expectation of higher rates discourages foreign investment, which pushes the currency lower; a lower currency causes still more inflationary concerns, pushing bond prices lower. Only when the consensus of global opinion deems that rates have risen enough to both dampen domestic inflationary prospects and produce inflation-adjusted returns competitive with other debt markets will the flow of funds resume and the currency begin to stabilize. The difficulty experienced by many developing nations, however, is that the price of maintaining a strong currency through high interest rates is politically unpalatable because of the sedating effect high capital costs usually have on economic growth.

• **Budget deficits.** When a government spends more than it takes in, the resulting revenue gap is plugged by either borrowing or creating money. All other factors being equal, both solutions are poison to a nation's currency. The excessive creation, or printing, of new money obviously devalues a currency if the monetary aggregates expand faster than the nation's output and productive capacity. And if a country borrows to finance its fiscal deficit, a different set of problems ensues. Nations with large financing needs are often dependent on foreigners for at least a portion of those funds, especially if the internal savings rate is low. Interest is then due on the debt, of course, and if the amount of interest paid to foreigners exceeds the amount coming into the country, the net outflow creates a drag on the currency. (For the first time in its history, the United States had a negative net-interest position in 1994.) Heavy dependence on short-term foreign investment to plug a budgetary shortfall also destabilizes a currency because of the fear that the foreign benefactors will bail out at any moment, thus exerting a massive sell program on the currency. Besides complications resulting directly from the deficit, fiscal imprudence has other ramifications as well. When a government has its snout buried too deeply in the public trough, private investors have difficulty getting their share of the capital feed necessary to make the kinds of investments that could enhance productivity and output over the long haul. Massive governmental demand for financing also raises the cost of funds (interest rates) for everyone. The increased capital costs are then passed along to consumers in the form of higher prices. As noted earlier, the fear or the reality of inflation undermines the value of financial assets, which will then discourage foreign investment and lower demand for a nation's currency.

• **Barriers to foreign investment.** Besides having the desire to buy the equity or debt offerings of a foreign country, investors must have the ability to do so. The deregulation of global securities markets—including liberalization of the amount of investments that can be made by foreigners—is one of the key trends of the 1990s. Yet despite progress, significant obstacles to foreign investment remain, especially in many of the smaller or emerging markets that, until recently, have not felt the need or desire for large influxes of foreign capital to finance internal growth. Cultural and political considerations may also play a role in limiting the desire for outside financing. To the extent that a nation constricts the amount of foreign investment permitted in its securities markets, an artificial cap is placed on demand for that nation's currency, which will have the effect of limiting the currency's upside potential. One of the reasons that the government of South Korea, for example, has only gradually begun to lift restrictions on foreign investments in its equity markets is its concern that an unregulated inflow of portfolio investment would push up the value of the Korean won, therefore making its exports more expensive—and less competitive—in global markets. Yet another reason for restrictions on foreign portfolio investment is the belief that such capital flows are both fickle and not necessarily related to productivity enhancement, a concern more than borne out by developments in Mexico.

Both Cause and Effect

What makes the comprehension of currency fluctuation even more slippery is the fact that not only does a nation's economy affect its currency, but its currency affects its economy in a kind of circuitous chicken-or-the-egg conundrum. In 1994, for example, inflationary worries in the United States forced its bond prices lower, which, in turn, discouraged foreign investment in bonds. The diminished foreign investment pushed the dollar lower, resulting in even greater inflationary worries. The heightened inflationary expectations then further depressed bond prices, which in turn only reinforced the determination of foreigners to avoid U.S. credit. And on and on the cycle went until long-term Treasury securities had fallen by roughly 25 percent from October 1993 through September 1994, the worst four-quarter performance for the U.S. bond market since the 1920s. The currency markets were, in effect, functioning as a kind of inflationary vigilante force, pushing interest rates north and causing an eventual slowdown in the U.S. economy. (The slowdown in U.S. economic growth finally began to appear in the first half of 1995.) And not only does currency affect overall economic health, but a currency's exchange rate is more than occasionally manipulated by governments as a weapon to mask structural economic inadequacies or to level the playing field to correct alleged unfair international practices. A partial listing of the many ways a nation's currency can impact its economy includes the following:

• **International investment.** If a currency is seriously weak, cross-border capital flows will begin to ebb, robbing a country of the type of direct investment required to improve output and productivity, which cause its economy to grow and its living standards to increase. Americans considering an investment in Russia, for example, may be dissuaded by the weak ruble, which has plunged amid the hyperinflation of the post-Communist era. If an American investor buys a Russian asset and the dollar proceeds to rise relative to the ruble, when the American eventually repatriates the investment, the number of dollars received will be proportionately smaller, cutting into any profit or perhaps even turning a profit into a loss. The crisis in the Mexican peso was made all the more serious because of its implications for a similar exit of foreign capital from that country. The 50 percent fall in the peso against the American currency beginning in December 1994 wiped out billions of dollars of gains by American investors, clearly sating the appetite for further Mexican adventures. To a significant extent, weak currencies are both a cause and an effect of economic underperformance because of the disincentives a weak currency creates for direct and portfolio foreign investment.

• **Balance of trade.** Nowhere is the paradox of currency more obvious than in the area of international trade. For the reasons just noted, a weak currency tends to hurt a nation's exports in the long run by discouraging direct foreign investment, thus starving a country of the kinds of productivity-enhancing capital needed to make its products competitive in a global marketplace. But over the short term, a weak currency can actually enhance a country's balance of trade by making exports cheaper (and therefore more competitive) abroad while making imports more expensive at home. Because popular pressure often bends political will to its ways, governments with chronic trade deficits usually seek to solve the problem by fostering a gradually declining currency. The United States, which has run trade shortfalls for over 20 years, is a fine example of political pressure forcing government officials to devalue its currency. Owing to the burgeoning trade deficits with Japan, the Reagan, Bush, and Clinton administrations each acquiesced to an unofficial "weak-dollar" policy, in which the United States allowed the dollar to slip ever lower against the yen. From 1984 through May 1995, the dollar fell from 250 yen to just 82 yen, making U.S. exports progressively cheaper in Japan while making Japanese imports in the United States increasingly expensive. The weak-dollar policy was used as a political weapon by U.S. officials to force Japan to open its markets to American goods and services. (Ironically, the strong yen was a contributing factor to a severe Japanese recession, which had the completely unintended effect of actually limiting internal Japanese demand for U.S. products, quite apart from any price attractiveness.) While the long-term wisdom of a weak-currency policy can be debated, there is evidence that a falling currency can mitigate the effects of a weak-trade position. Since the mid-1970s, the size of the U.S. trade deficit, expressed as a percent of the GDP, has loosely tracked the exchange value of its currency (see Figure 2.2).

· **Inflation.**   As discussed earlier, a weak currency will tend to exacerbate inflationary fears, whereas a strong currency can offset cost pressures otherwise building within an economy. If the U.S. dollar were to fall 10 percent against a trade-weighted basket of currencies, for example, the cost of imported goods and services in the United States would rise by 10 percent, assuming foreign companies did not simply absorb their lower revenues by cutting profit margins. And because Americans spend roughly 10 percent of their incomes on foreign goods, a 10 percent fall in the dollar would translate into about a 1 percent rise in the

Figure 2.2.   Currency and Trade
Trade-weighted value of U.S. dollar (line graph, right scale). U.S. merchandise trade deficit, as percent of nominal GDP (bar graph, left scale).

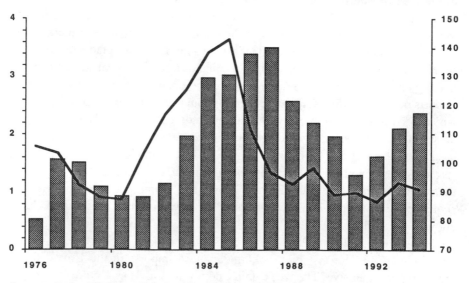

Sources: Federal Reserve; U.S. Bureau of the Census; Commerce Department.

consumer price index (10 percent × 10 percent = 1 percent). Higher costs for imported goods and services also provide cover for domestic firms to raise their own prices without compromising competitiveness. A weak currency further stimulates a domestic economy because the increased revenue from exports is frequently reinvested in domestic plants or equipment. Conversely, a strong currency tends to subdue inflation by making imported goods cheaper, curtailing overseas profits and limiting the ability of domestic corporations to raise prices without sacrificing cost advantage. The price of crude oil, for example, crashed at roughly nine dollars a barrel shortly after the U.S. Federal Reserve's dollar index peaked at over 162 in 1985. For all of 1985 and 1986—the years of the so-called "Super Dollar"—consumer-price inflation in the United States averaged just 2.45 percent, the lowest two-year level since the early 1960s.

• **Profits.** While a strong currency is an effective tool for controlling infla-tion, the downside is the depressant effect it can have on corporate profits. A strong currency hurts exports and limits the ability of domestic concerns to raise prices, thus compressing profit margins. Foreign earnings, limited as they are, are further reduced by repatriation losses after conversion from the local cur-rency. On the other hand, a weak currency stimulates exports by making them less expensive abroad and creates a financial windfall for firms when foreign revenues are repatriated into the home currency. The increased cost of imports that usually accompanies a weak currency also permits companies to raise prices without losing business to foreign competitors, thereby expanding profit mar-gins. The performance of large-capitalization U.S. stocks—stocks from compa-nies that tend to do a disproportionately large amount of business overseas and, therefore, profit from a weak dollar—underscores this relationship. Large-capitalization (large-cap) stocks tend to outperform their small-cap cousins in a nearly exact inverse relationship to the strength of the U.S. dollar. In other words, large-cap American equities tend to beat the performance of small-cap stocks during periods when the U.S. dollar is falling and to underperform small-caps when the dollar rises.

Central Bank Interventions

Most of the world's major currencies are known as "free-float" or "managed-float" currencies, meaning either that governments do not fix exchange rates or that, if they do, the rates are within broad target ranges. Only if a currency ex-ceeds those ranges do governments usually step in, either buying or selling their currency to force it within the desired range. But even if a currency is allowed to float more or less freely on world exchanges, governments can still affect the value of their currency in several ways:

- Political leaders wanting to push their currency lower (to stimulate exports, for example) could direct their central bank to sell its own currency and/or buy the currency of the nation with whom a trade imbalance exists.

- A government, again acting through its central bank, could keep interest rates low relative to another country or countries, fostering a negative flow of funds between financial assets, again with the effect of lowering demand—and, therefore, the price—for its currency.

- A government could strongly imply that it will not intervene to support its currency in the event of a decline, giving traders carte blanche to take the currency wherever markets want to take it without fear of being trapped by a central bank intervention.

The ramifications of each of these actions could be intensified if they are coordinated with actions from the governments or central banks of other nations. In 1985, for example, when the U.S. dollar reached record high levels against most major currencies, it became in the national interest for the United States to want the dollar lower (to improve exports) and for U.S. trading partners to want their own currencies higher (to lower the inflationary implications of expensive U.S. imports). What followed was the so-called "Plaza Accord" (named after the New York City hotel where the agreement was reached) in which finance ministers of several industrialized economies agreed to work in concert to push the dollar lower.

It is highly unusual, however, for central banks to foster a currency intervention that is both effective and long term. Intervening with enough power to hold in check an avalanche of free-market money determined to take an asset to its natural level requires not only the will but also considerable financial means. The cost of extended interventions, in fact, can actually offset most of the gains achieved. A coordinated central-bank intervention might involve as much as $50 billion but, even at that amount, would represent only a tiny fraction of the more than $1 trillion sloshing around the world's foreign-exchange markets on any given day. It is even more unusual for the legislative branch of governments to intervene with favorable fiscal, trade, or loan programs intended to improve the currency position of another nation. Legislative bodies, being closely attuned to popular will, generally oppose expensive foreign-policy bailouts. The issue of global economics is usually entirely too abstract to elicit anything other than a yawn and simultaneous determination to hold close to the fiscal purse strings.

The Mexican currency crisis of 1994 and 1995 is a clear example of popular resistance to expensive interventions. Because of a massive rupture in its current-account position, the Mexican government was forced to devalue the peso by 31 percent in December 1994. Market forces proceeded to take the currency another 20 percent lower over subsequent months. The devaluation wiped out billions of dollars in foreign investment in Mexico, threatened to push the Mexican economy into recession (disturbing a growing export market for U.S. goods), and undermined confidence in the concept of global investing in general and emerging markets in particular. President Clinton first proposed a $40 billion program of loan guarantees, a plan that was endorsed by former U.S. presidents Ford, Carter, and Bush; six former secretaries of state; and a bipartisan group of leaders from the U.S. Congress. Despite the high-powered endorsements, however, Mr. Clinton was forced to withdraw the proposal when support among the American people evaporated as the costs became known. In its place, Clinton advanced a scaled-back $20 billion line of credit, a plan that he could carry out without Congressional approval.

Because popular sentiment almost always opposes spending money on any type of foreign-currency rescue mission, nations will generally act in their own best economic and political interest. If those interests happen to coincide with those of another nation (as was the case of the Plaza Accord), then coordinated and effective action may be taken. The disparate economies and political priorities of nations, however, argue against frequent or extended periods of synchronous national interest. Investors looking for help from the world's monetary and fiscal authorities, therefore, should expect little more than brief interventions when extreme conditions develop, with the maximum positive benefit being the stability created when currency speculators are temporarily sent to the sidelines for fear of being trapped by the actions of a central bank. Any hard-earned stability in the currency, however positive, will generally allow only for the longer-term trend to reemerge. In the final analysis, currency-exchange rates will be set in global markets by global investors, not governments or central banks.

Living with the Problem

Given that currency fluctuations are a reality that can have potentially significant effects on the value of foreign holdings, you are correct to wonder how the currency issue should influence your approach to owning foreign stocks. Should you only buy into markets with strong currencies relative to the dollar? Should you attempt to time the movement of the currency to coincide with the holding period of your investment? Should you hedge your financial asset in the currency options or futures markets, thereby offsetting any losses in your foreign stock portfolio caused by a strong dollar? Or should you ignore the problem completely and take the same kind of long-term view of currency moves that you might take to the underlying equity market?

The answers to these questions will vary from investor to investor, but there are two ways that investors have often tried to deal with the currency problem:

- **Short-term timing.**   Attempting to time an international equity investment would involve divining both when the foreign stock market itself and the currency of the foreign country are set to appreciate. This is not an enterprise suitable for most individual investors. In fact, trying to guess the short-term swings of a currency is at least as difficult as forecasting the near-term movements of equities, which is itself nearly impossible. Gurus who profess such prescience abound, but, in reality, if anyone could predict the short-term price swings of any asset, they clearly would have no incentive to tell you about it. (Some experts believe that the only reason to make short-term predictions is to create demand for the other side of the trade.) Jumping in and out of markets is usually a fool's game and will generally cause more harm than good for the overwhelming majority of players. It is not necessary to predict the short-term course of a market to succeed as an investor. Learn to ignore the short-term outlook for all markets, including currencies.

- **Hedging.**   The practice known as hedging involves the purchase or sale of one security for the purpose of offsetting risks taken in another. Usually the securities being hedged are in different markets, such as equity and currency exchanges. If you are concerned about the effects of currency fluctuation on your investments, you could buy a financial futures contract that would lock in the prevailing exchange rate at the time of your investment. A perfectly executed hedge would guarantee that the impact of any currency-related gain or loss upon your stock investment would be exactly offset by a corresponding gain or loss on your futures position. Investors who buy stocks directly on foreign exchanges or who buy "country" mutual funds that do not hedge might consider hedging to eliminate all or a portion of the currency risk. Keep in mind, however, that hedging can have drawbacks. First, because the U.S. dollar has fallen more than it has risen against many of the world's more important currencies, hedging would often have been counterproductive. Second, hedging can be expensive—transaction costs will usually eat up a few percentage points per year from your return, while the hedge itself will effectively incapacitate a portion of your investment by tying up funds. Finally, a viable futures market does not exist for some of the currencies that carry the most risk for U.S. investors. For these reasons, many of the mutual funds that invest internationally, including some that invest only in the securities of a single nation, either are unable to hedge or choose not to hedge any or a significant portion of their portfolios

Over the long haul, the best strategy for the average individual investor to follow in dealing with the reality of foreign-exchange fluctuations is to buy mutual funds that have a dollar-denominated track record that can be carefully scrutinized or simply to confine international investments to those countries that have had a strong currency. The country chapters list the historical return of a nation's currency relative to the dollar, the long-term return of the country's stock market in dollar terms, the names of mutual funds that invest exclusively in that country, and whether those funds hedge currency risk. Regardless of how you choose to treat the issue of currency fluctuations, however, understanding the dynamics behind those fluctuations is vitally important. The value of a nation's currency speaks volumes about the economic circumstances of the country itself. In fact, for most investors, the greatest benefit of a thorough understanding of currency movements can be found in the light it might shed on the underlying financial strength of the country in which they are contemplating an investment.

CHAPTER 3

Mutual Funds

For many investors, the most efficient way to access the growth from international stock markets is through mutual funds. Information in this chapter should give you the tools to make informed decisions about fund selection, as well as presenting the top-performing funds from the rapidly expanding international sector.

Mutual funds are pools of money from investors seeking the same objective through the same market or markets. This type of money management offers investors the following important advantages over buying individual foreign securities:

• **Diversification.** Most mutual funds hold at least 100 different issues, often from several markets across varying industry and capitalization sectors. Such diversification is beyond the means of all but the wealthiest of individual investors. Assuming a position of just $3,000 per security, owning 100 stocks would require a total investment of $300,000, or more than 27 times the average portfolio size indicated by a recent New York Stock Exchange (NYSE) share-ownership study. Diversification, of course, is always important because it lowers overall risk; but it is even more vital in the highly combustible environments that characterize non-U.S. stock markets.

• **Professional management.** If ever there was a case to be made for the importance of professional, hands-on selection, it would be in the area of foreign-stock picking. Evaluating investment opportunities overseas requires an in-depth knowledge of vastly diverse accounting and business principles, economies, markets, cultures, and politics. It would be difficult for the average investor to ep up with the huge quantities of information required to make consistently oit individual stock picks in foreign markets.

- **Efficiency.** Even if an American investor had the requisite time and expertise to play the foreign-stock game on his or her own, many foreign bourses make it virtually impossible to do so in anything resembling an economically justifiable way. A few large U.S. brokerage houses now allow customers to buy and sell individual stocks and bonds on foreign markets, but high commissions and restrictions on non-institutional ownership of foreign securities will often render such participation impractical. Some non-American markets give mutual funds access to securities otherwise off limits to foreign investors, and brokerage firms usually give large institutional investors, such as mutual funds, price breaks on commissions, which can make the buying and selling of foreign securities vastly more profitable.

- **Accountability.** Mutual funds have readily available track records that can be examined by individual investors. If a fund manager has a poor record relative to an applicable market benchmark or to other managers working in the same area, investors are free to simply avoid the fund. There is no place an inept manager can hide from a potential customer armed with the kind of information found on a timely basis in virtually every corner of the American financial press.

What's in a Name?

Americans shopping for funds that invest in non-U.S. markets will find the shelves generously supplied. There are over 300 international mutual funds; of those, roughly half are known as *foreign* stock funds, meaning that virtually all fund assets are placed into non-U.S. markets. Another quarter are *world* or *global* funds, which invest in foreign markets but also may place a significant percentage of assets in the U.S. market. The remaining quarter are *single-country* or *regional* funds, which invest only in a designated nation or area of the globe, such as Singapore or Asia. To complicate matters, a handful of newcomers call themselves *emerging market* funds, which refers to investments in countries whose per capita gross domestic product (GDP) is less than roughly $8,000. (As of 1995, per capita GDP in the United States was nearly $24,000.) Clearly, an overlap in terms is possible between emerging and regional or country funds, because many countries and sometimes all the nations of an entire region may qualify under that definition of *emerging market*. For purposes of organization, only foreign and regional funds are covered in this chapter; single-country funds are listed in the specific chapter dealing with the country in which the particular fund invests. (So-called global funds are not covered in this book—such funds put a significant portion of assets in the U.S. market, placing them outside the province of non-U.S. investing.)

Several criteria were applied to the process of selecting the top foreign and regional funds. Over the long haul, understanding and applying the following criteria might be at least as important as buying any of the specific funds listed because fund rankings will change as new holding periods are measured.

• **Low cost.**   All mutual funds pass along to investors the cost of doing business. These costs include legal and administrative overhead; transaction expenses, such as brokerage commissions on the securities bought and sold; research department salaries and travel; shareholder services; and the fee charged by the portfolio manager. According to Morningstar, Inc., a Chicago-based mutual-fund-tracking company, the average expense ratio for all categories of international funds is roughly 1.8 percent per year. These charges, of course, are deducted directly from fund earnings and, therefore, lower the total return to investors.

It may seem like a small matter, but a mutual fund's annual expense ratio can make a huge impact on your total return over the long haul; for example, assuming a $20,000 initial investment into each of two funds earning 15 percent per year before expenses, a fund with a 2.5 percent annual expense ratio would return $45,000 less after 20 years than would a fund with just 1.5 percent in average annual costs.

It is important to recognize that the expense ratios for international funds will tend to be somewhat higher than those of domestic funds. International funds have increased costs associated with research and management, as well as generally higher transaction expenses related to doing business on foreign exchanges. Still, it is vitally important to shop carefully for funds that make a priority of keeping expenses down. Only funds with annual expense ratios below 1.75 percent are listed among the top funds in this chapter.

• **No sales load.**   All of the funds listed in this chapter are available without front- or back-end load, meaning that the funds can be bought and sold without sales charges. While the performance of the fund's portfolio is in no way related to its marketing strategy (managers are not compensated by sales fees), the amount of any charge can significantly impact the return on your investment: Suppose you put $20,000 into an international mutual fund with a front-end sales charge of 4.75 percent. That means that $950 would be siphoned off and given to the broker who sold you the fund, with only the remaining $19,050 of your original investment actually going to work. Over time, the impact of starting with a smaller initial investment would be dramatic. Assuming a 12 percent annual return on your purchase of $20,000, the 4.75 percent "one-time" sales charge of $950 would actually cost you $28,461 over 30 years, compared to what you would have made had the fund not charged a load. The drastically lower long-term return results from the diminished benefits of compounding from the smaller base investment. Realizing the true cost of front-end loads is your best defense against succumbing to brokers pitching load funds.

• **No 12b-1 fee.** Technically included in the expense ratio of a fund, a 12b-1 fee (named after the Securities and Exchange Commission directive that gave it legal sanction) is a charge levied against earnings to compensate funds for the cost of marketing. The majority of funds now charge a 12b-1 fee, although the size of the fee varies from as little as 0.25 percent to over 1 percent per year. The most onerous of the fees will be found among funds that impose a contingent deferred sales charge, or back-end load. A back-end load is a sales fee imposed on liquidations of fund assets held for less than a prescribed amount of time, usually five years or less. Since at least some buyers of back-end load products will hold the funds long enough to entirely sidestep the load, funds need some means of raising money to pay the brokers who sell the product to clients. In these cases, the 12b-1 functions as a kind of hidden commission that goes on charging every year. Some no-load funds also impose a 12b-1 fee, although the amount is usually small. None of the funds listed in this chapter impose a 12b-1 fee.

• **Limited downside volatility.** Losing money is always difficult to swallow, even if an investment is performing well over the long haul. While any investment in stocks or bonds will have down months and down years, it is possible through careful selection to pick managers who have been able to at least dampen the inevitable cyclical losses through some combination of deft stock picking or nicely timed asset allocation, either to cash entirely or to markets that might be somewhat healthier. As noted in Chapter 1, the traditional yardstick of volatility is a mathematical equation known as standard deviation, which measures the average of how far each data point in a series strays from the mean. Funds with annual returns that vary widely from year to year will have high standard deviations and, by implication, the greatest volatility. And to the extent that volatility is often equated with risk, a high standard deviation is usually viewed as a sign of vulnerability to losses. But since standard deviation makes no distinction between upside volatility (which is good) and downside volatility (which is bad), it often fails to tell investors what they want to know about potential losses.

The best way to measure risk is to add the number of losses an investment experiences over time, and then to divide that sum by the number of years being measured, for example, If a fund lost money twice in the past 10 years and the aggregate losses of those 10 years was 15 percent, the fund would have an average annualized loss of 1.5 percent (15 percent / 10 = 1.5 percent). By comparing that figure to other funds in the same category or to an applicable market benchmark, prospective investors can get a better feel for the ability of an investment or manager to sidestep risk. All of the funds listed in this chapter have average annualized losses below that of the relevant market index.

• **Superior performance.**   Simply reducing downside volatility, of course, is not an end in itself. If all an investor wanted was to be free from risk, that objective could easily be accomplished by hiding in the safety of U.S. Treasury bills or bank certificates of deposit. Reducing downside risk acquires value only when it is accompanied by superior performance. Each of the top funds listed in this chapter has outperformed an applicable market benchmark—the Morgan Stanley Capital International (MSCI) Europe, Australia, Far East (EAFE) index—over the past 10 years. The outperformance of the EAFE is both a theoretical and a practical measure of skill and value for foreign-stock funds; a manager unable to outperform the EAFE not only is returning less than a theoretical average, but also is earning below what an investor could get by purchasing the unmanaged EAFE directly through the Vanguard no-load mutual fund group. (Unmanaged or index international funds will be discussed later in this chapter.)

Open-End and Closed-End Funds

Before listing the top-performing funds, a further refinement of the data is required. Regardless of investment objective, mutual funds of all shapes and sizes are classified as either open-end or closed-end. *Open-end funds* are those that issue new shares as additional investor money comes in, usually resulting in the size or net assets of the fund increasing over time. Even after the initial offering period, open-end investments and liquidations are made through the fund itself, with all buys and sells occurring at the net asset value (NAV) of the fund. (A fund's NAV is the aggregate dollar value of all its holdings divided by the number of shares outstanding.) *Closed-end funds* fix the number of shares at the initial offering, after which prospective investors must buy from existing shareholders wanting to sell. Because the number of shares of a closed-end fund is predetermined, any change in the amount of money the fund must manage will be solely the result of the performance of the portfolio itself.

Advantages and Disadvantages

There are distinct advantages and disadvantages to each type of fund, and investors should be aware of each before plunging ahead. The primary benefit to owning an open-end fund is the guaranteed ability to buy or sell shares at the fund's NAV; for example, if you wanted to buy 2,000 shares of no-load, open-end Fund XYZ, you would be able to do so at the fund's exact NAV. If you then decided to sell your 2,000 shares of Fund XYZ, you would again be assured of receiving the full value of XYZ's assets, prorated to your percentage of ownership.

Closed-end funds are an entirely different animal. Because the size of the fund is limited by the terms of its initial offering, shares must be exchanged between prospective buyers and sellers in a secondary market such as the NYSE. The price a seller might get is a reflection not only of how well the fund's investments are faring, but also of the relative balance of supply and demand for fund shares themselves—if the number, or dedication, of buyers for closed-end Fund ABC exceeds the number of sellers, ABC's share price could increase even if the NAV of the fund were to fall. Suppose, for example, that closed-end Fund ABC invests in Malaysian stocks. And suppose that over a one-month period the Malaysian market is flat and that ABC's portfolio manager equals the overall market's performance, meaning that the NAV of ABC remains unchanged. If, however, the aggregate of investment opinion regarding the Malaysian market or of Fund ABC's portfolio-management skills were to decline over that month, the demand for ABC shares would probably fall, resulting in a lower per-share price.

Unlike their open-end cousins, then, closed-end funds do not necessarily trade at their NAV. In fact, nearly all closed-end funds usually sell at a premium to or a discount from their NAV. The amount of the premium or discount varies from fund to fund, depending on the outlook for whatever market a particular fund invests in and on the consensus of global opinion about the ability of the fund's manager to exploit opportunities in that market. It is not unusual, however, for the same closed-end fund with the same portfolio manager to cycle from a 20 percent premium to a 20 percent discount to NAV over the course of just a few years.

Demand for Closed-End Shares

Since closed-end shares rarely trade at their precise NAV, swings in the discount/premium factor of a fund can seriously complicate investment decisions. There are four general scenarios that result from changes in investor demand for closed-end shares:

1. Enhance a capital gain. When investor demand for closed-end shares increases at the same time the stocks in the portfolio are going up, owners enjoy a financial windfall; for example, if Fund ABC's NAV increases by 20 percent while its NAV premium widens from 20 percent to 25 percent, existing shareholders would make a 25 percent gain.

	From	To	Change
Net asset value	$10	$12	+20%
Discount (–) / Premium (+)	+20%	+25%	+5%
Total: Per share price	$12	$15	+25%

2. Limit a capital gain. The same tailwinds that enhanced the size of your gain can just as quickly change into headwinds that slow you down. If your fund's NAV increases by 20 percent but its premium to NAV falls from 20 percent to just 5 percent over the same period, the size of your net gain would be cut by three quarters.

	From	To	Change
Net asset value	$10	$12	+20%
Discount (–) / Premium (+)	+20%	+5%	–15%
Total: Per share price	$12	$12.60	+5%

3. Increase a capital loss. If you own a closed-end fund, having your NAV fall while the discount expands is your worst nightmare. Unfortunately, the problem of discount/premium slippage exacerbating losses in underlying NAVs is a fairly common bear-market trait. When prices in a given market begin to fall suddenly and quickly, the NAV of a fund investing in that market will almost always decline as well. And as the losses mount, investor sentiment toward the overall market and the fund itself usually becomes negative, lowering overall demand and pushing the discount/premium position lower. Such double whammies can be especially lethal in single-country funds, in which underlying markets are themselves more volatile and investor sentiment especially sensitive to sudden and precipitous swings.

	From	To	Change
Net asset value	$10	$8	–20%
Discount (–) / Premium (+)	+20%	–20%	–40%
Total: Per share price	$12	$6.40	–47%

4. Mitigate a capital loss.   Occasionally, a decline in the NAV of a closed-end fund will be cushioned by a simultaneous improvement in its discount/premium position. This is most likely to occur as markets stabilize, allowing for the NAV to level off as investor sentiment picks up. If a fund's NAV falls while its discount/premium position improves, the actual paper loss experienced by shareholders would be reduced.

	From	**To**	**Change**
Net asset value	$10	$8	–20%
Discount (–) / Premium (+)	–20%	–10%	+10%
Total: Per share price	$8	$7.20	–10%

Although changes in a closed-end fund's discount or premium can obviously spell at least short-term disaster for investors, closed-end funds also have certain benefits. Besides the fact that discount/premium swings can potentially work to your advantage, the limitation on the number of shares outstanding makes it easier for the closed-end manager to achieve superior results. This is especially important for funds investing in only the securities of a single country, where the number of stocks available to foreigners is often limited and the liquidity of the stocks that are available is perhaps less than ideal. For that reason, most single-country funds are of the closed-end variety.

Unlike open-end fund managers, who frequently find themselves inundated with additional capital to invest precisely as prices are moving higher and the number of available values shrinking, closed-end fund managers do not need to choose between chasing inflated share prices or earning paltry returns in the cash market. Empirical data on the relationship of fund size and performance is mixed, but it should be almost intuitive that, to the extent that managers are required to make fewer correct decisions and avoid diluting returns in a cash equivalent, results should be enhanced, all other factors being equal.

Additional Costs

There is one last item to consider in choosing between open- and closed-end funds. Because open-end funds can be purchased or liquidated directly from the fund itself, there are no additional transaction costs, assuming the fund is a no-load. The open-end, no-load fund investor can complete a round-trip trade (a buy and a sell) without incurring *any* transaction costs. Closed-end funds, however, trade on stock exchanges and, thus, can only be purchased through the services of a broker performing in the usual role of matching buyers and sellers. Brokers, of course, do not work for free, so you will find yourself paying commissions ranging from 1 percent to 3 percent on each side of the trade, depending on the size of your transaction and the type of broker you use. If you are not relying on a full-service broker's advice, it obviously makes no sense to execute your trade at the full-service broker's higher rates. Buy your closed-end funds through whichever discount broker gives you the desired balance between service and low cost.

When to Buy Closed-End Funds

Depending on when you get in or out, changes in a closed-end fund's price relative to its NAV can be either a blessing or a curse. If you hold a fund long enough, of course, it will almost certainly be both. In terms of knowing when to buy a closed-end fund, it is generally not a good idea to invest when the fund is selling toward the high-end of its historical discount/premium cycle. In other words, if a closed-end fund has sold for as low as a 25 percent discount to NAV and as high as a 25 percent premium to its NAV, it might be foolhardy to chase after the fund when it is selling at or near a 25 percent premium, regardless of your outlook for the market in which the fund invests. Remember that discount/premium cycles are largely a reflection of sentiment and that sentiment is usually a contrary indicator, meaning that the risk of a severe market downturn is often greatest when investors are most bullish. (Sentiment is a contrary indicator because, when investors are optimistic, they presumably have already purchased their shares, pushing prices higher while depleting future buying power. Conversely, overwhelmingly bearish sentiment indicates large cash reserves and, thus, the potential for new buying power.)

Because changes in investor sentiment can make already choppy markets still choppier, it is often prudent for individual investors not to get their foreign-stock exposure through closed-end funds, *if they can avoid it*. In other words, the overwhelming majority of investors might want to disregard closed-end funds from consideration for purchase unless no open-end funds exist to take advantage of a given investment opportunity. Because numerous open-end funds are available in the foreign- and regional-market sectors, only at the country-fund level does it become necessary to buy closed-end funds. For each of the closed-end funds listed in the country chapters, you will find data indicating its historic discount/premium range. Before buying these or any other closed-end funds, however, call the fund or consult a financial publication to determine the fund's most recent discount or premium.

There is no shortage of readily available sources to supply you with the latest information about mutual funds, including the most recent 5- and 10-year track records, expense ratios, 12b-1 fees, sales charges, and possible changes in fund management and investment strategy. Financial publications such as *The Wall Street Journal, Barron's, Money,* and *Forbes* publish updates on the entire universe of funds shortly after the end of each fiscal quarter (in January, April, July, and October). For a more detailed analysis, Morningstar, Inc., a Chicago-based financial-research company, offers publications on open- and closed-end funds, plus a service for investors who are interested only in no-load open-end funds. Figure 3.1 shows a sample of a Morningstar Mutual Funds fact sheet. (For subscription information and a full listing of its services, call Morningstar at 800-876-5005.)

The Top-Performing Foreign Funds

The four top-performing mutual funds from the foreign-sector universe are T. Rowe Price International Stock, Vanguard International Growth, Vanguard Trustees' Equity International, and Scudder International. A $10,000 investment divided evenly among the four funds on January 1, 1985, would have grown to $48,338 by the end of 1994, compared to less than $41,000 for the EAFE and "just" $38,332 for Standard & Poors (S&P) Composite Index of 500 Stocks. As noted earlier, these funds were chosen on the basis of superior long-term results, below-average downside volatility, open-end structure, and consumer friendliness. Figures 3.2, 3.3, 3.4, and 3.5 illustrate how $10,000 grew in each fund individually. The bars indicate the year-end value. All data refers to the 10-year period 1985 through 1994.

Figure 3.1. *Morningstar Mutual Funds* Sample Page

Volume 24, Issue Number 6, March 3, 1995. Reprinted with permission.

T. Rowe Price New Asia

				Ticker	Load	NAV	Yield	SEC Yield	Assets	Objective
				PRASX	None	$7.19	0.9%	N/A	$1768.7 mil	Pacific Stock

T. Rowe Price New Asia Fund seeks capital appreciation.

The fund invests primarily in the common stocks of large- and small-capitalization companies domiciled, or with primary operations, in Asia and the Pacific Basin (excluding Japan). At least 65% of its assets will be invested in the equity securities of Asian companies, excluding Japan. The fund may invest in countries such as China, Sri Lanka, Laos, Vietnam, or Cambodia, as their markets become more accessible. The fund may purchase up to 35% of its assets in non-U.S.-dollar-denominated high-grade debt securities.

Portfolio Manager(s)

Martin G. Wade. Since 9-90. MA'65 Cambridge U. Wade is president and chief investment officer of Rowe Price-Fleming International, his employer since 1979. Previously, he spent 11 years in various positions with the Robert Fleming Group and the Jardine Fleming Group.

Performance 01-31-95

	1st Qtr	2nd Qtr	3rd Qtr	4th Qtr	Total
1990	...	...	...	1.60	1.60 *
1991	19.05	-2.08	-1.96	4.40	19.32
1992	3.55	10.95	-6.19	3.20	11.24
1993	7.49	7.78	15.25	33.88	78.76
1994	-20.14	0.79	13.33	-11.36	-19.15

Trailing	Total Return %	+/- S&P 500	+/- MSCI FE ex-Jpn	% Rank All Obj	Growth of $10,000
3 Mo	-20.04	-20.37	-2.11	99 69	7,996
6 Mo	-14.25	-18.41	-2.62	98 47	8,575
1 Yr	-23.72	-24.24	-8.12	99 74	7,628
3 Yr Avg	11.70	3.85	-1.58	5 27	13,935
5 Yr Avg	...	...	...	...	...
10 Yr Avg	...	...	...	...	...
15 Yr Avg	...	...	...	...	...

Most Similar Funds in MMF

Dean Witter Pacific Growth	Strong Fit
Fidelity Emerging Markets	Fair Fit
Newport Tiger	Fair Fit

Historical Profile

Return	High
Risk	High
Rating	★★★★ Above Avg

Risk Analysis

Time Period	Load-Adj Return %	Risk %Rank All Obj	Morningstar Return Risk	Morningstar Risk-Adj Rating
1 Yr	-23.72			
3 Yr	11.70	97 59	2.48 [3] 1.63	★★★★
5 Yr	...			
Incept	13.73		4.6 ★ s	

Average Historical Rating   (17 months)

[1] 1=low, 100=high [2] 1.00 = Equity Avg [3] 0.00 = 90-day T-bill return

Portfolio Analysis 10-31-94

Total Stocks: 153
Total Fixed-Income: 8

	Share Chg (04-94) 000	Amount 000		Value $000	% Net Assets
	532	5614	United Overseas Bank	61547	2.67
	905	5146	Bangkok Bank	55743	2.42
	1928	6683	Swire Pacific Cl A	51025	2.22
	15092	30000	Renong	46967	2.04
	3139	11000	Technology Resources	42838	1.86
	11769	11769	Telecom New Zealand	41000	1.78
	628	7574	United Engineers	40909	1.78

History

	1984	1985	1986	1987	1988	1989	1990	1991	1992	1993	1994	01-95
							92%	92%	93%	89%	92%	93%
NAV	...	...	...	...	...	...	5.04	5.91	6.34	11.10	8.01	7.19
Total Return %	...	...	...	...	...	...	1.60 *	19.32	11.24	78.76	-19.15	-10.24
+/- S&P 500	...	...	...	...	...	...	-7.36 *	-11.17	3.62	68.70	-20.47	-12.83
+/- MSCI FE ex-Jpn	...	...	...	...	...	...		6.21	5.05	-7.26	-10.25	0.60
Income Return %	...	...	...	...	...	...	0.80	2.05	1.66	0.37	0.86	0.00
Capital Return %	...	...	...	...	...	...	0.80	17.26	9.58	78.39	-20.01	-10.24
Total Rtn %Rank All	...	...	...	...	...	...		45	17	1	99	99
Total Rtn %Rank Obj	...	...	...	...	...	...		16	13	22	77	60
Income $	...	...	...	...	...	...	0.04	0.10	0.10	0.04	0.07	0.00
Capital Gains $	...	...	...	...	...	...	0.00	0.00	0.13	0.19	0.89	0.00
Expense Ratio %	...	...	...	...	...	...	1.75	1.75	1.51	1.29	1.22	...
Income Ratio %	...	...	...	...	...	...	2.10	1.75	1.64	1.02	0.85	...
Turnover Rate %	...	...	...	...	...	...		49	36	40	63	...
Net Assets ($mil)	...	...	...	...	...	...	80.0	102.9	314.5	2234.4	1987.6	1768.7

Objective
Pacific Stock

Investment Style History
Equity
Average Stock %

Growth of $10,000
Investment Value ($000)
Strength Relative to S&P 500

▼ Manager Change
▽ Partial Manager Change
▲ Avg Unknown After
◄ Avg Unknown Before

Performance Quartile (Within Objective)

Tax Analysis	Tax-Adj Return %	% Pretax Return
3 Yr Avg	9.92	84.8
5 Yr Avg	--	--
10 Yr Avg	--	--
Potential Capital Gain Exposure	-17% of assets	

Other Measures		Standard Index S&P 500	Best Fit Index M-SPacxJp
Standard Deviation	2?.64	Alpha	5.4	-1.3
Mean	12.41	Beta	1.05	0.97
Sharpe Ratio	0.45	R-Squared	15	93

Analysis by Daniel O'Keefe 02-17-95

Diversification didn't soften the blow to T. Rowe Price New Asia Fund.

Investors might have expected this fund to hold up better than it did in 1994's bear market. After all, the fund has decent-size stakes in Australia and New Zealand, both of which posted relatively strong performances in 1994. (Almost all the fund's ex-Japan peers shy away from these developed markets.) What's more, management astutely cut back considerably on the fund's Hong Kong and Malaysian stakes during 1993, and they were two of the region's biggest losers in 1994. Yet the fund still slid more than many of its Pacific ex-Japan peers--even those with significantly more exposure to poor-performing Hong Kong and Malaysia.

That's because the fund invests far more in small- and mid-cap stocks than do many of its competitors. Blue-chip standbys such as Hang Seng Bank and Hong Kong Telecommunications don't show up in this fund's top

holdings; the fund's quest for double-digit earnings growth generally leads it to the stocks of much smaller companies. As its smaller companies took a big beating, especially in Hong Kong and Taiwan, the fund was lined up for especially grueling losses. Management-team member Chris Alderson, however, says the fund remains committed to its picks. With so many fast-growing small companies now selling for as little as five times earnings while paying out attractive yields, he thinks the market is bound to turn their way.

This is still a very attractive Pacific ex-Japan offering. Over the long term, it has been a top performer. Moreover, its emphasis on small caps and its investments in Australia and New Zealand set it apart from its Pacific ex-Japan peers. As with most all emerging-markets funds, though, shareholders must have a great tolerance for volatility. Quarterly losses of 20% or more are not unusual.

Address	100 E. Pratt Street	Minimum Purchase	$2500	Add: $100	IRA: $1000
	Baltimore, MD 21202	Min Auto Inv Plan	$50	Systematic Inv: $50
Telephone	800-638-5660 / 410-547-2308	• Date of Inception	03-28-90
Advisor	Rowe Price-Fleming International	**Expenses & Fees**
Subadvisor	None	Sales Fees	No-load
Distributor	T. Rowe Price Investment Services	Management Fee	0.50% flat fee +0.46%G
States Available	All plus GU,PR,VI	Actual Fees	Mgt: 0.85%	Dist: N/A
Report Grade	A+	Expense Projections	3Yr: $41	5Yr: $71	10Yr: $156
Income Distrib	Annually	Annual Brokerage Cost	0.75%

				40267	1.75
				39962	1.74
Thai Farmers Bank	1173	4562		37504	1.63
Hutchison Whampoa	2201	8650			
Western Mining	701	6020		36176	1.57
Gucco Group	2351	7659		35966	1.56
Golden Plus Holdings	3827	7411		35555	1.54
Carter Holt Harvey	1220	14661		33892	1.47
Aokam Perdana	954	4104		33874	1.47
Hysan Development	6432	12707			
Westmont	980	4613		32679	1.42
Fletcher Challenge (NZ)	908	11992		32330	1.40
Hopewell Holdings	8610	31248		32148	1.40
Siam Cement	-88	556		3092	1.39
Singapore Land	4877	4877		31384	1.36

Investment Style

Style: Value Blend Growth

Size: Large Med Small

	Stock Portfolio Avg	Rel MSCI EAFE	Rel Objective
Price/Earnings Ratio	25.9	0.71	0.80
Price/Book Ratio	3.0	1.16	1.02
Price/Cash Flow	21.4	1.37	1.13
5 Yr Earnings Gr %	18.2#	--	1.64
Return on Assets %	9.0#	1.93	1.11
Debt % Total Cap	24.4	0.72	0.98
Med Mkt Cap ($mil)	1990	0.17	0.44

figure is based on 50% or less of stocks

Country Exposure 12-31-94	% of Stocks		Sector Weightings	% of Stocks	Rel Obj
Malaysia	21		Utilities	1.9	0.31
Hong Kong	20		Energy	1.0	0.65
Singapore	15		Financials	39.9	1.56
Australia	12		Industrial Cyclicals	28.8	1.25
Thailand	11		Consumer Durables	5.9	0.44
Total number of countries:	12		Consumer Staples	0.7	0.22
Hedging Policy:	Occasional		Services	17.4	1.38
			Retail	1.5	0.31
			Health	0.0	0.01
			Technology	2.9	0.38

Special Securities	% of assets		Composition	% of assets 12-31-94	
○ Private/Illiquid Securities	0.0		Cash	4.9	Bonds	0.0
○ Structured Notes	0.0		Stocks	92.9	Other	2.2
● Emerging-Markets Secs	78.4				
● Options/Futures	Yes				

M⊙RNINGSTAR Mutual Funds

T. Rowe Price International Stock

Address: 100 East Pratt Street, Baltimore, MD 21202
Phones: (800) 638-5660 / (410) 547-2308
Compound average annual return: +18.0%
Average annualized loss: −1.31%
Largest one-year loss: −8.89%
Front-end load: No
Back-end load: No
Redemption fee: No
12b-1 fee: No
Expense ratio: 1.08%
Assets: $5.46 billion
Minimum initial investment: $2,500
Minimum IRA (Individual Retirement Account) purchase: $1,000

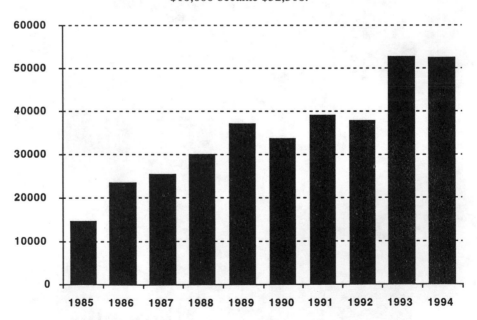

Figure 3.2.   T. Rowe Price International Stock
$10,000 became $52,318.

Vanguard International Growth

Address: Vanguard Financial Center, P.O. Box 2600, Valley Forge, PA 19482
Phones: (800) 662-7447 / (215) 669-1000
Compound average annual return: +17.16%
Average annualized loss: –1.78%
Largest one-year loss: –12.05%
Front-end load: No
Back-end load: No
Redemption fee: No
12b-1 fee: No
Expense ratio: 0.67%
Assets: $2.7 billion
Minimum initial investment: $3,000
Minimum IRA purchase: $500

Figure 3.3. Vanguard International Growth
$10,000 became $48,756.

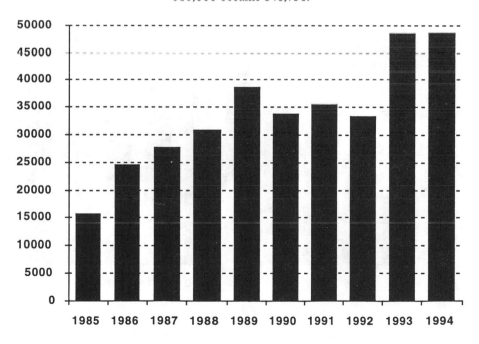

Vanguard/Trustees' Equity International

Address: Vanguard Financial Center, P.O. Box 2600, Valley Forge, PA 19482
Phones: (800) 662-7447 / (215) 669-1000
Compound average annual return: +16.84%
Average annualized loss: –2.10%
Largest one-year loss: –12.26%
Front-end load: No
Back-end load: No
Redemption fee: No
12b-1 fee: No
Expense ratio: 0.45%
Assets: $1.0 billion
Minimum initial investment: $10,000
Minimum IRA purchase: $500

Figure 3.4.   Vanguard/Trustees' Equity International
$10,000 became $47,439.

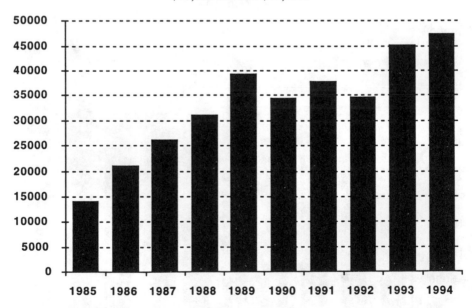

Scudder International

Address: 175 Federal Street, Boston, MA 02110
Phones: (800) 225-2470 / (617) 439-4640
Compound average annual return: +16.19%
Average annualized loss: −1.45%
Largest one-year loss: −8.92%
Front-end load: No
Back-end load: No
Redemption fee: No
12b-1 fee: No
Expense ratio: 1.17%
Assets: $2.3 billion
Minimum initial investment: $1,000
Minimum IRA purchase: $500

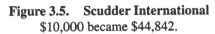

Figure 3.5.   Scudder International
$10,000 became $44,842.

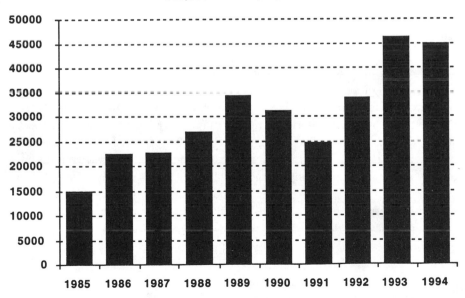

Regional Funds

There is yet another category of mutual funds, namely those that invest only in the equities of a specified region, such as Europe, Latin America, or the Pacific/ Oceania area, sometimes called the Pacific Rim. Because the idea of foreign investing in general and precisely targeted foreign investing in particular is a relatively recent phenomenon, there are few such funds (open- or closed-end) that have 10-year track records. Most regional funds, in fact, began operations later than 1990, giving them less than even a 5-year track record. Of the open-end regional funds that have been around for at least 10 years, none have been able to meet the selection criteria established earlier, namely outperformance of an applicable market benchmark (in this case, the regional subcomponent of the EAFE) over a trailing 10-year period. While this is likely to change over time as funds improve performance and acquire a meaningful history, as of now, investors should consider playing regional markets through the funds set up to mimic the appropriate subcomponent of the EAFE. These types of investments are known as index funds, because their construction is based entirely on that of a market index.

The Case for Index Funds

While each of the four funds profiled earlier in this chapter beat the return of the average foreign stock (as measured by the EAFE) by a wide margin, such outperformance is often more the exception than the rule. In the U.S. market, for example, a substantial majority of money managers are usually unable to beat a standard market benchmark such as the S&P 500, especially when long time periods are measured. The reasons for the consistently below-average returns have to do with the fact that, at any moment, securities prices already reflect consensus expectations. In order to outperform the average return, a manager will need to be more correct than the consensus, a difficult proposition that becomes ever more difficult over the long haul. Because the majority of managers are, by definition, average and because they must pay transaction costs to execute their strategies, the net effect is a median return approximating that of a broad-market index less expenses, which usually range from 1 to 2 percent per year. So-called index funds often outperform managed funds because they buy only those stocks comprising a given index (thus matching the average return) but have a vastly reduced expense ratio due to the "no-brainer" aspect of the fund. Since the transaction expenses for index funds are less, the return will often be more than that of a managed fund.

The case for indexing your foreign-stock purchases, while still persuasive, is not as strong as that for the U.S. market. Foreign bourses are generally less efficient than their American counterpart, meaning that consensus expectations have a greater average error, making it more likely that a highly skilled (and perhaps somewhat fortuitous) money manager could be more correct than the consensus on a regular basis. Also, because buying an index fund locks you into a predetermined country weighting, foreign-index investors run the risk of being forced to stay in an inhospitable market, even when the country might be mired in a long-term bear market. Since Japan's stock market, for example, represents roughly 45 percent of the aggregate value of the world's non-U.S. equity markets, the EAFE correctly assigns a 45 percent weighting to Japan. But given such a high weighting, if Japan is in a bear market (as it has been for most of the 1990s), even phenomenal returns from other markets, such as Hong Kong or Singapore, will usually not be enough to offset the weakness. Of course, the opposite could also be true; when the Japanese market rebounds, its huge relative weighting could be more than enough to offset declines in other markets.

The following is a listing of no-load, open-end funds that attempt to track the return of a predetermined foreign-market index.

Index: Morgan Stanley Capital International EAFE and Sub-EAFE

Fund(s)	Sponsor	Phones
International Equity Index Pacific (55%)	Vanguard	(800) 662-7447 (215) 669-1000
International Equity Index European (45%)	Vanguard	(800) 662-7447 (215)-669-1000

Each of the Vanguard funds is built on a component of the EAFE index. Investors wishing to replicate the entire EAFE would put 55 percent of their money into the Equity Index Pacific and 45 percent into the Equity Index European. In other words, given $10,000 to invest, placing $5,500 into the Equity Index Pacific fund and $4,500 into the Equity Index European portfolio would create holdings designed to track the MSCI EAFE. Investors wishing to buy only European stocks, of course, would invest only in the European fund, while those wanting only Asian exposure would purchase only the Pacific fund. The EAFE index itself is capitalization-weighted, with country portfolios carefully constructed to accurately reflect the sector and individual stock makeup of an overall market. Country weightings within EAFE are dominated by the established markets of Japan (45 percent), the United Kingdom (16 percent), and Germany and France (6 percent each). The well-known but smaller markets of Singapore, Malaysia, and Hong Kong combine to account for barely 6 percent of the EAFE's relative size. The Vanguard funds do not actually own all of the roughly 1,200 securities comprising the EAFE, but instead employ a sophisticated statistical sampling procedure designed to achieve the same return while avoiding the less liquid, smaller-cap segment that could add substantially to operational costs, thus defeating the purpose of an index fund. Since their inception in 1990, both EAFE subset funds have very nearly matched their respective EAFE proxies, less transaction costs of 0.32 percent per year. Vanguard does not hedge its funds for currency fluctuation (the heavy Japanese yen exposure has often led to a net foreign-exchange benefit for American investors) and imposes a 1 percent transaction fee to buy each fund. Despite the small charge, the Vanguard EAFE funds are still technically no-load because proceeds from the fees are added to the fund's NAV, thus aiding existing shareholders. The purpose of the fees is to offset the relatively high cost of brokerage on foreign bourses, thus putting new investors on a pay-as-you-go basis. Aside from new money, of course, there is negligible additional share turnover in an index fund because the makeup of the index itself changes relatively little over time.

Index: Morgan Stanley Select Emerging Markets Free Index

Fund(s)	Sponsor	Phones
International Equity Index Emerging Markets	Vanguard	(800) 662-7447
		(610) 669-1000

If you find the EAFE a bit too concentrated in Japanese and large-cap issues, this foreign index fund could give you more of the country diversification and small-market participation you might be after. The International Equity Index Emerging Markets portfolio attempts to mimic a bogy designed especially for Vanguard by MSCI. The index resembles MSCI's Emerging Markets Index, but it excludes stocks from those nations whose equity markets lack sufficient liquidity or that impose undue restrictions on foreign portfolio investment. As of May 1995, 66 percent of the fund's assets were deployed in such Pacific Rim bourses as Hong Kong (14.9 percent), Singapore (6.9 percent), Malaysia (21.6 percent) and Thailand (11.6 percent). The fund has no Japanese or United Kingdom exposure. Mexico, Brazil, and other Latin American exchanges account for about 25 percent of the fund's assets. In all, the fund held positions in 12 markets, including Greece, Portugal, and Turkey. A 2 percent portfolio charge to purchase the fund is added to the fund's NAV, as is a 1-percent charge on redemptions. Proceeds from the fees are added to the fund's NAV, benefiting existing shareholders. The fund does not hedge for foreign-exchange fluctuations.

Index: Schwab International Index

Fund(s)	Sponsor	Phone
Schwab International Index	Charles Schwab	(800) 526-8600

The Schwab International Index fund is a large-cap play on non-U.S. markets, which results in a heavy weighting in the developed bourses of Europe and Japan. The fund invests in more than 300 of the world's largest companies, making it somewhat comparable to the MSCI EAFE, though the index on which the fund is based does not attempt to precisely reflect overall world equity-market weightings. The Schwab International Index fund limits exposure in any one country to 35 percent of assets, meaning that its Japanese portion will underweight EAFE by at least 10 percent. The fund's low expense ratio will save investors roughly 1 percent per year over managed funds. Like the Vanguard funds, the Schwab International Index fund does not hedge its currency exposure.

Separate Accounts

No discussion of managed investments could be complete without mention of yet another form—the separate, or private, account. Separate accounts are similar to mutual funds in that they are managed by an investment advisor who is paid on a fee-only basis, thereby eliminating the potential for conflicts of interest. Like mutual funds, these accounts have the additional advantages of professional management and economy of scale, with institutional investors trading at brokerage rates vastly reduced from those available to individual investors. Unlike mutual funds, however, separate accounts are just that—accounts into which money is placed that is separate from monies invested by others, making each account private. Some separate accounts may also have individually designed portfolios if a particular investor has a special need not addressed by the advisor's general portfolios. For these reasons, the separate account has some attraction for many investors.

Along with the benefits of a separate account, however, come some drawbacks. Reporting requirements are generally less stringent for separate accounts than for mutual funds, meaning that an investor might feel less secure that the information being received from a separate account is comparable (derived from the same accounting standards and procedures) to that received from mutual funds. And because separate accounts are generally smaller, there is usually somewhat less operational efficiency, creating higher expense ratios than in most mutual funds. Perhaps most important for the average investor is the purely practical issue of minimum investment size. The overwhelming majority of separate accounts require minimum investments of from $1 million to as high as $10 million, effectively pricing them out of range for most individuals. When these factors are combined with track record relative to an applicable market benchmark, there are few investment advisors that offer separate accounts—especially foreign-based separate accounts—that would be affordable and desirable for a significant portion of the investing public.

One exception to the rule, however, is Brandes Investment Partners Inc., of San Diego, California. Over the years 1985 through 1994, Brandes International Equity accounts averaged a 22.21 percent compounded annual return, as compared to 16.70 percent for the EAFE. Equally impressive was Brandes' relative lack of downside volatility, outperforming the EAFE in both up and down quarters over that period. The minimum investment size for opening a Brandes account is $100,000, putting it within range of many individual investors. Figure 3.6 shows how a $100,000 investment in the average Brandes International Equity account in 1980 would have grown to more than $1.9 million by year-end 1994, versus $785,332 for the unmanaged EAFE.

The historical ability of the Brandes International Equity account to hold up better than even the large-cap EAFE index in down markets is an indication of Brandes' so-called value approach to stock selection, which seeks out companies that are cheap relative to earnings, cash flow, dividends, or book value. By avoiding those companies whose stock prices already reflect extreme optimism and institutional coverage, Brandes at least partially insulates its accounts from the frequent lurches that unfortunately are a characteristic of non-U.S. equity markets. In addition to its International Equity account, which is comprised only of foreign securities, Brandes offers a Global account (which holds at least some U.S. stocks) and a Balanced account, made up of stocks and bonds from domestic and foreign companies. Both the Global and Balanced accounts have also outperformed applicable benchmarks. (For more information, call Brandes at 800-237-7119.)

Figure 3.6.   Brandes Investment Partners Inc.

Return of average Brandes International Equity account (line graph) and MSCI EAFE (bar graph), in U.S. dollars. Assumes initial investment of $100,000 on December 31, 1979.

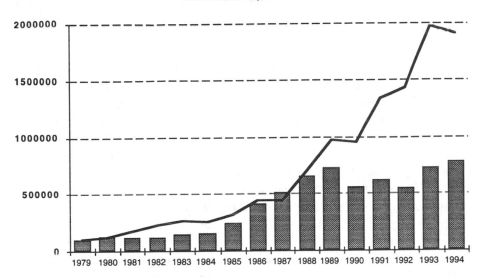

Source: Brandes Investment Partners, Inc.

Beware the Wrap Account

In their desire to participate in separate accounts managed by investment advisors, many financial consumers have fallen for the so-called "wrap" account that is offered by full-service stockbrokers. The wrap structure evolved as the brokerage industry came to realize that the more sophisticated end of its clientele was not always satisfied with the investment qualifications of its salespeople/brokers or with the built-in conflicts of interest they face. To mollify these concerns, brokers entered into partnership with a number of investment advisory firms on mutually beneficial terms: The broker brings the advisor new business in exchange for an ongoing piece of the action. The minimum investment size is often reduced to as low as $25,000 as part of the deal. (Such help you don't need!) Whereas the typical advisor fee might begin at 1 percent of assets under management and decline as the size of the portfolio increases, the brokerage wrap account usually hits the customer with a total fee of 3 percent each year, *triple* the usual charge. Even allowing for the fact that the 3 percent fee includes all commissions (the advisor-only fee structure of a separate account does not include commissions), the wrap fee will at best break even with the overall expenses of a private account and will usually run about 1 percent more each year. If, for example, an advisor earns an average of 12 percent annually on a client's portfolio, less a 1 percent management fee and another 1 percent for commissions, the client would earn a net 10 percent per year; if, however, that same advisor were managing a client's money through a wrap account with the customary 3 percent annual charge, the net return for the client would fall to just 9 percent (12% − 3% = 9%), or a full 1 percent per year less than under the non-wrap arrangement. While a 1 percent per year differential in return may not seem like much at first, consider the long-term effects. Given two $100,000 portfolios, each earning 12 percent per year before costs, the portfolio paying just 2 percent per year (a 1 percent advisory fee plus 1 percent transaction expenses) would have $221,163 more after 25 years than would the portfolio paying the net 3 percent annual charges of a brokerage wrap account. No matter how good a money manager may be, no referral is worth more than twice the original value of your entire investment. The weakness of the wrap structure is that it takes a good idea—matching investors with professional money managers who are free from conflicts of interest and who will work with a reasonable minimum amount—and weakens it by turning what should be a one-time finder's fee into an annual charge. Given the paramount importance of reducing overall costs to a successful long-term investment program, the wrap structure is usually too expensive to benefit most investors. For the overwhelming majority of individuals, mutual funds and the ADRs discussed in the following chapter are the most accessible and efficient ways to gain exposure to the growth in foreign economies.

CHAPTER 4

American Depositary Receipts

In spite of their potential advantages, mutual funds don't appeal to everyone. Some investors like to retain the ability to pick their own stocks, to decide when to buy and sell, and to allocate their funds among the various international markets based on their own outlooks and risk tolerance levels. Many investors also prefer to own individual stocks instead of the essentially blind pool of securities making up a mutual fund portfolio.

If you count yourself among this type of more independent investor, American depositary receipts (ADRs) may offer you the best way to get the foreign diversification you want and need. ADRs are certificates evidencing ownership of a foreign-based corporation. The certificates are denominated in U.S. dollars and trade as regular shares of stock on the NASDAQ (National Association of Securities Dealers Automated Quotation system), the NYSE (New York Stock Exchange), or the over-the-counter (OTC) market. An ADR has several advantages over buying shares of the same company on a foreign exchange. Because the shares are traded in the United States, nearly all domestic brokerage firms are able to execute your buy-and-sell orders at their regular commission rates. The minimum investment amount will usually be the same as for any American stock. And because the ADR is bought and sold in U.S. dollars, there is never a need to subject your purchase to foreign exchange. (ADRs do not insulate an investment from currency risk, however; more about that later in this chapter.)

Foreign corporations have several motivations for wanting to sell their shares in the United States through ADRs. First, ADRs provide global diversification of a company's shareholder base, at least partially reducing the vulnerability of its stock price to domestic cyclical conditions. Second, local restrictions on the amount of stock that may be held by foreigners makes overseas listing the only

61

way for many non-U.S. companies to efficiently access American capital. Finally, despite advances in the general level of sophistication of the world's stock exchanges, some countries nonetheless remain seriously behind the curve in matching their economy's need for capital with foreign investors hungry for opportunity.

For all those reasons, a foreign-based company may apply for a listing as an ADR on a U.S. securities exchange, such as the NYSE or the NASDAQ. In order to qualify, the corporation must convert its books from the accounting practices used in its own country into what is known as U.S. GAAP (U.S. generally accepted accounting principles). Depending upon the content of the GAAP figures, the NYSE or NASDAQ may then grant the foreign company a listing as an ADR. The corporation deposits a portion of its outstanding shares with a local bank, which keeps possession of the shares and performs the requisite paperwork, including the issuance of certificates of ownership, distribution of dividends, and the mailing of annual reports and other shareholder correspondence. In some cases, foreign corporations willing and able to meet even more rigorous initial and ongoing disclosure standards may be given a so-called direct listing, putting the foreign-domiciled corporation on the same level as such American corporate icons as General Motors and IBM. Most of the directly listed companies are Canadian, and each of the country chapters in this book carries a separate compilation for this class of security.

It is important to understand a few vital distinctions in the types of ADRs trading on U.S. securities markets. The kind of ADR described in the previous paragraph is known as a *sponsored* ADR, because the company itself applied for the ADR listings. Other ADRs are *unsponsored*: Before the idea of gaining a foreign listing became especially popular in recent years, it was not uncommon for the listing process to be initiated by a bank, which would simply buy shares of the company on its home securities market and proceed to perform the same function for foreign shareholders as it would had the entire process been initiated (sponsored) by the company itself. However, because such unsponsored ADRs by definition involve companies not choosing to participate in the process, most fail to meet the U.S. GAAP standards required by the NYSE and NASDAQ and, thus, trade only on the OTC market on so-called broker "pink" sheets. These OTC-traded ADRs often do not achieve the level of financial disclosure to which most investors are accustomed. Equally important is the fact that unsponsored ADRs are not necessarily adequately liquid—an insufficient number of shares may be available to maintain a healthy equilibrium between potential buyers and sellers. The imbalance of orders can result in large spreads between bid and asked prices, creating the potential for customers to be badly burned on their trade executions. Additionally, investors wanting to follow the performance of their

Table 4.1. Foreign Companies Available on Major U.S. Stock Markets

Country	NYSE	NASDAQ	Total
Argentina	8	1	9
Australia	9	10	19
Bermuda	2	0	2
Brazil	1	0	1
British West Indies	1	0	1
Canada	33	0	33
Chile	15	1	16
China	3	0	3
Columbia	1	0	1
Denmark	3	0	3
Finland	1	1	2
France	5	4	9
Germany	1	0	1
Greece	0	1	1
Hong Kong	6	0	6
Indonesia	1	1	2
Ireland	2	3	5
Israel	2	2	4
Italy	8	0	8
Japan	11	15	26
Korea	2	0	2
Liberia	1	0	1
Luxembourg	1	1	2
Mexico	23	2	25
Netherlands	11	3	14
New Zealand	2	0	2
Norway	2	1	3
Panama	2	0	2
Peru	1	0	1
Philippines	2	0	2

(continued)

Table 4.1.   (Continued)

Country	NYSE	NASDAQ	Total
Portugal	1	0	1
Singapore	1	0	1
South Africa	1	15	16
Spain	7	0	7
Sweden	0	7	7
United Kingdom	37	33	70
Venezuela	1	0	1
Totals	208	101	309

ADR on a daily basis will usually be unable to do so when it trades only on the OTC market. For reasons relating to disclosure, liquidity, and convenience, only direct listings and ADRs trading on the NYSE or NASDAQ will be included in the country chapters of this book.

Excluding OTC-traded ADRs from consideration for purchase will reduce the quantity but certainly not the quality of the foreign corporations available to U.S. investors. While many of the smaller ADRs are traded only via OTC pink sheets, nearly all of the large, blue-chip foreign corporations meet U.S. GAAP requirements for NYSE or NASDAQ listing. Several of the more popular foreign markets—including Japan, Canada, the United Kingdom, Chile, and Mexico—have an ADR or direct-listing menu large enough to represent a substantial portion of the capitalization of each country's home exchange. And the number of listed ADRs is only likely to increase in the coming years as both the NYSE and NASDAQ aggressively scan the globe for companies with an interest in tapping the U.S. capital market.

During 1994, nearly 150 ADRs (including those traded OTC) came to market, and volume was more than five times the amount of just seven years earlier. As of mid-1995, more than 300 companies from 37 countries were either directly listed or were trading as an ADR on the NYSE or the NASDAQ stock market. Table 4.1 shows a breakdown of 309 companies by country and exchange.

The return of ADRs has roughly equaled the return of U.S. equities over the last 10 years. As illustrated in Figure 4.1, a $10,000 investment into the average ADR and direct listing on January 1, 1985, would have grown to $35,185 by year-end 1994, compared to $36,577 for the average U.S. stock. The non-U.S. stock data are an unweighted average of the return from all ADRs and foreign

Figure 4.1.   American Depositary Receipts: How $10,000 Would Have Grown
Annual return of Wilshire 5000 index of U.S. common stocks (bar graph) and
unweighted average of ADR and direct listings (line graph).

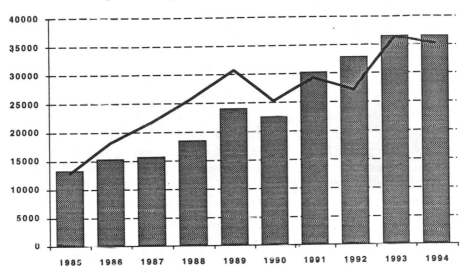

Sources: Morningstar, Inc.; Wilshire Associates.

direct listings tracked by *Morningstar American Depositary Receipts* in a given
year. As of 1995, 708 such securities were included in the Morningstar database.
(More information on a Morningstar publication that tracks and reports on ADRs
and direct listings will be found at the end of this chapter.)

Why They Do What They Do

Before diving into the ADR marketplace, investors should disabuse themselves
of one of the more widely held myths regarding this class of security. Because
ADRs are dollar-denominated—they are bought and sold in the U.S. currency—
many investors believe that this absence of foreign exchange protects them from
the kinds of currency risks described in Chapter 2. It does not. In fact, ADRs
(and directly listed foreign-based securities) are just as subject to the effects of
foreign-exchange fluctuation as any non-U.S. investment. This was a lesson made
painfully obvious to holders of Mexican ADRs in late 1994 and early 1995 when
a 50 percent fall in the peso only exacerbated a painful decline occurring on the
Mexican Bolsa. Regardless of whether you are looking at one day, one month,
or one year, the price change of an ADR will track the foreign-exchange adjusted

value of the underlying stock trading on its home market; for example, if you owned a Sony ADR and if the dollar/yen relationship stayed unchanged while Sony stock in Tokyo went up 10 percent, the value of your Sony ADR on the NYSE would also appreciate by 10 percent. If, however, the U.S. dollar lost 5 percent of its value against the yen while Sony stock in Tokyo was gaining 10 percent, the size of your gain would be increased by 5 percent, or the amount of the dollar's depreciation. (Remember from Chapter 2 that currency fluctuation is a double-edged sword. American investors benefit when the dollar falls and lose when the dollar rises relative to the currency of the company's home country.)

The value of an ADR on the NYSE or NASDAQ is determined entirely by a combination of foreign-exchange and stock-price changes occurring on a foreign stock exchange. The reason ADRs track the currency-adjusted performance of the same stock trading on its home market is because, if price differentials greater than aggregate transaction costs ever appeared between a stock trading on different exchanges, arbitrageurs would immediately swoop in and drive up or down the price in one of the markets to exploit the momentary price differential. The arbitrageur essentially functions as a kind of global-market vigilante to keep an ADR price from straying too far from the currency-adjusted value of the underlying stock as it trades on its home securities market. Because of the currency risk, however, investors should be careful to consider not only the merits of the company and economy of the country in which the stock trades, but also the historical record of that country's currency against the U.S. dollar. Each of the country chapters in this book contains additional historical information on the performance of a given nation's currency relative to the American dollar.

Buying ADRs

There are several ways to play the ADR game. You might want to invest in all or most of the ADRs of a given country in an attempt to replicate the return of the average stock from that country. This would seem especially appropriate if a country is enjoying either a strong cyclical or secular bull market. (Trying to match the median return of a country whose equity market is currently performing poorly or that has an unattractive long-term track record would obviously not be a good idea.) Those countries with the largest number of ADRs will naturally give you the best chance for equaling the dollar-denominated return of a particular foreign market, because the return of just one or even a handful of stocks can diverge from the average by a substantial amount. If, for example, a country has just a single ADR available, individual circumstances relating to that company's industry sector or its own position within that sector could result in its stock trading far better or far worse than the average of all stocks from that market. The more

ADRs you own from a particular country—preferably including companies from the widest possible array of industries—the greater your chances of earning an average return.

Of course, you may not want to put all your chips into a single country's ADRs or direct listings, either because that nation's overall stock market has been a below-average performer or because you would prefer to diversify across a wider swath of countries or industries. In that case, you could build your portfolio of ADRs on a "bottom-up" basis, that is, looking only at the prospects for each individual company and more or less ignoring the company's home equity market. Or you could use ADRs to build a globally diversified portfolio of companies from a particular industry, such as gold or autos or telecommunications or high-technology. Though sector-relative strength ebbs and flows, at any given moment there are enormous differences between the performance of stocks from one industry versus another, even as all stocks function in the same global economic environment. As of May 1995, for example, global semiconductor stocks were up 49 percent for the year to date, whereas the steel and auto sectors were each off more than 6 percent, according to Dow Jones & Company's World Industry indexes. A more than 50 percent range between the best- and worst-performing groups is hardly unusual, although the identity of the winners and losers is always difficult to determine in advance and will change over time.

The access to foreign stocks through ADRs or direct listings makes it possible to own virtually all of the major players from a given industry, regardless of where the company is domiciled. And, finally, income-oriented investors can use ADRs to generate a steady flow of dividend income in much the same way they might use U.S. stocks. Assuming, of course, that the foreign corporation actually pays a dividend (many do not, choosing instead to reinvest profits in their own company), the depositary institution simply takes the amount of the dividend, converts it to U.S. dollars, and sends you a check. Unlike their American counterparts, which pay cash dividends quarterly, most foreign businesses usually pay their dividends on a semiannual basis to both domestic and overseas investors. Tax requirements in most foreign countries generally require a 15 percent withholding, but U.S. investors can file Form 6166 with the IRS to qualify for an offsetting U.S. tax credit.

New Developments

Two nascent developments could further contribute to the increasingly global nature of capital markets into the twenty-first century. The NYSE is in the early stages of a plan that would allow foreign-based corporations to trade stocks on the Big Board *in their local currencies*. Although still several years away from

Figure 4.2. Morningstar American Depositary Receipts Sample Page

Placer Dome

Placer Dome is a precious-metals mining firm. In 1994, gold production totaled 2 million ounces, 1.7 million attributable to Placer Dome, at cash-production costs of US$198 per ounce. In 1993, the company also produced 48,655 lbs of copper, 10,316 ounces of silver, and 14,630 lbs of molybdenum. The group has interests in 16 mines located in North America, Australia, Chile, Papua New Guinea, and the Philippines. The company's 50%-owned Zaldivar operation in Chile holds South America's richest undeveloped copper deposits.

Chairman Robert M. Franklin — Tel 604-682-7082, Fax 604-682-7092
President & CEO John M. Wilson — US Tel N/A, US Fax N/A
Address 1600-1055 Dunsmuir St. Vancouver, BC V7X 1P1
US Exchange NYSE — US Ticker PDG — Dep. Bank — Employees 6,231

	Price (US$) 21.75	P/E 49.4	P/B N/A	P/Sales 5.8	Yield% 1.24	Industry Gold Mining	Country Canada

Valuation Ratios

	Country	Industry	US
P/E	49.4	30.1	28.9
P/Sales	5.8	3.1	4.7
Price/Book	N/A	2.64	2.54
Yield%	.24	1.00	0.90

Growth Rates

Avg annual %	3 Yr	5 Yr	10 Yr
Sales	2.3	6.0	-3.1
Earnings	NMF	5.1	-4.8
Net Worth	N/A	N/A	N/A
Dividends	7.5	4.3	4.0

Calculated per share in local currency.

US Accounting

	FY93	1 Yr %Chg
Net Inc ($mil)	100.6	10.7
Earn/sh ($)	0.43	13.2
Net Worth ($mil)	161.7	1.8

Profile

Size	Large Cap
Style	N/A
Risk	Average

	Country Index	Best Fit JSE Gold
Alpha	32.2	20.3
Beta	1.20	0.49
R²	24	34

Lower Line: Relative Strength (vs Country Index)

Sales Breakdown

Segment Sales %	12/91	12/92	12/93
Gold	85.1	85.2	87.1
Silver	3.6	4.8	4.6
Molybdenum & Other	4.4	3.9	4.6
Copper	6.8	6.1	3.7

Operating Margins %	12/91	12/92	12/93
Gold	22.9	28.7	29.8
Silver	--	(Loss)	(Loss)
Molybdenum & Other	5.5	(Loss)	(Loss)
Copper	6.1	8.1	(Loss)

Interim Result

Sales (US$mil)	3/31	6/30	9/30	12/31	Year
1992	248.0	259.0	264.0	249.0	1,020.0
1993	213.0	234.0	219.0	251.0	917.0

	1985	1986	1987	1988	1989	1990	1991	1992	1993	1994	1995
	1.39	1.33	1.23	1.18	1.17	1.15	1.21	1.29	1.37	1.40	
		21.4	15.8	19.8	21.5	16.8	12.4	25.6	28.3	21.9	
		10.9	10.9	12.1	13.4	9.6	9.0	10.5	18.1	18.4	
Vol (mil)											
Currency Change vs US$	-5.7	1.4	5.3	9.2	3.4	0.0	1.8	-10.9	-3.8	-5.0	0.7
Sales (US$mil)	309.0	313.4	628.2	639.0	763.7	926.5	968.8	1,020.0	917.0	899.0	1,078.0
Operating Income	53.9	66.7	168.7	113.1	114.0	106.3	-271.1	124.0	120.0	N/A	215.8
Operating Margin %	17.4	21.3	26.9	17.7	14.9	11.5	NMF	12.2	13.1	N/A	20.0
Tax Rate %	24.0	NMF	19.5	23.0	42.3	44.6	NMF	16.4	16.9	35.6	37.0
Net Income	25.8	50.5	119.2	212.8	93.7	63.0	-242.3	111.0	107.0	105.0	140.7
Net Margin %	8.3	16.1	19.0	33.3	12.3	6.8	NMF	10.9	11.7	11.7	13.1
Long-Term Debt	117.3	96.1	37.0	136.8	159.3	309.8	249.5	69.0	230.0	N/A	230.0
Net Worth	479.8	588.7	1,134.2	1,580.4	1,651.2	1,761.8	1,480.8	1,459.0	1,514.0	N/A	1,582.6
Return on Equity %	5.5	9.5	13.8	15.5	5.8	3.7	NMF	7.6	7.2	N/A	8.9
Return on Assets %	4.5	6.8	12.2	12.0	4.5	3.0	NMF	6.3	6.3	N/A	6.8
Shares Outstanding (mil)	43.2	46.4	219.4	234.5	234.8	236.4	236.7	237.1	238.1	238.4	239.0
Payout Ratio %	36.7	19.3	25.5	19.1	62.5	96.3	NMF	55.3	57.8	61.4	52.5

Per Share

	1985	1986	1987	1988	1989	1990	1991	1992	1993	1994	1995
Sales (US$)	7.16	6.99	2.88	2.82	3.25	3.94	4.09	4.31	3.66	3.77	4.51
Cash Flow	2.02	2.70	0.90	1.45	0.89	0.95	-0.47	1.17	1.10	N/A	1.19
Earnings	0.60	1.14	0.55	0.94	0.40	0.27	-1.02	0.47	0.45	0.44	0.59
Capital Expenditure	2.27	1.68	0.55	1.57	1.24	2.01	0.96	0.96	0.61	N/A	1.26

C$/US$ High 30 — Low 20

Calendar Year

										03/09/95
Net Worth	11.10	12.68	5.17	6.74	7.32	7.45	5.26	6.15	6.36	N/A	6.62
Dividend	0.22	0.22	0.14	0.18	0.25	0.26	0.26	0.25	0.26	0.27	0.31
Average Price to Earnings	—	—	19.6	17.3	22.6	50.9	NMF	NMF	42.0	50.0	39.0
Average Price to Book	—	—	1.86	2.18	2.20	2.32	1.86	1.73	3.09	7.07	3.07
Average Price to Cash Flow	—	—	9.24	10.82	13.63	19.73	NMF	21.40	16.11	N/A	17.05
Average Yield %	—	—	1.37	1.06	1.21	1.50	2.06	2.44	1.41	1.17	1.34
Total Return %	—	—	-23.50	-2.46	41.33	-5.21	-33.53	8.05	116.22	-12.30	0.00
Market Capitalization (US$mil)	—	—	3,345.5	3,078.0	4,285.1	4,018.7	2,604.1	2,756.5	5,922.8	5,186.3	5,186.3

Earnings/share (US$)

1992	0.05	0.05	0.10	0.14	0.18
1993	0.05	0.16	0.08	0.06	0.26
1994		0.09	0.08	0.11	

Dividend/share (US$)

1992	0.07	0.07	0.07	0.07
1993	0.07	0.07	0.07	0.07
1994	0.07	0.07	0.08	

1994	216.0	242.0	210.0	231.0	899.0	0.47
						0.45
						0.44

Balance Sheet

Assets (US$mil)	12/92	12/93	% Chg Local Cur
Cash & Short-Term Inv	477.0	777.0	62.9
Accounts Receivable	157.0	119.0	-24.2
Inventory (Avg Cost)	123.0	98.0	-20.3
Other	0.0	0.0	0.0
Current Assets	757.0	994.0	31.3
Tangible Assets	1,138.0	1,031.0	-9.4
Net Investments	81.0	64.0	-21.0
Other	91.0	139.0	52.7
Total	2,067.0	2,228.0	7.8

Liabilities (US$mil)	12/92	12/93	% Chg Local Cur
Accounts Payable	98.0	107.0	9.2
Short-Term Debt	46.0	21.0	-54.3
Other	57.0	25.0	-56.1
Current Liabilities	201.0	153.0	-23.9
Long-Term Debt	69.0	243.0	252.2
Other	338.0	318.0	-5.9
Shareholders' Equity	1,459.0	1,514.0	3.8
Total	2,067.0	2,228.0	7.8

Capital Structure as of 12/93

Equity/Assets %	68.0	Int Exp (US$mil)	22.0
Debt/Assets %	32.0	Int Coverage	9.0x

As of 12/94, equity consists of 238,448,674 common shares. As of 12/93, options represent 2,053,000 common shares. Long-term debt includes US$182.7 mil in 7.125% unsecured bonds (ex. 5/15/03). 7.8% of long-term debt is due in '95, 9.9% in '96, and 82.3% after '99.

Analysis by Andrew Clarke   03/09/95

Placer Dome is a solid, if somewhat pricey, gold-mining investment.

Although the numbers came up short in 1994, this senior precious-metals producer remains a good long-term option for most portfolios. Since the late 1990s, Placer Dome has consistently increased gold production, while a strong exploration and development program has kept reserves steady near 19 million ounces. In 1994, however, production declined because of seismic disturbances at the company's Golden Sunlight Mine in the United States. Profits followed suit, sinking a penny to US$0.44 per share.

Even so, the market didn't punish Placer Dome severely. While these shares have shed 13% of their value over the past year, many gold-mining stocks have fared far worse. The widely followed JSE Gold Index is down 25% for the same period. Placer Dome expects production to pick up this year, now that its Golden Sunlight is up and running again. There's a good chance that the company will make a substantial addition to gold reserves, too, as work continues at sizable advanced-stage exploration properties in Venezuela and the U.S. By the end of the decade, Placer Dome aims to mine 2.5 million ounces of gold annually, up from 1.9 million currently, and raise mineral reserves to 25 million ounces.

Those targets are ambitious, but the market probably isn't overpaying for a stake in Placer Dome's future, at least not relative to other North American majors such as Barrick Gold. Down 20% from its 52-week high, Placer Dome's market cap sits just above US$5 billion. At that level, an ounce of its gold reserves costs US$245. Because total production costs stand at about US$260 per ounce, investors are buying an ounce of gold for a little more than US$500.

There are certainly cheaper ways to invest in gold mining--South African producers, for example, or small North American operations. Some of these stocks such as Glamis Gold haven't proven as risky, either. Among North American giants, however, Placer Dome's valuation is par for the course.

Ownership

Major Owners %
N/A

Mutual Funds (thous shares)

Benham Gold Eq Index	4,222.0
20th Century Ultra Invst	3,200.0
New Perspective	1,500.0
Van Eck Int Invest Gold	1,280.0
Fidelity Sel Amer Gold	990.0
Franklin Gold	938.8
Dreyfus Capital Val A	912.8

Insiders %   0.4

Notes *Italics* = Morningstar estimates. The company reports according to Canadian accounting standards. ➊ In '87, Placer Development, Dome Mines, and Campbell Red Lake merged to create Placer Dome. Data prior to '87 are for Placer Development. ➋ In '91, the company reported a write-down of mining interests of US$343.5 mil. ➌ Data for '94 are preliminary and unaudited. ➍ Net income and earnings per share exclude nonrecurring gains of US$100.5 mil ('90) and US$11.9 mil ('89).

Data Editor J. Plotnick

Source: *Morningstar American Depositary Receipts*, Morningstar, Inc., 225 West Wacker Drive, Chicago, IL 60606, 312-696-6100.

implementation, the plan would have the effect of bringing more foreign capital to American markets by removing currency-transaction expenses from certain investments. Perhaps more importantly, a newfangled derivation of the ADR, known as the GDR (global depositary receipt), is now trading in Europe. The GDR offers companies from smaller or emerging markets the same advantages as a listing in the United States but accessing European money instead. Both the NYSE plan for home-currency trading and the new GDR security give fair indication that the process of globalizing the world's securities markets is sprinting ahead, with the promise of an ever-expanding array of opportunities for the globe-trotting investor.

Additional information regarding ADRs or directly-listed foreign stocks is available from Morningstar, Inc., the same Chicago-based company that publishes the open- and closed-end mutual fund reports described in the previous chapter. *Morningstar American Depositary Receipts* is a biweekly publication containing comprehensive data and analysis on roughly 700 foreign companies with stocks trading in the United States. It also contains timely summaries on the factors influencing the home equity market of each foreign stock, as well as sector overviews. (A one-year subscription to *Morningstar American Depositary Receipts* costs $295; a three-month trial is available for just $45. More information is available by calling 800-876-5005.) Figure 4.2 shows a sample from *Morningstar American Depositary Receipts*.

CHAPTER 5

Principles of Sound Foreign Investing

As profitable as overseas investing can be over the long haul, adhering to a few simple rules can help to insure that your financial house will not be blown down by the inevitable price twisters that hit all markets from time to time. Investing in any asset class with resale-price fluctuation carries with it the potential for significant financial bloodletting, and, if done improperly, buying foreign stocks can turn into a disaster. Following are *Ten Principles of Sound Foreign Investing* that could make your venture into overseas equities a rewarding experience:

1. **Don't invest any money in foreign stocks that cannot remain invested for at least three years.** The so-called three-year rule is a good idea in any market, but it becomes absolutely essential if you are going to venture abroad in search of greater returns. Along with those greater returns will come increased volatility. The 21 stock markets covered in this book have a median downside volatility of 2.57 times that of the U.S. equity market. Even the relatively placid stock markets of Europe carry nearly double the downside risk of the U.S. market. And remember that American stocks—over the short term, at least—can be plenty risky in their own right. Your best protection against waking up one morning and suddenly finding yourself missing a healthy chunk of the money you had planned on using for a new car, a down payment on a house, or some other big-ticket item is simply to avoid placing or keeping in a market any funds that will be needed within a three-year period. In other words, constantly evaluate if the money you have invested abroad will be needed at any time in the next three years. If the answer ever becomes "yes," sell the investment (even if it is at a loss) and place the proceeds into a cash-equivalent investment, such as a money market fund, bank

certificate of deposit, or U.S. Treasury bill. The lower return you are likely to receive in those types of financial parking lots is the price you will have to pay to keep your money safe and available for your important purchases.

2. **Diversify.** Regardless of how impressive a given market's historical return might have been, it is never a good idea to put too many chips on a single bet. All countries experience cyclical downturns, and, if you happen to be in the wrong place at the wrong time, you could find yourself down 50 percent or more in a single year. Or you could end up missing the overall uptrend that a broadly diversified portfolio of international equities is likely to capture. While it is not necessary that you construct a foreign portfolio that exactly reflects proper country weightings (such as Morgan Stanley Capital International's EAFE [Europe, Australia, Far East] index, for example), do resist the urge to concentrate all your holdings in the securities of one country, region, or industrial sector of the global equity market.

3. **Trust history more than promises.** Countries are a lot like people. They often speak of changing their ways, but, in reality, few do. If change were easy, it would have been done already, and, if it has not already been done, it probably will not be easy. In the absence of a track record to the contrary, it is usually safer to simply assume that things will continue as they have been, with allowances for normal cyclical fluctuations. If a country has a chronically weak current account, for example, or if its stock market has been weak over the long term, chances are good that the current account will remain weak, and its stock market will remain an underachiever. Over the long haul, you will lose far more money than you will gain by trying to anticipate turnaround candidates. This principal also applies to the selection of money managers. Your best bet is to hire individuals who have proven that, over an extended period of time, they are able to deploy assets in a way that beats what you get either on your own or by simply placing your money in an index fund that matches the non-U.S. return. A successful track record may be no guarantee of future results, but it is worth considerably more than promises.

4. **Don't try to "time" any equity market.** No one can predict with certainty when and where markets will move. By definition, market movements must be generally unexpected, because, if the consensus of global players had known a move was coming, they would have already acted, thus preempting or canceling the move altogether. Accept the fact—unpleasant as it may seem—that no one can help you know exactly when it is best to get in and

out of markets. Everyone will have an opinion, of course, and usually those opinions will seem sharply at odds with each other. But keep in mind that markets require buyers and sellers, and clearly the two sides will not agree. Not only is trying to guess exactly when to buy or sell a given stock or market impossible, but such deliberations necessarily entail excessively short-term focus that will only divert your attention from the more important task of accessing the long-term investment potential of various markets. After you have reached the conclusion that a country or region's long-term economic and equity-market record merits your investment, take a position and stick with it. A long-term, buy-and-hold strategy will cost less and almost always return more than a schizophrenic approach of guessing market tops and bottoms.

5. **Dollar-cost average.** Rather than guessing when it is best to buy or sell a given market or fund, try a technique known as dollar-cost averaging. Under this plan, you would carefully choose which funds or investments you want to make over time, then allocate a small portion of new investment money into the investments on a monthly basis. If there is more than one investment, simply rotate your monthly payments. Dollar-cost averaging virtually guarantees that you will not be buying only at market tops, and, if prices decline, you will be buying more shares, thus lowering your overall cost basis. Investors who use dollar-cost averaging are often astonished at the size of the nest egg they have accumulated over time, even when the investments themselves were not necessarily the optimum way to play a given market.

6. **Keep one-quarter of your money in foreign stocks.** While a proper weighting of non-U.S. stocks would be about 58 percent of your total equity portfolio, the vastly enhanced downside risk of foreign markets argues against an asset allocation of that magnitude. Because foreign stocks are more than twice as risky as their U.S. counterparts, a more prudent weighting would be to put about 25 percent of your money into foreign stocks. Even at that underweighting of the non-U.S. equity sector, you would still be increasing by fivefold the amount of foreign stocks held by American investors. If you are willing to take an exceptionally long-term, buy-and-hold approach to a broadly diversified portfolio—one that does not concentrate assets in any region or country—and if you are willing to live with the heightened risk, you could consider placing as much as 50 percent of your assets in foreign equities, thus probably adding a few percentage points to your long-term return. But even a long-term, buy-and-hold approach does not entirely compensate for downside volatility because, at some point, you will need to sell

your investment. If that time happens to coincide with one of the inevitable price drops, you would be selling into a buyer's market. The three-year rule thus becomes even more important for investors pushing the envelope of foreign-asset allocation closer to its natural 58 percent weighting.

7. **Avoid closed-end funds trading near the top end of their historical discount/premium cycle.** Investors need to be even more careful with closed-end funds than with other types of foreign securities because of the factors described at length in Chapter 3. The closest you should come to any type of market timing is to avoid buying closed-end country funds when they are trading at or near the top of their historical discount/premium cycles or when they are at a substantial premium to their net asset values, even if the amount of the premium is well below the historical top. It is usually an invitation to disaster to buy a closed-end fund that is trading with a significant premium, even if that premium is well within its historical range. Similarly, avoid the tendency to view deep discounts in closed-end funds as an overpowering invitation to buy, *regardless of all other factors*. If a fund, for example, over the past five years has traded for as low as a 20 percent discount to its net asset value and as high as a 20 percent premium, resist the urge to buy the fund just because it might be available at or near the 20 percent discount. A deep discount is a sign of investor contempt for a market and, thus, is a contrary indicator; but there are no guarantees that the market itself will not go significantly lower while the discount stays the same or that the market will not need to put in a prolonged base before rebounding. Only if the fund carrying the deep discount is an investment you would otherwise want to make on a long-term, buy-and-hold basis should the fact of the deep and historically wide amount of the discount play a role in your decision to accumulate fund shares.

8. **Don't be misled by cyclical rebounds.** Even countries whose stock markets have relatively poor long-term track records will enjoy brief periods of above-average or even spectacular results. These upside bursts will usually occur shortly after global sentiment regarding the market's prospects becomes so pessimistic that subsequent events cannot possibly be as bad as everyone had expected, setting up the likelihood of what is known as a "positive surprise." These periodic rebounds from deeply undervalued levels are often purely cyclical and not worthy of a play for most long-term investors. Resist the urge to chase a rapidly moving market, especially if that market is in a country that has a long-term record of equity underperformance versus the

United States and an equally lengthy record of mismanagement of its economy.

9. **Don't judge a country only by its currency.** Currency can be a double-edged sword. While a strong currency can be a sign that a nation has its economic house in order, it does not necessarily mean that an investment in its stock market will be as profitable—even after conversion back into dollars—as those you might find elsewhere. Japan, Germany, and Switzerland, for example, have traditionally had strong currencies against the U.S. dollar; yet the stock markets in those three countries combined to underperform the U.S. market by an average of 68 percent over the 1988 to 1994 period. As discussed at length in Chapter 2, when a nation's currency is appreciating too rapidly, the profits of its exporters—an increasingly important segment of virtually every country's economy—will usually be seriously impacted. And when a nation's exporters are hurting, it often sets in motion a chain reaction that ultimately squeezes profits throughout the economy. Additionally, keep in mind that maximizing economic growth may not necessarily be the top priority of a nation's monetary and fiscal authorities. If a country has a small or nonexistent economic lower-class and a substantial component of individual wealth, the economic best interests of the nation might be to foster an appreciating currency, thereby preserving or adding to the buying power of its wealthy citizens. And, as American equity investments in Japan, Germany, and Switzerland have demonstrated, a falling U.S. dollar is not necessarily enough to make up for disappointing returns in a country's stock market. On the other hand, nations with a historically dreadful currency—Argentina, Mexico, and Brazil come quickly to mind—might offer few reasons to believe the dollar-denominated value of investments in their markets will hold over the long term, regardless of how fast the underlying economy may be growing. In piecing together a long-term portfolio of international investments, look for countries that have been able to foster a *stable* currency and for those whose long-term dollar-denominated return beats what you could have earned by just staying home.

10. **Avoid the temptation to bail out when prices fall sharply.** Just as bad investments sometimes go up, good investments sometimes go down. There are no equity markets—even those that have beaten the United States over the long haul—that have not experienced the cyclical downturns known as bear markets. These declines tend to occur before changes in a country's business cycle, when inflation threatens to pick up (implying a hike in inter-

est rates), or when optimism has become excessive, thus drying up buying power and setting up the potential for negative earnings surprises. Bear markets can perform a healthy function of clearing excesses from a market, allowing for another advance to take prices beyond old highs. If the fundamental long-term reasons for investment in a country or region remain solid, use the inevitable cyclical declines as a buying opportunity, not as a reason to bail out. Similarly, do not suspend your long-term buying program just because foreign markets in general might be falling. There is considerable evidence, however, that American investors do exactly that. In 1993, while the EAFE was soaring 33 percent, U.S. investors poured a record $63 billion into foreign equities. But the next year, as the EAFE meandered mostly sideways and tremors in emerging markets got plenty of press, U.S. investors suddenly lost interest, cutting back on foreign purchases by 25 percent. The key to a successful investment program is to ignore sentiment and price swings and to stick to the carefully chosen investments you have made, regardless of what might be happening on a short-term basis.

Handled with sufficient care, foreign stocks can play a positive and significant role in building your financial nest egg. By increasing your total takedown of foreign equities to about 25 percent of your total stock holdings, by investing only long-term money, by diversifying across a number of regions and countries, and by using a dollar-cost averaging approach to accumulating more shares, chances are good that, over the long haul, you will match and probably even exceed the U.S. market's 10 percent annual compounded return by at least another 1 or 2 percent annually. And while it may not seem like much at first, adding just another 1 or 2 percent each year to your return can make a huge difference over time. Assuming you are starting with a $20,000 investment, improving your annual compounded return by just 2 percent per year (from 10 percent to 12 percent) would enhance the size of your nest egg by $124,000 over 25 years.

CHAPTER 6

Understanding the Data

The centerpiece of this book is the economic and financial-market data found in Chapters 7 through 27, the country chapters. Following is an explanation of where the data for a particular chapter section originated, how certain computations were made, what time periods are included, and what the graphics represent.

Financial Strength

Data in this section is from the International Monetary Fund (IMF), except for external debt, which was referenced from the *CIA World Factbook*. Where the most recent IMF data was not yet available, figures from the *Europa World Yearbook* or various financial media were used. All percentages listed are averages for the 1964 to 1994 period or 1964 through the most recent date for which data is available; for example, the listing of a country's merchandise-trade account would be the average of 1964 through 1994, unless 1994 data was unavailable, in which case the average of 1964 through 1993 data was used. (In some cases, especially for government budget deficits or surpluses, information is often one or two years late in being published.) Gross domestic product (GDP) is converted to U.S. dollars (the currency in which most IMF flow-of-funds data are computed) by using average annual exchange rates, except for 1994, which uses year-end exchange rates. The Balance of Payments graphic found in each country chapter displays the surplus or deficit of a country's budget and current account, expressed as a percentage of nominal GDP. The key point of reference in the graph is the "zero line," which is represented as a solid black line to stand apart from other horizontal grid lines.

Currency

Except for 1994 exchange rates, all information in this section is from the IMF.
Money supply and consumer price index information are annual averages beginning with 1964 data and continuing through the most recently reported period,
which in most cases is 1994. Exchange rates are annual averages, except for 1994,
which is the year-end figure published in *Barron's*. The graphic found in each
country chapter displays the amount of a foreign currency that could be purchased
by one U.S. dollar. The scale is inverted; that is, higher numbers are found at the
lower or bottom end of the axis because an appreciating currency would be indicated by the U.S. dollar being able to purchase fewer units of the foreign currency. Thus, an ascending pattern of bars would indicate an increasing value of
the foreign currency relative to the dollar. When the range of data is extreme, a
logarithmic scale is used, which creates a more accurate visual representation by
putting figures in proportion. A logarithmic scale is especially important in graphics for the Latin American currencies, some of which have experienced value
changes of millions or even billions of percent over the past 30 years.

Economic Output

Figures are derived from IMF data, except for 1994 information, which was
published in various financial media. GDP is listed in U.S. dollars using year-
end 1994 currency-exchange rates. Where 1994 information is unavailable, 1993
data was used. Similarly, per capita GDP uses 1994 figures, unless unavailable.
GDP growth rate is the average annual change in inflation-adjusted GDP over
the 1964 to 1994 period, unless 1994 data is unavailable, in which case 1964 to
1993 averages are used. In all cases where 1993 information is used, relative
computations were made off 1993 data in the United States. The economic output graphic uses a combination of line and bar data representation. The bars
measure the annual percentage change in a country's real GDP, while the line
represents the cumulative output of that country's real GDP relative to the U.S.
economy. When this type of line (known as a relative strength line) is climbing,
it means that the economy of the particular country is growing faster than—or at
least not shrinking as fast as—the U.S. economy. GDP is represented in U.S.
dollars using average annual currency-exchange rates, except for 1994, which
uses year-end currency values.

Stock Market

Data pertaining to market capitalization, number of issues traded, and primary indexes are supplied by the Federation Internationale des Bourses de Valeurs (FIBV) in Paris, France. Total return, volatility, bull/bear cycles, and correlation information is derived from Wilshire Associates, Inc., proprietary country indexes, which are compiled in both local-currency and U.S. dollar terms. The Wilshire data is monthly, covering 1988 through 1994.

The relative volatility ratio is computed by comparing each country's standard deviation, total monthly losses, average monthly loss, number of monthly losses, and number of monthly losses greater than 5 percent with the same category of information from the U.S. market. The five foreign-U.S. ratios are then averaged to produce a single relative volatility ratio. A relative volatility ratio of 2.00 would indicate that a foreign market has exactly twice the downside volatility of the U.S. market.

The U.S. equity market is referenced by the Standard & Poor's Composite Index of 500 Stocks (S&P 500), a widely quoted benchmark of 500 large-capitalization companies that, in the aggregate, comprise about three-quarters of the value of the American equity market. Data from the Country Funds section of each chapter is from Morningstar, Inc., which publishes a comprehensive evaluation of open- and closed-end mutual funds (see Chapter 3). Total return figures for closed-end funds refer to changes in the fund's net asset value (NAV), which, because of discount/premium cycles in its per share price, is usually different from that experienced by many investors. The NAV-based return, however, is the best measure of a fund's basic money-management ability, because fund management is not responsible for discrepancies relative to NAV that may appear on securities exchanges.

Information on American Depositary Receipts (ADRs) and Direct Listings of foreign securities is from the New York Stock Exchange (NYSE) and the National Association of Securities Dealers Automated Quotation system (NASDAQ), with supplemental information from *Morningstar American Depositary Receipts*.

The stock market graphic uses three lines, one to show the cumulative monthly return of the Wilshire country index in local currency (black), another to show the monthly total return of the Wilshire index when converted to U.S. dollars (gray), and another to show the monthly cumulative return of the U.S. equity market (dotted) as represented by the S&P 500 index. In cases where extremes of data ranges are found, a logarithmic scale is used to put price changes in proportion.

CHAPTER 7

Commonwealth of Australia

Overview

Australia's democratic system of government and high degree of political stability represent significant pluses for foreign investors considering Australian portfolio investment. Over the remainder of the 1990s, Australia could also benefit from the increasing attention the country receives as the 2000 Summer Olympic Games—scheduled to be held in Sydney—draw near. Australia's per capita income of nearly $16,000 makes it the second wealthiest nation in the Asia/Oceania region. The Aussie economy, however, is not without its weaknesses. Because of a relatively high concentration of natural-resource companies, Australia is vulnerable to commodities price swings and coincident slowdowns in overall global economic growth. The Aussie current account is also seriously in deficit, primarily because of large and chronic shortfalls from income and services trade. The current-account deficits have exerted, in turn, downside pressure on the Australian currency and upward pressure on domestic interest rates. Australian stocks have roughly equaled the return of U.S. equities in local-currency terms since 1988, but they have fallen behind when measured in U.S. dollars as a consequence of Australia's downward drifting currency. The significant commodities exposure in the Aussie market, however, could offer important portfolio diversification for U.S. investors. Natural-resource plays will generally do well when the global economy is nearing a full-scale expansion, a condition that could cause U.S. interest rates to rise, thus depressing American stocks. If nothing else, a booming Australian equity market could be an early warning signal of an impending monetary tightening in the United States.

Geography

Area: 2,966,150 square miles
Size relative to United States: 78%
Capital: Canberra
Population density per square mile: 6
Population density relative to United States: 0.08x

Demographics

Population: 18 million
Population relative to United States: 7%
Average annual rate of natural increase: 0.8%
Projected population by 2025: 23 million
Population change by 2025: +28%

Government

Type: Federal Parliamentary State
Head of State: Paul Keating, Prime Minister (1991)
Political System: Under a constitution promulgated in 1901, the Commonwealth of Australia is governed according to a system combining elements of British parliamentary and American federal tradition. Legislative power is vested in a bicameral Federal Parliament consisting of a House of Representatives and a Senate. The prime minister serves as the executive head of government and is chosen from the majority party in the House. All members of the Australian legislature are popularly elected; voting is compulsory. The Senate consists of 76 members (10 from each of the six states, and two apiece from the eight territories) who serve six-year terms. Half of the Senate comes up for reelection every three years. The House of Representatives is made up of 176 members who serve three-year terms. Like the U.S. House, representation in the Australian lower legislative body is proportional to the population in the states and territories. Additional executive power—most of it of the ceremonial variety—resides in the British monarch through the governor general and the six state governors. (Most of the original European settlers of Australia were transported British convicts, and over 90 percent of the country's current population is of British descent.) Australian politics in the post-World War II period has been dominated by the Liberal and Labor parties, with the latter holding power since 1983. Labor

was led by Robert Hawke from 1983 through 1991, when an economic recession led to an intraparty leadership struggle eventually won by Paul Keating. The Labor Party and Keating were most recently returned to power through elections in 1993.

Economy

Financial Strength
(Historical data, relative to GDP)

Merchandise trade: +0.53%
Services: −1.35%
Income: −2.53%
Current account: −3.16%
Portfolio investment: +0.69%
Direct investment: +1.19%
Overall balance of payments: +0.24%
Budget: −1.40%
External debt: 46%
Investment/consumption ratio: 0.33

Figure 7.1. Australian Balance of Payments
Surplus/deficit of Australian budget (black) and current account (gray), as percent of GDP.

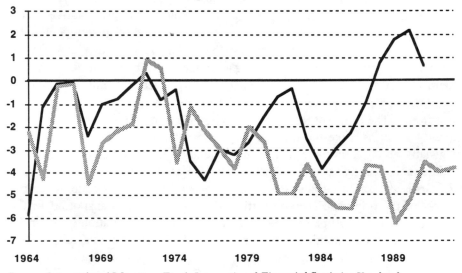

Source: International Monetary Fund, *International Financial Statistics Yearbook.*

Figure 7.2. Australian Currency
Australian dollars per U.S. dollar (inverted scale).

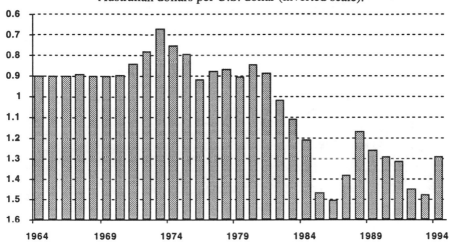

Source: International Monetary Fund, *International Financial Statistics Yearbook.*

Currency
(Historical data)

Money supply growth: 12.01%
Consumer price index: 7.13%
Monetary unit: Dollar
Monetary unit against U.S. dollar: −39%

Economic Output
(Historical data)

GDP: $283 billion
GDP relative to U.S. GDP: 4.85%
GDP growth rate: 3.72%
GDP growth rate relative to U.S. GDP growth rate: 1.30x
Per capita GDP: $15,726
Per capita GDP relative to U.S. per capita GDP: 69%

Economic Summary

Since the end of World War II, Australia has transformed itself from a nation dependent almost entirely on agricultural exports to a diversified, industrial economy with a total output approaching $300 billion. Over the past 30 years,

Figure 7.3.   Australian Economy

Annual percentage change in Australian real GDP (bar graph, left scale). Growth in Australian real GDP relative to U.S. real GDP, 1963 = 100 (line graph, right scale).

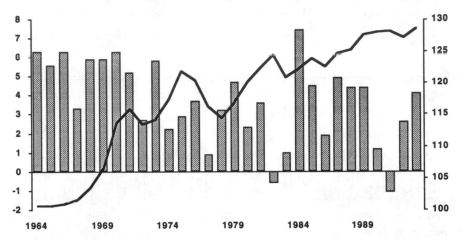

Source: International Monetary Fund, *International Financial Statistics Yearbook.*

Australian GDP has grown at an average rate of 3.72 percent, roughly one-third faster than the United States. Per capita income at nearly $16,000 gives the country a standard of living second only to Singapore among Asia/Oceania states. The Aussie economy has successfully emerged from a significant recession in 1991 to resume trend-level growth over the 1992 to 1994 period.

Although agricultural exports remain important to the Australian economy, manufacturing is now the greatest source of income. Most of the country's manufacturers are located in the more urbanized states of New South Wales, Victoria, and Queensland and include food processing and metallurgical industries. Three-quarters of all Australian exports are primary products, such as wool, meat, wheat, iron ore, and coal. Australia is rich in natural resources, including bauxite, zinc, lead, tin, copper, nickel, and uranium. In the late 1800s, a gold rush at Broken Hill, located near the Outback region in western New South Wales, uncovered a lode of silver, lead, and zinc. Today, a company known as the Broken Hill Proprietary Company is Australia's largest corporation, with operations across a wide range of natural-resource industries, including steel, energy, and mining. Because of the country's large representation of such natural-resource companies, however, a slump in worldwide commodities prices tends to disproportionately hurt the Australian economy. Fortunately, Aussie exports are becoming increasingly diversified, with more trade and investment occurring with many of the rapidly growing Asian nations and less with European nations, especially with the United Kingdom.

The major weakness in the Australian economy is the large shortfall in its current account, which has averaged a 3.16 percent of gross domestic product (GDP) annual deficit since 1964. The sources of the current-account problem are deficits in both income and services trade, which together have posted annual deficiencies of nearly 2 percent of GDP over the past 30 years, more than offsetting the country's 0.53 percent average surplus in merchandise trade. On the fiscal front, Aussie budgets have averaged a 1.40 percent annual deficit since 1964, but surpluses have become common in the 1990s. Despite the fiscal improvement, however, the current-account deficit—estimated in 1994 to have reached nearly 5 percent of GDP—puts downward pressure on the Australian dollar, making Australian stocks and bonds less attractive for American investors. The resulting lack of foreign-portfolio investment, in turn, pushes up Aussie real and nominal interest rates, threatening to slow its economy. Over the past three decades, the Aussie currency, which is allowed to float freely, has fallen by more than one-third against the U.S. dollar.

Australian Stock Market

Exchange

Classification: Developed
Capitalization: $200 billion
Capitalization relative to U.S. stock market: 4%
Number of issues: 1,107
Primary index: All Ordinaries
Total return in local currency, 1988–1994: +122%
Total return in U.S. dollars, 1988–1994: +106%
Total return in U.S. dollars relative to U.S. stocks, 1988–1994: –28%

Volatility
(Historical)

Standard deviation: 5.59
Total monthly losses: 145%

Average monthly loss: 3.54%
Number of monthly losses: 41
Number of monthly losses greater than 5 percent: 11
Number of monthly losses greater than 10 percent: 1
Number of monthly losses greater than 15 percent: 0
Maximum monthly loss: 13.35%
Relative volatility ratio: 2.00

Price Cycles

Phase	From	To	Total return
Bull	January 1988	December 1989	+51%
Bear	January 1990	April 1990	−17%
Bull	May 1990	July 1990	+16%
Bear	August 1990	December 1990	−18%
Bull	January 1991	May 1992	+36%
Bear	June 1992	November 1992	−20%
Bull	December 1992	December 1994	+59%

Figure 7.4.　Australian Stocks

Return of Australian stocks in local currency (black), U.S. dollars (gray), and S&P 500 (dotted); Dec. 1987 = 100.

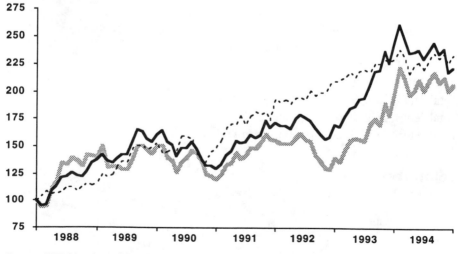

Source: Wilshire Associates Incorporated.

Correlations

New Zealand 0.61
United Kingdom 0.51
Sweden 0.49
Canada 0.45
Hong Kong 0.42
Singapore 0.38
Indonesia 0.33
France 0.33
United States 0.31
Germany 0.26
Japan 0.25

Malaysia 0.22
Thailand 0.22
Philippines 0.20
Switzerland 0.16
Korea 0.14
Taiwan 0.11
Mexico 0.11
Brazil 0.07
Argentina –0.02
Chile –0.05

Country Funds

Name	Originated	Hedging	Structure	Discount/ Premium	Phones
First Australia	Dec. 1985	Possible	Closed end	–27 / +21	(212) 214-3334 (800) 451-6788

Source: Morningstar, Inc.

American Depositary Receipts

Name	Exchange	Symbol	Industry
Amcor	NASDAQ	AMCRY	Paper
Australia and New Zealand Banking Group	NYSE	ANZ	Banking and financial services
Boral	NASDAQ	BORAY	Building materials
Broken Hill Proprietary Co.	NYSE	BHP	Mining, steel
Coles Myer	NYSE	CM	Retailer
FAI Insurance	NYSE	FAI	Property and casualty insurance
Memtec	NASDAQ	MMTCY	Industrial machinery
National Australia Bank	NYSE	NAB	Banking
News Corporation	NYSE	NWS	International communications
Orbital Engine	NYSE	OE	Manufacturing
Pacific Dunlop	NASDAQ	PDLPY	Marketing, manufacturing
Santos	NASDAQ	STOSY	Oil and gas exploration and production
Western Mining Corp.	NYSE	WMC	Mining
Westpac Banking Corp.	NYSE	WBK	Banking

Direct Listings

None

Stock Summary

Australia's stock market has been hampered by its relatively slow growth economy, the large current-account deficit, and its heavy natural-resource orientation, which accounts for roughly one-third of the market's capitalization. (Global natural-resource and commodities plays have been underperformers for most of the worldwide disinflationary cycle of the 1980s and 1990s.) Over the 1988–1994 period, Australian equities gained 122 percent in local currency terms but just 106 percent in U.S. dollars, resulting in a 28 percent underperformance of the American market over that period. With a downside volatility ratio of only 2.00, however, the Australian stock market has the lowest risk quotient of any Asia/Oceania bourse. The three bear markets that Aussie stocks have endured since 1988 have not been particularly bloody, with the average stock declining by a relatively mild 18 percent over five months. The Australian exchange is best correlated with nearby New Zealand, as well as equities in the United Kingdom, Sweden, and Canada (which also has a high concentration of commodities plays). At 0.31, U.S. stock movements correlate only modestly with the Aussie market, implying the potential for an average amount of portfolio diversification.

Fairly reflecting the importance of natural resources to the Australian economy, a number of commodities-based ADRs are available on the NYSE and NASDAQ exchanges. As noted earlier, Broken Hill Proprietary, which accounts for one-tenth of the entire Aussie market's capitalization, is engaged in mining, energy exploration, and steel production on a global basis. The company's stock has outperformed the overall Australian equity market by a wide margin since late 1988. Other natural-resource or deep-cyclical plays include Amcor (paper), Boral (building materials), Western Mining (gold mining), and Santos (oil and gas exploration). A number of smaller commodities-based companies, including Poseidon Gold, trade over the counter. Investors preferring the country-fund approach will find one such offering, the First Australia fund, which began operations in December 1985. Since 1988, First Australia has significantly underperformed the Wilshire Index: Australia on a dollar-denominated NAV basis (60 percent versus 106 percent), with approximately the same magnitude of downside volatility. The fund generally trades at a steep discount to NAV. As of October 1995, First Australia's assets were available on the American Stock Exchange for just 85 cents on the dollar.

Australian equities, on balance, are a global cyclical play due to their large natural-resource weighting. In 1993, for example, a year in which gold stocks and other cyclical issues began to shoot higher as investors began to discount accelerating economic recoveries in the United States, Japan, and Germany, the average Aussie stock climbed more than 42 percent in U.S. dollar terms. Increasing diversification with smaller Asian markets should give the Australian economy some insulation from cyclical downturns in the world's more established economies. American investors using Australia to play the commodities game, however, need to recognize the historical weakness in the Australian currency, which has declined by 39 percent against the dollar since 1964, primarily because of the country's chronic current-account deficits.

CHAPTER 8

Hong Kong

Overview

In both symbolic and strategic terms, Hong Kong represents the purest play on the opening of the Chinese economy. Along with its magnificent natural harbor and ideal location at the southern tip of the most prosperous Chinese provinces, Hong Kong has the largest equity market in Asia. With per capita gross domestic product (GDP) of more than $15,000, the British crown colony has a standard of living second only to Singapore among Asian nations. Investors in Hong Kong equities have also been suitably rewarded, earning 268 percent in U.S. dollar terms over the 1988 to 1994 period, roughly double the return of the U.S. market.

Despite its clear advantages, however, Hong Kong also comes with serious potential drawbacks. Because government officials peg its currency to the American dollar, the Hong Kong stock market—which is heavily overweighted in property and finance issues—is hostage to U.S. interest rates. Investors also fear that wildly inflated real estate prices in the colony may cause a classic boom/bust cycle similar to that presently convulsing the Japanese economy. Beyond the economic concerns, however, are the huge political questions arising from the territory's reunification with China in July 1997. Despite assurances that Hong Kong's capitalist economy will be allowed to grow without interference from the mainland, the specter of Tiananmen Square lurks just out of sight and never out of mind. Developing economic problems in China itself, including a looming slowdown and near hyperinflation, are also reasons to give investors pause. Over the long term, however, investors in Hong Kong are likely to reap the benefits flowing from the inevitable development of the world's largest untapped market.

Geography

Area: 416 square miles
Size relative to United States: 0.01%
Capital: Victoria
Population density per square mile: 13,943
Population density relative to United States: 191x

Demographics

Population: 6.07 million
Population relative to United States: 2.3%
Average annual rate of natural increase: 0.92%
Projected population by 2025: 6.9 million
Population change by 2025: +14%

Government

Type: Dependent Territory of the United Kingdom

Head of State: Christopher Patten, Governor (1992)

Political System: Much of present-day Hong Kong was ceded by China to the British in the aftermath of the Opium Wars of the mid 1800s. The area north of the Kowloon peninsula on the adjoining mainland (known as the New Territories) was leased to Britain in 1898 for a period of 99 years. After intense negotiations, the United Kingdom and China agreed in 1984 that the entire British crown colony of Hong Kong would revert to Chinese control upon the termination of that lease on June 30, 1997. Under the terms of the agreement returning Hong Kong to Chinese sovereignty, the People's Republic of China agreed to allow Hong Kong's capitalist economic system and the lifestyle of its people to remain unchanged for 50 years after the agreement goes into effect. It further agreed to allow full freedom of speech, assembly, travel, and worship. The territory will be considered a special administrative zone of China and will be known as "Hong Kong, China."

Despite the assurances contained in the Sino-British Joint Declaration of 1984 and those found in the new Basic Law or constitution for Hong Kong, which will take effect on July 1, 1997, Hong Kong businesses are demonstrating concern over the return to Chinese control. Roughly half of the companies trading on the

Hong Kong Stock Exchange have changed their legal domiciles to Bermuda or the British West Indies. Attempts by the British to institutionalize democratic procedures in the colony have been resisted by Chinese authorities, and the status of Hong Kong's legal system—considered to be among the finest in Asia—remains in question as officials debate the appropriate jurisdiction of a court of final appeal.

Economy

Note: IMF data on currency, balance of payments, and economic output is not available.

Hong Kong Stock Market

Exchange

Classification: Developed
Capitalization: $269 billion
Capitalization relative to U.S. stock market: 4.4%
Number of issues: 529
Primary index: Hang Seng
Total return in local currency, 1990–1994: +261%
Total return in U.S. dollars, 1990–1994: +268%
Total return in U.S. dollars relative to U.S. stocks, 1990–1994: +134%

Volatility
(Historical)

Standard deviation: 7.50
Total monthly losses: 170%
Average monthly loss: 4.88%
Number of monthly losses: 35
Number of monthly losses greater than 5 percent: 12
Number of monthly losses greater than 10 percent: 6
Number of monthly losses greater than 15 percent: 1
Maximum monthly loss: 18.08%
Relative volatility ratio: 2.45

Figure 8.1. Hong Kong Stocks
Return of Hong Kong stocks in local currency (black), U.S. dollars (gray), and S&P 500 (dotted); Dec. 1987 = 100.

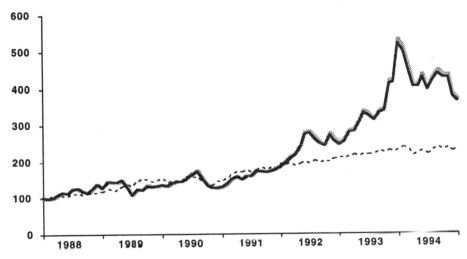

Source: Wilshire Associates Incorporated.

Price cycles

Phase	From	To	Total return
Bull	January 1988	April 1989	+50%
Bear	May 1989	June 1989	−28%
Bull	July 1989	July 1990	+61%
Bear	August 1990	November 1990	−28%
Bull	December 1990	December 1993	+318%
Bear	January 1994	December 1994	−31%

Correlations

Singapore 0.56
Malaysia 0.55
Indonesia 0.48
United Kingdom 0.46
Australia 0.42
Canada 0.41
Philippines 0.40
Thailand 0.40
Sweden 0.39
United States 0.38
France 0.31

Germany 0.29
New Zealand 0.27
Taiwan 0.27
Chile 0.22
Japan 0.17
Korea 0.16
Switzerland 0.15
Brazil 0.11
Mexico 0.08
Argentina −0.06

Country Funds

Name	Originated	Hedging	Structure	Discount/Premium	Phone
China Fund	July 1992	No	Closed end	−14 / +40	(212) 808-0500 (800) 421-4777
Greater China	July 1992	No	Closed end	−11 / +19	(212) 713-2000
Jardine Fleming China	July 1992	No	Closed end	−16 / +32	(800) 638-8540
Templeton China World	Sept. 1993	Possible	Closed end	−14 / +14	(800) 292-9293

Sources: Morningstar, Inc.; Barron's.

American Depositary Receipts

Name	Exchange	Symbol	Industry
Brilliance China Automotive Holdings	NYSE	CBA	Automotive manufacturer
China Tire Holdings	NYSE	TIR	Tire manufacturer
Concordia Paper Holdings	NASDAQ	CPLNY	Pulp and paper products
EK Chor China Motorcycle	NYSE	EKC	Motorcycle manufacturing and sales
Great Wall Electronic	NASDAQ	GWALY	Consumer electronics
Hong Kong Telecommunications	NYSE	HKT	Telecommunications

Direct Listings

Name	Exchange	Symbol	Industry
Amway Asia Pacific Ltd.	NYSE	AAP	Amway distributor
DSG International	NASDAQ	DSGIF	Household products
Nam Tai Electronics	NASDAQ	NTAIF	Consumer electronics
Pacific Basin Bulk Shipping	NASDAQ	PBBUF	Shipping
Tommy Hilfiger Corporation	NYSE	TOM	Sportswear

Stock Summary

Despite a significant bear market in 1994, Hong Kong stocks have usually been friendly to American investors over the past seven years, appreciating by 268 percent in U.S. dollar terms, or by 134 percent more than the Standard & Poor's 500 over the identical period. The Hong Kong market has also been among the least volatile of all non-U.S. bourses, with a relative downside volatility reading of 2.45, the second-lowest figure for any Asian exchange. And because the Hong Kong currency (also known as the dollar) is pegged to the U.S. dollar, Americans venturing into the Hong Kong market can take some comfort in the knowledge that foreign exchange will likely not be a problem, unless, of course, Chinese officials decide to allow the Hong Kong dollar to float.

The stable Hong Kong currency, however, is a double-edged sword for American investors. To keep the Hong Kong dollar moving in tandem with the U.S. dollar, Hong Kong officials generally raise interest rates whenever the Federal Reserve hikes U.S. rates. All equity markets are interest-rate sensitive to some degree, but increasing capital costs especially menace the Hong Kong equity market because roughly 50 percent of its market capitalization is in the property and finance sectors. (In this regard, the makeup of the Hong Kong stock exchange is somewhat unrepresentative of the Hong Kong economy as a whole, where property and finance combine for only about one-quarter of GDP.) Much of the fall in Hong Kong stocks occurred after the American Fed began to raise rates in February 1994.

Besides its vulnerability to U.S. interest-rate moves, two other factors serve to keep equity prices in Hong Kong on a leash. There is the ever-present uncertainty regarding the political and attendant financial-market consequences of Hong Kong's reunification with mainland China in 1997. Despite its apparent commitment to open markets and a Western-style economy, there are serious questions regarding China's aging political leadership, as well as its possible choice of Shanghai over Hong Kong as the nation's financial center. Additionally, skyrocketing real estate prices in Hong Kong gave many investors the scary feeling that they might be looking at a replay of the asset-price deflation that occurred in Tokyo in the aftermath of an astronomical speculative frenzy in real estate in that country during the late 1980s. Indeed, the timing and magnitude of the Hang Seng decline off its early January 1994 top does seem to closely parallel the early stages of the Tokyo bourse's fall after its secular peak in January 1990.

Relative to other Asian markets, Hong Kong equities tend to be a bit of a bargain, trading at price/earnings multiples of roughly half of those found in nearby Asian/Oceania markets. Part of the reason for the relative undervaluation of Hong Kong equities results from the overweighting of the property sector in the Hang Seng index, but relatively slower economic growth in Hong Kong is a factor as well. Over the past 10 years, the Hong Kong economy is estimated to have grown at close to a 5 percent annual rate, somewhat below the level of growth in neighboring Korea, Thailand, Malaysia, and Singapore. Additionally, because of uncertainties over China's handling of its serious inflation problem, questions have developed as to the possible spillover effect of a slowdown in the Chinese economy that may result from a monetary tightening in that country. Given the large and growing economic interdependence between Hong Kong and China, any slow-down in the rate of growth on the mainland will almost certainly negatively impact Hong Kong itself.

None of the four country funds listed earlier are pure Hong Kong plays. Al-though each of the funds allocated at least half of their assets to Hong Kong as of mid-1995, most of the remaining portions were divided among Taiwan and China itself. For investors wanting a more concentrated dosage of Hong Kong stocks, several Hong Kong ADRs and direct listings are available, including Hong Kong Telecommunications, a relatively stable play on the developing Chinese infrastructure, which already accounts for more than 7 percent of the value of the entire Hong Kong exchange.

CHAPTER 9

Republic of Indonesia

Overview

Indonesia's economic selling points for foreign investment are political stability; abundant natural resources; and a large, low-wage population. With per capita gross domestic product (GDP) of just over $700, the nation remains substantially behind Asia's "Little Tiger" economies of Hong Kong, South Korea, Taiwan, and Singapore in elevating the living standards of its people. A rapidly expanding population is a major contributing factor to the general poverty of the world's fourth-most-populous country. Despite its problems, however, Indonesia has made substantial progress over the past 25 years in transforming itself from an agricultural, energy-driven economy to one that is in the early stages of becoming a major industrial center. At present, Indonesia's main economic advantage is a low wage scale, one that is just a fraction of those in more prosperous Asian countries. As such, Indonesia has become a "final-assembly" location for many Asian corporations—high-tech components are manufactured domestically and then shipped to Indonesia to capitalize on the low labor costs for assembling the components into final products.

Indonesia's stock market is a mere infant, making its disappointing five-year track record somewhat misleading. Capitalized at just $46 billion as of year-end 1994, the Jakarta Stock Exchange represents less than a third of the nation's economy. Investors in Indonesian equities would have shown a net negative return over the first half of the 1990s. Despite the disappointing start, however, the Indonesian government seems committed to developing an open, high-tech equity market, and investors with a long time frame and a strong stomach could eventually be nicely rewarded.

Geography

Area: 735,268 square miles
Size relative to United States: 19%
Capital: Jakarta
Population density per square mile: 271
Population density relative to United States: 3.68x

Demographics

Population: 194 million
Population relative to United States: 75%
Average annual rate of natural increase: 1.6%
Projected population by 2025: 275 million
Population change by 2025: +42%

Government

Type: Republic
Head of State: General Haji Mohamed Suharto, President (1967)
Political System: The 1,000-member People's Consultative Assemble, or MPR (Majelis Permusyawaratan Rakyat), convenes at least once every five years to formulate the broad outlines of state policy, to rule on constitutional matters, and to elect government officials, including the president and vice president. Incorporated within the MPR is the 500-member House of Representatives, which meets at least once each year and functions as the legislative branch of the government. Four hundred of the House members are chosen by the Indonesian people through general election; the remaining 100 members are appointed by the armed forces and the president.

In the aftermath of Japanese occupation of the islands during World War II, Indonesian nationals led by General Sukarno declared the nation independent, a claim that was eventually granted by the Netherlands in 1949. (The islands had been a Dutch colony since the early nineteenth century.) During his 20-year reign, Sukarno established increasingly close ties with Communist movements and the Indonesian military. As the economy weakened in the mid-1960s, however, armed conflict between communist and anticommunist factions erupted, culminating in pro-Western General Haji Mohamed Suharto assuming power. Shortly after taking control of the government in 1967, Suharto returned the nation to a representative democracy and has presided over nearly a quarter century of political stability. Suharto's term expires in 1998, however, and he has not announced his intentions regarding reelection.

Economy

Financial Strength

Merchandise trade: +4.96%
Services: –4.14%
Income: –3.83%
Current account: –2.69%
Portfolio investment: +0.04%
Direct investment: +0.63%
Overall balance of payments: +0.60%
Budget: –2.07%
External debt: 36%
Investment/consumption ratio: 0.30

Figure 9.1. Indonesian Balance of Payments
Surplus/deficit of Indonesian budget (black) and current account (gray), as percent of GDP.

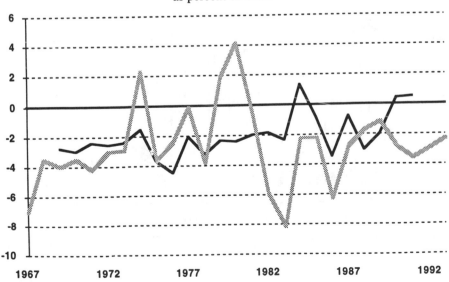

Source: International Monetary Fund, *International Financial Statistics Yearbook.*

Currency

(Historical data)

Money supply growth: 34%
Consumer price index: 70% (12% since 1970)
Monetary unit: Rupiah
Monetary unit against U.S. dollar: -88%

Economic Output

(Historical data)

GDP: $141 billion
GDP relative to U.S. GDP: 2.42%
GDP growth rate: 6.29%
GDP growth rate relative to U.S. GDP growth rate: 2.20x
Per capita GDP: $728
Per capita GDP relative to U.S. per capita GDP: 3%

Figure 9.2.   Indonesian Currency
Rupiahs per U.S. dollar (inverted scale).

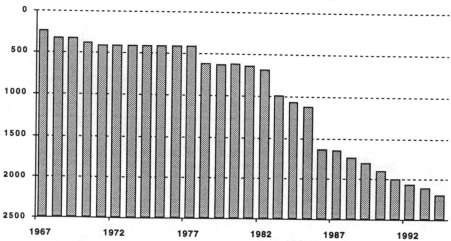

Source: International Monetary Fund, *International Financial Statistics Yearbook.*

Figure 9.3.   Indonesian Economy
Annual percentage change in Indonesian real GDP (bar graph, left scale).
Growth in Indonesian real GDP relative to U.S. real GDP, 1963 = 100
(line graph, right scale).

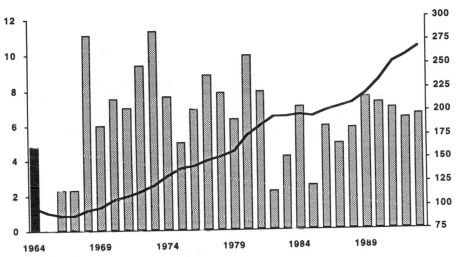

Source: International Monetary Fund, *International Financial Statistics Yearbook.*

Economic Summary

Indonesia is in the midst of its sixth five-year plan since President Suharto came
to power in 1967. Known as Repelia VI, the government-designed economic
blueprint for the years 1994 to 1998 sets goals of 6.2 percent annual real GDP
growth with vastly increased public spending for transportation infrastructure and
telecommunications. The plan also calls for an eventual hike in personal and
corporate income taxes. Presently, only about 4 million individual and corporate
tax returns are filed in a nation of nearly 200 million people. The government
envisions the new taxes to gradually replace oil and gas revenues, which it has
come to see as unreliable in the aftermath of the commodity-price crash of the
1980s.

The mere existence of Repelia VI, of course, gives sufficient indication of the
continuing attempts by the Indonesian government to macro-manage its economy.
Despite substantial liberalizations over the first half of the 1990s, foreign investment in Indonesia remains somewhat restricted. Direct foreign investors in Indo-

nesia, for example, may hold 100 percent equity for only the first 10 years, after which 51 percent ownership must begin to pass to the Indonesian government or to the domestic private sector through a stock offering. Despite the remaining restrictions, however, Indonesia also offers substantial benefits to foreign investors. Wages in Indonesia are just half of those in Malaysia and Thailand, and a full 20 times lower than those in Japan. In an attempt to increase per capita incomes, the Indonesian government plans to increase the minimum wage from $1.80 to $2.30 *per day.*

Indonesian economic growth has averaged 6.29 percent annually over the past 30 years (roughly 2.5 times the U.S. growth rate), aided by a generally accommodative monetary policy that has resulted in a healthy 33 percent yearly increase in the money supply. Along with abundant rupiahs, however, has come abundant inflation, with the nation's consumer price index increasing by an average of 12 percent annually since 1970. (Indonesia's 30-year average inflation rate of 70 percent is distorted by the more than 1,000 percent inflation in 1966.) Indonesia is a member of the Organization of Petroleum Exporting Countries (OPEC) and is the world's largest producer of liquefied natural gas. A sharp fall in energy prices during the mid-1980s, however, led to an economic slowdown, inspiring the government's attempts to diversify its export base away from energy products. Since 1983, non-energy goods have grown from 25 percent to 67 percent of total exports. As the government deregulated the financial-services sector as part of its economic diversification plan in the late 1980s, rapid credit expansion led to a resurgence of inflation, resulting in a tight-money policy from the Indonesian Central Bank during much of 1990 and 1991. When money growth and inflation fell below trend in 1993, the government loosened monetary policy, resulting in increased economic growth and corporate profits in 1994.

Indonesia's financial position is a mixed bag. The country is heavily in debt, with external public IOUs totaling 40 percent of GDP as of 1992. Indonesia's current account is also usually in deficit, averaging a 2.69 percent annual shortfall since 1969, despite modest improvement in recent years. On the plus side, Indonesia runs consistent merchandise-trade surpluses, led by large exports of wood products (Indonesia is the world's largest exporter of plywood), petroleum and natural gas, palm oil, and textiles. The most hopeful sign for Indonesia's future is the steady and spectacular improvement in its investment-to-consumption ratio. Over the past 30 years, investment in Indonesia has grown from a mere 4 cents for every dollar consumed to nearly 60 cents, double the world pace.

Figure 9.4. Indonesian Stocks

Return of Indonesian stocks in local currency (black), U.S. dollars (gray), and S&P 500 (dotted); Dec. 1987 = 100.

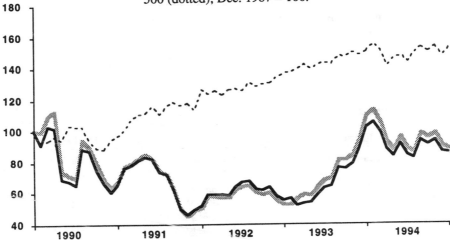

Source: Wilshire Associates Incorporated.

Indonesian Stock Market

Exchange

Classification: Emerging
Capitalization: $47 billion
Capitalization relative to U.S. stock market: 0.75%
Number of issues: 217
Primary index: Jakarta Stock Exchange (JSX) Composite
Total return in local currency, 1990–1994: –15%
Total return in U.S. dollars, 1990–1994: –12%
Total return in U.S. dollars relative to U.S. stocks, 1990–1994: –63%

Volatility
(Historical)

Standard deviation: 10.18
Total monthly losses: 210%

Average monthly loss: 6.57%
Number of monthly losses: 32
Number of monthly losses greater than 5 percent: 16
Number of monthly losses greater than 10 percent: 7
Number of monthly losses greater than 15 percent: 2
Maximum monthly loss: 34.25%
Relative volatility ratio: 4.79

Price Cycles

Phase	From	To	Total return
Bear	January 1990	June 1990	−30%
Bull	July 1990	July 1990	+35%
Bear	August 1990	November 1990	−33%
Bull	December 1990	April 1991	+35%
Bear	May 1991	October 1991	−47%
Bull	November 1991	July 1992	+42%
Bear	August 1992	December 1992	−19%
Bull	January 1993	January 1994	+116%
Bear	February 1994	December 1994	−22%

Correlations

Hong Kong 0.48
Singapore 0.44
Thailand 0.43
Australia 0.33
Germany 0.31
Malaysia 0.30
Sweden 0.30
Canada 0.29
New Zealand 0.29
Philippines 0.27
Brazil 0.26

Taiwan 0.25
United Kingdom 0.22
United States 0.22
Chile 0.15
Mexico 0.13
Switzerland 0.12
France 0.10
Korea 0.07
Japan -0.04
Argentina -0.08

Country Funds

Name	Originated	Hedging	Structure	Discount/ Premium	Phone
Indonesia Fund	March 1990	No	Closed end	−21 / 41	(212) 832-2626
Jakarta Growth	April 1990	No	Closed end	−30 / 34	(212) 509-8181

Source: Morningstar, Inc.

American Depositary Receipts

Name	Exchange	Symbol	Industry	Listed
Indonesian Satellite Corp (Indosat)	NYSE	IIT	Telecommunication	October 1994
Tri Polyta Indonesia	NASDAQ	TPIFY	Chemicals	July 1994

Direct Listings

None

Stock Summary

Prior to the government's ambitious deregulation of the financial services sector in late 1988, the Jakarta Stock Exchange (JSX) was mostly a rumor to foreign investors. During 1988, only 6.94 million shares were traded, barely 0.1 percent of the turnover rate in 1994. Over the same period, the market's capitalization increased 618-fold to $46 billion, while the number of listed companies grew from 24 to 217. In 1992, the JSX was itself privatized.

Because the JSX listed few securities before its deregulation, returns prior to the 1990s are mostly meaningless. Unfortunately, over the period for which significant data is available—the Wilshire Index: Indonesia begins in January 1990—the returns do not tell a profitable story for equity investors. From 1990 through 1994, investors in the average Indonesian stock would have shown a net loss of roughly 12 percent, for a dollar-denominated underperformance of the U.S. market of 63 percent over that period. Indonesian equities did have their moment of glory, however, with the JSX Composite climbing 114 percent in 1993, the third-largest advance of any global market in that year. Overall, however, five bear markets in five years, each taking the average stock lower by 30 percent, kept Indonesian equities on their heels. The frequent and substantial losses put the Jakarta market's relative-volatility ratio at 4.79, indicating a nearly fivefold increase in downside volatility compared to the U.S. market.

Despite the fact that foreigners are involved in 76 percent of the trading by value on the JSX, foreigners are limited to a 49 percent share of Indonesian corporations, a ceiling that may be raised in coming years. Governmental efforts are also underway to increase domestic participation in the Indonesian equity market, but the country's low average per capita income may keep progress to a minimum. Americans interested in getting an early play on the Indonesian economy can choose among two closed-end country funds and two American Depositary Receipts (ADRs). Both the Indonesia Fund and Jakarta Growth fund came public in Spring 1990. Over the first four full years of operations, Jakarta

Growth outperformed Indonesia Fund with significantly less downside volatility. Partly because of the restrictions on foreign investment, the two funds often trade at substantial premiums to their NAVs. In the ADR arena, NYSE-listed Indosat, the country's primary telecommunications provider, which was part of a widely anticipated privatization in 1994, is a relatively inexpensive play on the enormous potential growth in the Indonesian infrastructure. Tri Polyta Indonesia, trading on the NASDAQ, is a chemical producer whose stock price gyrates not only with the mercurial Indonesian market itself, but also with the price of the raw materials it requires.

The disappointing results from the Jakarta equity market over the first few years of its operations should be viewed in the light of several developments. First, market indexes were created just as the country began a period of monetary tightening, which ultimately had the intended effect of slowing the economy and, thus, reducing corporate profits. Additionally, the market's entirely normal correction after its huge run-up in 1993 was suddenly accelerated by global uncertainty over the viability of emerging markets in general in the wake of the Mexican government's decision to devalue its currency. Finally, the earthquake in Kobe threatened to divert badly needed Japanese investment from the Indonesian economy. According to the Indonesian government, Japan is the largest investor in the country, accounting for roughly 25 percent of foreign investment. Jakarta's -0.04 correlation to the Japanese equity market gives fair indication that funds often flow from Japan when few opportunities are found in that market. Price swings in Indonesian equities are moderately correlated with those in nearby Hong Kong, Singapore, and Thailand. Its relatively low correlation to the U.S. market (0.22) implies Indonesian equities could provide real portfolio diversification for American investors.

CHAPTER 10

Japan

Overview

Lingering deflation caused by the bursting of a speculative asset bubble (real estate) has kept the Japanese equity market mired in a long-term downtrend, which began in December 1989. Japan's economy, which once seemed the model for the Western world, is today often seen as an example of what can go wrong when governments and bureaucrats meddle excessively with free-market forces. The underlying problem in Japan remains an artificially inflated currency. Trade barriers once instituted to protect Japanese industry have boomeranged, creating merchandise-trade surpluses of such mammoth proportions that the resulting "Super Yen" now seriously undercuts Japan's export sector, depressing profits and keeping the economy in a slow-growth mode, at best. Profits growth has been so tepid that, despite currency-conversion benefits, American-equity investors in the Tokyo market would have barely broken even over the past seven years. A deeply entrenched bureaucracy has only frustrated the reform efforts of a series of weak Japanese governments. But although the strong yen undermines Japan's corporate profitability over the immediate term, it enhances the nation's overall power. Heaps of yen accumulating in Japanese financial institutions will need to be invested somewhere (earthquake-devastated Kobe will certainly be one beneficiary) and the weak dollar/yen relationship strongly argues that nearby Asian markets could stand to gain as well. Over the longer term, Japan will remain an economic superpower, and its equity market will still enjoy moments of glory; but those moments will shine a little less brightly and come a little less often.

Geography

Area: 145,874 square miles
Size relative to United States: 3.85%
Capital: Tokyo
Population density per square mile: 857
Population density relative to United States: 11.61x

Demographics

Population: 125 million
Population relative to United States: 48%
Average annual rate of natural increase: 0.3%
Projected population by 2025: 127 million
Population increase by 2025: 1.6%

Government

Type: Constitutional Monarchy

Head of State: Tomiichi Murayama, Prime Minister (1994)

Political System: Japan is governed by a constitution passed in 1946, during the U.S. occupation of the country in the aftermath of World War II. The constitution provides for a bicameral Diet (Parliament) made up of a House of Representatives, whose 511 members are elected concurrently to serve four-year terms, and a House of Councilors, made up of 252 lawmakers serving six-year terms.

Like those in the United States, elections in Japan tend to hinge on pocketbook issues. As long as the economy was booming, Japanese voters tolerated the bloated and archaic system of corruption, money politics, and bureaucracy fostered by its politicians. Japan's Liberal Democratic Party maintained a stranglehold on political power for most of the past four decades. In June 1993, however, among widespread public angst over a persistent economic recession, voters took a "throw the bums out" approach, electing a new coalition government led by Morihiro Hosokawa and spawning three new political parties. Hosokawa and his Japan New Party were elected on a platform of political reform, yet the new prime minister himself was forced to resign within a year amid charges of personal corruption.

From the perspective of an American trying to decide whether to buy Japanese stocks, the biggest drawbacks to the continuing political instability and weakness in Japan are that they increase the likelihood that needed regulatory reforms will fail, that fiscal and monetary medicines will be neglected, that trade talks with the United States will stall, and that internal Japanese demand for its stocks will suffer for a lack of confidence.

Economy

Financial Strength
(Historical data, relative to GDP)

Merchandise trade: +2.16%
Services: −0.84%
Income: +0.11%
Current account: +1.27%
Portfolio investment: −0.63%
Direct investment: −0.39%
Overall balance of payments: +0.29%
Budget: −3.25%
External debt: N/A
Investment/consumption ratio: 0.50

Figure 10.1.   Japanese Balance of Payments
Surplus/deficit of Japanese budget (black) and current account (gray),
as percent of GDP.

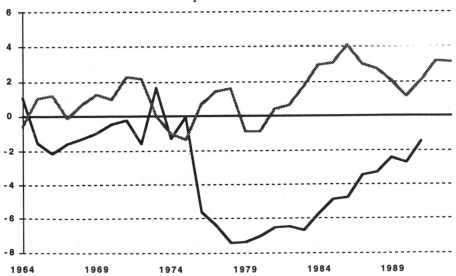

Source: International Monetary Fund, *International Financial Statistics Yearbook.*

Currency
(Historical data)

Money supply growth: 11.74%
Consumer price index: 5.19%
Monetary unit: Yen
Monetary unit against U.S. dollar: +220%

Economic Output
(Historical data)

GDP: $4.70 trillion
GDP relative to U.S. GDP: 75%
GDP growth rate: 5.46%
GDP growth rate relative to U.S. GDP growth rate: 1.91x
Per capita GDP: $33,528
Per capita GDP relative to U.S. per capita GDP: 148%

Figure 10.2.   Japanese Currency
Yen per U.S. dollar (inverted scale).

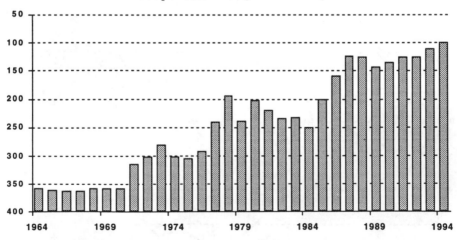

Source: International Monetary Fund, *International Financial Statistics Yearbook.*

Figure 10.3.   Japanese Economy

Annual percentage change in Japanese real GDP (bar graph, left scale). Growth in Japanese real GDP relative to U.S. real GDP, 1963 = 100 (line graph, right scale).

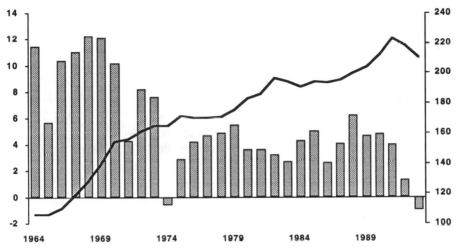

Source: International Monetary Fund, *International Financial Statistics Yearbook.*

Economic Summary

Japan enters the last half of the 1990s in the midst of its deepest slump of the postwar period. Though the growth rate of its economy has meandered slowly southward since the 1960s, the Japanese economy has adapted and rebounded from previous downturns and resumed healthy growth. Over the past 30 years, the Japanese real output has expanded at a 5.46 annual clip, roughly double the U.S. rate. Depending upon the dollar/yen relationship, Japan could actually have a larger economy than the United States (when measured in dollars) by as early as 1996—all this for a country roughly the size of Montana.

Japan's continuing inability to resume trend-level growth after a deep recession in the early 1990s, however, suggests that something is fundamentally wrong, or at least changing, in its economy. The country's extraordinary postwar success has been achieved through a combination of factors: an investment-to-consumption ratio nearly double the world average, a highly skilled and motivated work force, cooperative government/business partnerships, and protection for some of its key industries, such as automobiles, electronics, and agriculture. It is the last item that has led directly to the country's current economic malaise.

Aided by red tape and other assorted bureaucratic obstacles, Japan has amassed a huge trade surplus, currently running at $120 billion, roughly half of which comes at the expense of the United States. Over the past 30 years, Japan has never experienced a deficit in merchandise trade, averaging a 2.16 percent surplus since 1964. Since the yen began its latest climb against the dollar in the mid-1980s, however, the size of the merchandise-trade surpluses has shot up to an annual average of more than 3 percent of GDP. During the same period, the Japanese current-account surplus has increased to an average of 2.72 percent per year. (As of 1994, the U.S. current account stood at a –2.3 percent of GDP.)

The story of Japan's economic decline begins with its enormous prosperity of the 1980s. Awash in inflated yen, Japan's businesses needed a place to invest their wealth. Much of it found its way into domestic real estate and the Tokyo stock market, pushing prices to astronomical levels by the late 1980s. But when Japan's economy began a normal cyclical contraction shortly thereafter, the asset-inflation bubble was pierced, unleashing bank failures and a classic cycle of deflation. Because of its strong bureaucracy and weak political structure, Japan's government was unable to react quickly or effectively to the deepening crisis, delaying the application of badly needed monetary medicine and, more importantly, leaving in place most of the trade barriers that kept the yen artificially high. And as the yen kept climbing, profits of Japanese exporters kept falling, prolonging and intensifying the credit crunch and economic slowdown.

Japan now finds itself at a kind of economic crossroads. The protection of its industries has led to the loss of its low-cost edge. High wages—an inevitable byproduct of competitive atrophy—and the country's tradition of lifetime employment mean that Japan is no longer competitive with nearby Asian nations, such as Taiwan and Malaysia, in labor-intensive industries. Many of the Japanese corporations of the twenty-first century will likely farm out significant portions of their manufacturing processes, keeping in Japan itself only those areas that require a skilled workforce. And as employment begins to move offshore, Japan could suffer from a lack of the kind of consumer spending that its economy needs most.

History teaches never to underestimate the Japanese ability to adapt. It also teaches that stock prices bottom precisely when negative sentiment peaks. The possibility of a double-dip recession in fiscal 1996 has pushed sentiment still lower. The unrelenting pressures caused by the conundrum of its strong currency will at least mean that, when Japan does emerge from its current slump, its long-term growth rate will resemble more the economic senior citizen than the young hot shot, while its power will derive more from its ability to distribute and invest wealth than from the growth rate of its economic output.

Japanese Stock Market

Exchange

Classification: Developed
Primary location: Tokyo
Capitalization: $3 trillion
Capitalization relative to U.S. stock market: 60%
Number of issues: 1,775
Primary index: TOPIX
Total return in local currency, 1988–1994: 7%
Total return in U.S. dollars, 1988–1994: 14%
Total return in U.S. dollars relative to U.S. stocks, 1988–1994: –120%

Figure 10.4.   Japanese Stocks
Return of Japanese stocks in local currency (black), U.S. dollars (gray), and S&P 500 (dotted); Dec. 1987 = 100.

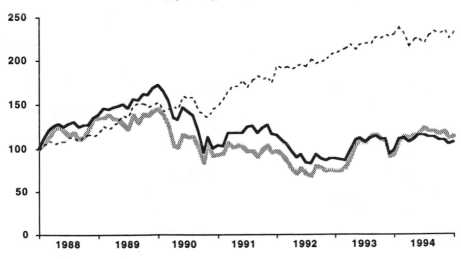

Source: Wilshire Associates Incorporated.

Volatility
(Historical)

Standard deviation: 7.9
Total monthly losses: 233%
Average monthly loss: 5.98%
Number of monthly losses: 39
Number of monthly losses greater than 5 percent: 18
Number of monthly losses greater than 10 percent: 6
Number of monthly losses greater than 15 percent: 3
Maximum monthly loss: 18.53%
Relative volatility ratio: 3.13

Price Cycles

Phase	From	To	Total return
Bull	January 1988	December 1989	+45%
Bear	January 1990	September 1990	–43%
Bull	October 1990	February 1991	+28%
Bear	March 1991	July 1992	–36%
Bull	August 1992	August 1993	+70%
Bear	September 1993	November 1993	–22%
Bull	December 1993	December 1994	+26%

Correlations

Sweden 0.53
United Kingdom 0.50
France 0.41
Singapore 0.41
Germany 0.37
Korea 0.35
Canada 0.33
Switzerland 0.26
New Zealand 0.26
Australia 0.25
United States: 0.25

Malaysia 0.24
Hong Kong 0.17
Brazil 0.16
Taiwan 0.12
Mexico 0.08
Philippines 0.07
Thailand 0.06
Indonesia 0.00
Argentina –0.10
Chile –0.20

Country Funds

Name	Originated	Hedging	Structure	Discount/ Premium	Phone
DFA Japanese Small Company	January 1986	No	Open end	Not applicable	(310) 395-8005
Japan Equity	August 1992	No	Closed end	−14 / +27	(800) 933-3440 (201) 413-6800
Japan Fund	April 1962	Possible	Open end	Not applicable	(800) 535-2726 (617) 439-4640
Japan OTC Equity	March 1990	No	Closed end	−26 / +42	(212) 509-7583
T. Rowe Price Japan	Dec. 1991	No	Open end	Not applicable	(800) 638-5660 (410) 547-2308

Source: Morningstar, Inc.

American Depositary Receipts

Name	Exchange	Symbol	Industry
Amway Japan	NYSE	AJL	Amway distributor
CSK Corporation	NASDAQ	CSKKY	Information services
Canon Inc.	NASDAQ	CANNY	Office equipment
Daiei, Inc.	NASDAQ	DAIEY	Retailer
Fuji Photo Film Co.	NASDAQ	FUJIY	Photographic equipment
Hitachi Ltd.	NYSE	HIT	Diversified manufacturing
Honda Motor Co.	NYSE	HMC	Motorcycles, automobiles
Ito Yokado Co.	NASDAQ	IYCOY	Supermarkets
Japan Air Lines	NASDAQ	JAPNY	Air carrier
Karin Brewery	NASDAQ	KNBWY	Brewer
Kubota	NYSE	KUB	Agricultural machinery
Kyocera Corporation	NYSE	KYO	Ceramic products
Makita Corp.	NASDAQ	MKTAY	Household products
Matsushita Electric Industrial Co.	NYSE	MC	Electronic products
Mitsubishi Bank	NYSE	MBK	Banking
Mitsui & Company	NASDAQ	MITSY	General trading
NEC Corporation	NASDAQ	NIPNY	Electronics
Nippon Telegraph & Telephone	NYSE	NTT	Telecommunications
Nissan Motor Co.	NASDAQ	NSANY	Automobiles
Pioneer Electronic Corp.	NYSE	PIO	High fidelity stereo

(continued)

Name	Exchange	Symbol	Industry
Sanyo Electric Co.	NASDAQ	SANYY	Consumer electronics
Sony Corporation	NYSE	SNE	Electronic products
TDK Corporation	NYSE	TDK	Electronics
Tokia Marine & Fire Insurance Co.	NASDAQ	TKIOY	Financial services
Toyota Motor Corporation	NASDAQ	TOYOY	Automobiles
Wacoal Corp.	NASDAQ	WACLY	Apparel

Direct Listings

None

Stock Summary

Beginning with the end of World War II and continuing through the 1980s, Japanese stocks enjoyed a secular bull market that only rarely was interrupted for even modest cyclical downturns. The long-term bull market was so powerful that Japanese equities outperformed their U.S. cousins by nearly 10-fold between 1950 and 1990, despite the fact that American stocks were themselves often in the midst of strong rallies. Beginning in December 1989, however, as the effects of asset-price deflation began to course through its economy, Japanese stocks abruptly changed course. For all of the 1990s, Japan has been in a classic secular bear market, with each cyclical upturn failing to break through previous highs and each cyclical decline making new lows. Over the 1988 to 1994 period, Japanese stocks returned a meager 14 percent in dollar terms, or roughly 120 percent below the coincident return of American equities. Like most long-term downtrends, the Japanese secular bear market began from highly inflated valuations, with price/earnings ratios reaching in excess of 60 times earnings in the late 1980s. As of the mid-1990s, those excesses were only partially exorcised, in part because of the slow growth of Japanese corporate profits, especially its export sector. Even on a cash-flow-per-share basis—the preferred method of valuation for some institutional investors—Japan's equity market has not become significantly less expensive now than it was before its decline.

Besides the drag of an excessively strong yen, other factors could work to constrain Japanese equities over the coming years. The internal Japanese savings rate—despite remaining high by world standards—is beginning to slip as labor and medical costs increase. More importantly, Japan's elaborate system of cross-holdings—corporations own shares of other corporations with which they have strong business ties—is likely to slowly unwind under global cost pressures. The gradual end of cross-holdings will increase the supply of shares, while less Japanese liquidity could dampen domestic demand for shares. More supply coupled with less demand will probably mean a downward pressure on Japanese multiples, even as its economy hits bottom and begins to heal.

There are currently no restrictions on foreign investment in the Japanese equity market, and no fewer than five Japanese country funds are available. U.S. investors can also partake of a wide menu of Japanese American Depositary Receipts (ADRs) from a representative cross section of industries, including many of Japan's corporate heavy hitters such as Canon, Honda, NEC, Nissan, and Toyota. American investors interested in buying foreign stocks to balance movements in the U.S. market might be especially interested in Japan; at 0.25, Japanese equities have the lowest correlation to American stocks of any developed market, providing potential global diversification during times when the U.S. market is weak or appears vulnerable.

CHAPTER 11

Malaysia

Overview

Malaysia sports a high-growth economy with minimal inflation and an improving balance sheet. Reflecting its underlying economic strength, the Malaysian equity market has been a star performer over the past seven years, significantly beating U.S. stocks in dollar terms, while subjecting investors to at least somewhat less volatility than many Asian bourses. Since emerging from a serious recession in the mid-1980s, the Malaysian economy has resumed trend-level growth in excess of 7 percent per year. Its transition from a largely commodity-based economy to one built on diversified manufacturing is continuing, spurred by several large industrial privatizations. The country is politically stable, with governmental policies tending to promote an above-average investment-to-consumption ratio. On the negative side, Malaysia has an above-average amount of external debt, is heavily dependent on exports, and must manage its currency in a way that keeps its products competitive in a global economy while still maintaining a safe environment for the kinds of direct foreign investment that enhance productivity. In order to keep its currency stable, Malaysian interest rates tend to loosely track those in the United States, resulting in stock market vulnerability during periods of American monetary tightening.

Geography

Area: 128,328 square miles
Size relative to United States: 3.39%
Capital: Kuala Lumpur

Population density per square mile: 152
Population density relative to United States: 2.06x

Demographics

Population: 20 million
Population relative to United States: 8%
Average annual rate of natural increase: 2.3%
Projected population by 2025: 32 million
Population change by 2025: +59%

Government

Type: Constitutional Monarchy .
Head of State: Azlan Muhibuddin Shah, Paramount Ruler (1989)
Political System: Malaysia's head of state, known as the Paramount Ruler, is a monarch elected to a five-year term by a vote of hereditary rulers from 9 of the country's 13 states. The monarch governs on advice from a cabinet and a parliament, which consists of a Senate (Dewan Negara) and House of Representatives (Dewan Rakyat). The Senate is made up of 40 members appointed by the Paramount Ruler and another 30 members added by popular election The 170 members of the House of Representatives are elected to five-year terms by universal adult suffrage. The cabinet is headed by the prime minister, who is appointed by the Paramount Ruler. Malaysian political power resides in the Barisan Nasional (National Front) coalition, which includes 13 parties. The Barisan Nasional has dominated each national election since its formation in 1973 from among the remnants of the so-called Alliance, a coalition that had governed the country during its struggle for independence in the 1950s until the temporary suspension of parliamentary democracy in 1969. The major political party in Malaysia is the United Malays National Organization (UMNO), of which the current prime minister, Dakut Seri Dr. Mahathir Mohamad, is a member. Dr. Mahathir has served as prime minister since July 1981. Communist parties are illegal in Malaysia, although small bands of communist guerrillas—most of whom are of Chinese origin—still hold bases in the mountainous border areas in northern Peninsular Malaysia.

Economy

Financial Strength
(Historical data, relative to GDP)

Merchandise trade: +7.5%
Services: -4.34%
Income: -4.15%
Current account: -1.34%
Portfolio investment: +1.12%
Direct investment: +3.33%
Overall balance of payments: +2.1%
Budget: -7.65%
External debt: 46%
Investment/consumption ratio: 0.37

Figure 11.1.   Malaysian Balance of Payments
Surplus/deficit of Malaysian budget (black) and current account (gray),
as percent of GDP.

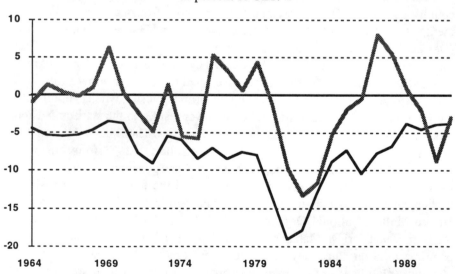

Source: International Monetary Fund, *International Financial Statistics Yearbook.*

Currency
(Historical data)

Money supply growth: 15.43%
Consumer price index: 3.71%
Monetary unit: Ringgit (M$)
Monetary unit against U.S. dollar: +13%

Economic Output
(Historical data)

GDP: $56 billion
GDP relative to U.S. GDP: 1%
GDP growth rate: 6.95%
GDP growth rate relative to U.S. GDP growth rate: 2.43x
Per capita GDP: $2,791
Per capita GDP relative to U.S. per capita GDP: 12%

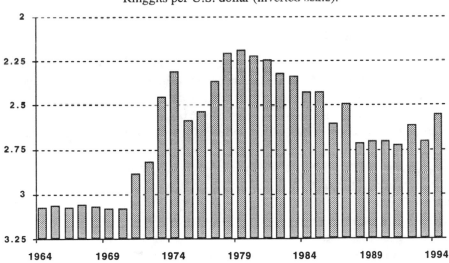

Figure 11.2.   Malaysian Currency
Ringgits per U.S. dollar (inverted scale).

Source: International Monetary Fund, *International Financial Statistics Yearbook.*

Figure 11.3. Malaysian Economy

Annual percentage change in Malaysian real GDP (bar graph, left scale). Growth in
Malaysian real GDP relative to U.S. real GDP, 1963 = 100 (line graph, right scale).

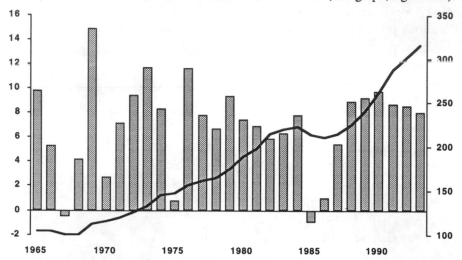

Source: International Monetary Fund, *International Financial Statistics Yearbook.*

Economic Summary

Sparked by a successful privatization program, strong foreign direct investment,
and robust export growth, the Malaysian economy grew by an annual average of
over 7 percent between 1971 and 1993, roughly double the U.S. rate over a similar period. Aided by a lessening dependence on imported energy, Malaysian
inflation has remained relatively subdued and its currency stable, despite repeated
efforts by its central bank (Bank Negara) to weaken the ringgit to mask trading
losses and protect exports. Malaysian economic policy walks a fine line between
two competing objectives. Foreign investment thrives on a strong Malaysian
currency, which has the effect of maintaining or even adding to the value of ringgit-
denominated assets. A strong ringgit, however, tends to work against Malaysian
exports, which currently account for almost 80 percent of Malaysian gross domestic product (GDP). The means used by Bank Negara to weaken its currency—
including abruptly changing banking laws to effectively lower the interest rates
paid to foreigners to zero or less—have been regarded in international financial

markets as heavy-handed, a view that could impact foreign confidence in Malaysian investments in coming years. Malaysia must also contend with the likelihood of significantly enhanced competition for international funds as neighboring economies such as China, Vietnam, India, and Indonesia begin to develop and require capital nurturing.

Malaysian financial strength is above average, especially for a developing economy. The basis of the country's economic health is a strong investment-to-consumption ratio and a positive overall balance-of-payments account. Over the past 30 years, Malaysia has invested an average of 37 cents for every dollar consumed, considerably above the world average of just 29 cents. Over the same period, Malaysia has averaged a 2.1 percent annual balance-of-payments surplus, due in large measure to a consistently positive merchandise-trade position and to substantial inflows of direct and portfolio investment. The merchandise-trade surpluses, which averaged 7.5 percent of GDP over the past three decades, have more than offset significant shortfalls in services trade and investment income, both of which have usually been in deficit. Malaysian merchandise exports are lead by electronics machinery (primarily semiconductor chips), textiles, rubber, palm oil, petroleum, and tin. More than half of aggregate Malaysian exports are to the United States, Japan, and nearby Singapore. The major weakness on the Malaysian balance sheet can be found in its fiscal policy: since 1964, budget deficits have averaged an astronomical 7.65 percent of GDP.

The Malaysian ringgit (formerly the Malaysian dollar) has generally been an ally of foreign investors. Over the past 30 years, large inflows of foreign capital have tended to put upside pressure on the ringgit, a condition that Bank Negara has sometimes tried to offset by intervening in the world's currency markets. Malaysia's export-driven economy can be hurt if the ringgit appreciates too severely. Aside from trying to trap speculators intent on bidding-up the ringgit, however, Bank Negara has in recent years played the currency-trading game itself, with occasionally disastrous results. In 1992 and 1993, the Malaysian central bank reportedly incurred losses in excess of $6 billion from ill-timed currency bets. Bank Negara's attempts at pushing down its currency in late 1992 and 1993 were clearly intended to mask and roll over its own currency-trading losses. Since 1964, the ringgit has been a small positive for U.S. equity investors, appreciating roughly 13 percent against the dollar. Most of the appreciation came before 1979, however, when the ringgit peaked at 2.18 against the dollar. Over the past 15 years, the Malaysian currency has been in a slow downward drift, trading in mid-1995 at 2.46 per U.S. dollar.

Malaysian Stock Market

Exchange

Classification: Emerging
Capitalization: $190 billion
Capitalization relative to U.S. stock market: 3%
Number of listed companies: 344
Primary index: Kuala Lumpur Stock Exchange (KLSE) Composite
Total return in local currency, 1988–1994: +526%
Total return in U.S. dollars, 1988–1994: +284%
Total return in U.S. dollars relative to U.S. stocks, 1988–1994: +150%

Volatility
(Historical)

Standard deviation: 7.25
Total monthly losses: 162%
Average monthly loss: 5.24%
Number of monthly losses: 31
Number of monthly losses greater than 5 percent: 9
Number of monthly losses greater than 10 percent: 4
Number of monthly losses greater than 15 percent: 2
Maximum monthly loss: 19.67%
Relative volatility ratio: 2.27

Price Cycles

Phase	From	To	Total return
Bull	January 1988	May 1990	+98%
Bear	June 1990	September 1990	–32%
Bull	October 1990	December 1993	+264%
Bear	January 1994	March 1994	–29%
Bull	April 1994	September 1994	+29%
Bear	October 1994	December 1994	–15%

Figure 11.4. Malaysian Stocks

Return of Malaysian stocks in local currency (black), U.S. dollars (gray), and S&P 500 (dotted); Dec. 1987 = 100 (logarithmic scale).

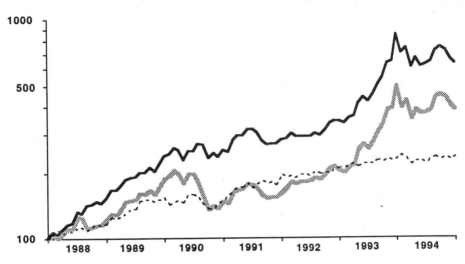

Source: Wilshire Associates Incorporated.

Correlations

Singapore 0.75	Japan 0.24
Hong Kong 0.55	New Zealand 0.24
Thailand 0.52	Sweden 0.24
Philippines 0.42	Australia 0.22
United States 0.37	France 0.22
Canada 0.33	Korea 0.21
Indonesia 0.30	Brazil 0.11
United Kingdom 0.30	Chile 0.09
Germany 0.29	Mexico 0.09
Switzerland 0.26	Argentina -0.06
Taiwan 0.26	

Country Funds

Name	Originated	Hedging	Structure	Discount/ Premium	Phones
Malaysia Fund	May 1987	No	Closed end	–31 / +67	(617) 557-8000 (212) 296-7200

Source: Morningstar, Inc.

American Depositary Receipts

None

Direct Listings

None

Stock Summary

Malaysian equities have generally been a boon for U.S. investors, with the Wilshire Index: Malaysia appreciating by 284 percent over the 1988 to 1994 period, more than double the coincident return for American equities. Accompanying the outperformance, of course, has been increased volatility; Malaysian stocks recorded a relative volatility score of 2.27, indicating slightly greater than double the price choppiness of the U.S. market. On two occasions, investors would have lost more than 15 percent in a single month, with the greatest one-month decline occurring in February 1994, when the market dived more than 19 percent. In fact, the performance of the Malaysian equity market in early 1994 underscores one of its vulnerabilities: When U.S. interest rates rise, Malaysian rates also tend to rise in order to maintain the value of the ringgit relative to the U.S. dollar and the Hong Kong dollar (which is pegged to U.S. currency). Not surprisingly, the Malaysian equity market is strongly correlated with that in Hong Kong, Singapore, Thailand, and the Philippines. Malaysian correlation to U.S. stocks, at 0.37, is the highest reading of any emerging market.

Malaysian equities have experienced five bull/bear cycles since 1988, with the largest move the 264 percent bull run between October 1990 and December 1993. (Underscoring the correlation with American equities, the 1990 low in Kuala Lumpur coincided with a major bottom in the U.S. market.) But whereas Malaysian stocks have been choppy on a month-to-month basis, the only three bear markets of the past seven years have been relatively mild, with the average decline of 25 percent being somewhat less the 33 percent long-term magnitude of bear-market falls in the United States. Reflecting the consistent growth in its economy and attendant increases in corporate profits, Malaysian stocks tend to be somewhat expensive. Over the past decade, market multiples have been roughly half again as high as those in the slower-growing U.S. market.

Although nearby Singapore may represent a healthier overall economic picture, the Malaysian equity market nonetheless offers investors a considerably larger menu of equities, in part because of a more advanced privatization program in Malaysia. Since 1990, several large government-owned businesses have floated shares, including Malaysian Airlines, Malaysian Industrial Shipping, and Tenega National, a large supplier of electricity. As of April 1995, however, no Malaysian American depositary receipts were listed on either the New York Stock Exchange or NASDAQ (National Association of Securities Dealers Automated Quotation system) markets, although a handful of stocks were trading on the U.S. over-the-counter market.

One closed-end country fund is available for investors wishing to target the Malaysian market: The Malaysia Fund, which came public in May 1987, has outperformed the Morgan Stanley Capital International Index: Malaysia in five of its seven full years of operation.

CHAPTER 12

New Zealand

Overview

New Zealand enters the last half of the 1990s in perhaps its best economic shape of the past 30 years, enjoying the fruits of a strong cyclical recovery and a decade-long series of deregulations and privatizations. The good times in the Kiwi economy are long overdue; New Zealand holds the dubious distinction of being one of the few non-Third World countries to underperform the U.S. economy over the past three decades. Since 1964, New Zealand's gross domestic product (GDP) has grown at just a 2.40 percent annual clip, losing roughly 13 percent relative to American output over that period. The country has also accumulated a massive external debt, currently more than two-thirds of GDP. Geographically isolated, New Zealand has traditionally relied upon exporting its diversified cache of agricultural goods, but export growth slowed dramatically as its leading trading partners suffered economic slowdowns in the early 1990s. As the Kiwi economy foundered, so did its equity market, returning 53 percent less than the average U.S. stock from 1988 to 1994. All that has changed recently, however, as the New Zealand stock market shot up 140 percent from its 1990 lows through year-end 1994. An improving currency—helped by long-term structural changes in New Zealand's fiscal position—has added to gains in Kiwi stocks for American investors. The newly bolstered Kiwi currency is a double-edged sword, though, because it threatens to slow exports. Like neighboring Australia, New Zealand offers equity investors a play on a variety of global commodities, plus a degree of political stability not found in most Asian nations. New Zealand may be one of the few countries whose long-term track record understates its future competitiveness.

128

Geography

Area: 103,884 square miles
Size relative to United States: 2.74%
Capital: Wellington
Population density per square mile: 34
Poopulation density relative to United States: 0.46x

Demographics

Population: 3.5 million
Population relative to United States: 1.3%
Average annual rate of natural increase: 0.9%
Projected population by 2025: 4.1 million
Population change by 2025: +17%

Government

Type: Parliamentary Democracy

Head of State: James Brendan Bolger, Prime Minister (1990)

Political System: New Zealand attained full independence within the British Commonwealth of Nations in 1947 The country is governed according to a parliamentary democracy system, with a unicameral legislature consisting of 99 members who serve three-year terms. Ninety-five of the members are elected by universal adult suffrage, with the remaining four legislators chosen by the country's small Maori population, an indigenous Polynesian people who first settled the islands in about A.D. 900. New Zealand still considers Britain's Queen Elizabeth II to be its sovereign and retains a British-appointed governor general.

Local politics are dominated by the Labor and National parties, which are roughly analogous to the American Democratic and Republican parties, respectively. Labor has generally promoted New Zealand's vast social welfare system but was also responsible for large-scale deregulation of business in the late 1980s. The National Party has consistently pushed its agenda of individual initiative and deregulation. Most recently, the Labor Party, under Prime Minister David Lange, led New Zealand from 1984 until 1990, when public discontent from several years of a downtrending economy contributed to Lange's ouster by the National Party and its leader, James Bolger. Bolger was reelected in 1993. A referendum passed in 1993 calls for legislative members to be elected on the basis of proportional representation, beginning with the 1996 general election. The new system could weaken New Zealand's strong two-party system, with smaller and more numerous parties forming governing coalitions.

Economy

Financial Strength
(Historical data, relative to GDP)

Merchandise trade: +1.33%
Services: −2.46%
Income: −3.26%
Current account: −4.11%
Portfolio investment: N/A
Direct investment: +0.87%
Overall balance of payments: −4.03%
Budget: −3.60%
External debt: 69%
Investment/consumption ratio: 32.30

Figure 12.1. New Zealand Balance of Payments
Surplus/deficit of New Zealand budget (black) and current account (gray), as percent of GDP.

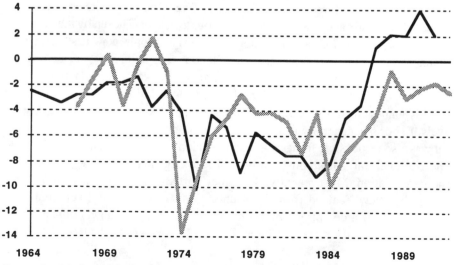

Source: International Monetary Fund, *International Financial Statistics Yearbook.*

Currency
(Historical data)

Money supply growth: 17%
Consumer price index: 8.97%
Monetary unit: New Zealand dollar
Monetary unit against U.S. dollar: –50%

Economic Output
(Historical data)

GDP: $56 billion
GDP relative to U.S. GDP: 0.8%
GDP growth rate: 2.40%
GDP growth rate relative to U.S. GDP growth rate: 0.83x
Per capita GDP: $16,034
Per capita GDP relative to U.S. per capita GDP: 62%

Economic Summary

Times have changed in New Zealand. Between 1986 and 1992, the Kiwi economy crawled along at a glacial pace, averaging annual growth of –0.2 percent. Over the past two years, however, New Zealand's economy has been positively ro-

Figure 12.2.   New Zealand Currency
New Zealand dollars per U.S. dollar (inverted scale).

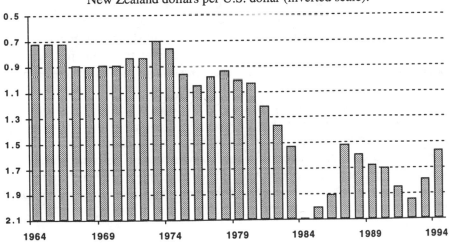

Source: International Monetary Fund, *International Financial Statistics Yearbook.*

Figure 12.3.   New Zealand Economy

Annual percentage change in New Zealand real GDP (bar graph, left scale). Growth in New Zealand real GDP relative to U.S. real GDP, 1963 = 100 (line graph, right scale).

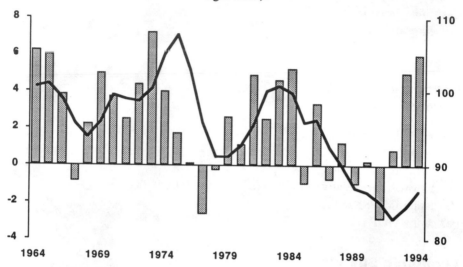

Source: International Monetary Fund, *International Financial Statistics Yearbook.*

bust, growing at an average of nearly 5.5 percent, more than double its historical average. The country is clearly reaping the benefits of its extensive deregulations and budgetary adjustments begun in the mid-1980s, as well as the buoyant economic recovery in the United States, which represents an important export market. An overbuilt commercial-real-estate sector is also showing signs of recovery. New Zealand's fiscal house has been made safe; since running massive budgetary deficits from 1964 through 1986, government surpluses have become common over the past decade. The most troubling aspect of the New Zealand economy is its current-account deficits, which have averaged 4.11 percent since 1964, with only modest recent improvement. The causes of the hemorrhaging current account are large shortfalls from income and services-trade positions, which wipe out consistent surpluses in merchandise trade. The country's healthy fiscal policy plus marginally improved balance of payments have helped to support the New Zealand currency, which has rebounded strongly against the U.S.

dollar in recent years. Over the past three decades, however, the New Zealand dollar has lost half its value relative to the U.S. dollar.

New Zealand Stock Market

Exchange

Classification: Developed
Capitalization: $27 billion
Capitalization relative to U.S. stock market: 0.43%
Number of issues: 187
Primary index: New Zealand Stock Exchange (NZSE) Gross Index
Total return in local currency, 1988–1994: +71%
Total return in U.S. dollars, 1988–1994: +81%
Total return in U.S. dollars relative to U.S. stocks, 1988–1994: –53%

Volatility
(Historical)

Standard deviation: 6.93
Total monthly losses: 189%
Average monthly loss: 4.61%
Number of monthly losses: 41
Number of monthly losses greater than 5 percent: 15
Number of monthly losses greater than 10 percent: 3
Number of monthly losses greater than 15 percent: 0
Maximum monthly loss: 13.24%
Relative volatility ratio: 2.53

Price Cycles

Phase	From	To	Total return
Bear	January 1988	February 1988	–17%
Bull	March 1988	August 1989	+65%
Bear	September 1989	December 1990	–45%
Bull	January 1991	December 1994	+140%

Figure 12.4.   New Zealand Stocks
Return of New Zealand stocks in local currency (black), U.S. dollars (gray), and
S&P 500 (dotted); Dec. 1987 = 100.

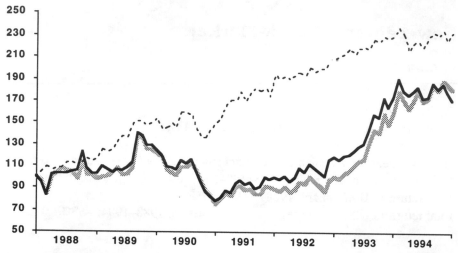

Source: Wilshire Associates Incorporated.

Correlations

Australia 0.61

Sweden 0.46

United Kingdom 0.37

Singapore 0.34

Canada 0.32

Indonesia 0.29

Hong Kong 0.27

Japan 0.26

United States 0.25

Malaysia 0.24

Germany 0.18

France 0.17

Switzerland 0.15

Thailand 0.15

Brazil 0.14

Philippines 0.14

Korea 0.10

Taiwan 0.07

Mexico 0.02

Argentina 0.01

Chile −0.15

Country Funds

None

American Depositary Receipts

Name	Exchange	Symbol	Industry
Fletcher Challenge	NYSE	FLC	Paper and construction
Fletcher Challenge Forestry Division	NYSE	FFS	Paper
Telecom Corporation of New Zealand	NYSE	NZT	Telecommunications

Direct Listings

None

Stock Summary

New Zealand equities have rebounded sharply since bottoming amid the ruins of a 45 percent bear market in December 1990. Beginning in January 1991, Kiwi stocks appreciated by 140 percent in U.S. dollar terms through December 1994. And the bull market kept right on coming in early 1995, with the All Ordinaries Index climbing another 17 percent through the first four months of the year. Through April 1995, the bull market in New Zealand had lasted 52 months, nearly as long as a coincident up move in the United States, a highly unusual occurrence for the generally shorter-cycled markets of Asia and Oceania. The recent strong gains, however, have not been enough to offset the serious declines of 1988 to 1990; and the Kiwi stock market finished 51 percent below American equities over the 1988 to 1994 period. The New Zealand exchange has a high correlation with Australian equities, and an average link with the U.S. market, primarily because of the American appetite for New Zealand's agricultural exports. Stocks in New Zealand have had roughly 2.5 times the downside volatility as U.S. equities.

While there are no country funds available on the New Zealand bourse, two large-cap American depositary receipts trade on the New York Stock Exchange: Telecom Corporation of New Zealand is the country's largest private business and is considered by many international investors to be *the* play on the Kiwi economy. The company provides cellular, domestic, and long-distance telephone service in a deregulated environment. Fletcher Challenge is a diversified, multinational company with operations in forestry, construction, and energy. Despite the limited menu of Kiwi stocks, Fletcher Challenge and Telecom Corp. NZ combine to represent roughly 25 percent of the value of the entire New Zealand market.

CHAPTER 13

Republic of the Philippines

Overview

Investors in Philippine equities could become the beneficiaries of one of the few examples of a government fundamentally changing and improving its long-term ways. Looking only at its historical record—or at least that portion before the ouster of former dictator Ferdinand Marcos—the Philippine economy represents one of the least attractive investment opportunities in Asia. Relatively slow growth along with high inflation and unemployment, an oppressive foreign debt, a string of natural disasters, and persistent political unrest often gave the Philippine equity market little positive reinforcement. An entirely inadequate infrastructure only compounded the difficulties.

But although many of the nation's economic problems remain, there is evidence of significant progress. During 1994 and 1995, the Philippine economy is projected to have grown by an average of roughly 6 percent per year, a nearly sixfold increase over the 1990 to 1993 pace and almost double its 30-year record. Growing political stability—accomplished without the heavy-handed tactics of various other Asian nations—has led to an avalanche of foreign direct and portfolio investment. Reflecting the improved economic climate, Philippine equities posted huge gains between October 1991 and December 1993 before correcting somewhat in 1994 and early 1995. While the nation still has serious long-term problems, including a high birth rate (the population of the Philippines is expected to grow by almost 50 percent by 2025) and vastly uneven distribution of wealth, its economy and equity market give solid evidence of shifting into a higher gear. Only time will tell, however, if the current improvement will be lasting or merely the cyclical peak before yet another downturn.

Geography

Area: 115,830 square miles
Size relative to United States: 3%
Capital: Manila
Population density per square mile: 593
Population density relative to United States: 8.05x

Demographics

Population: 67 million
Population relative to that of United States: 26%
Average annual rate of natural increase: 2.4%
Projected population by 2025: 101 million
Population change by 2025: +49%

Government

Type: Parliamentary Democracy

Head of State: Fidel V. Ramos, President (1992)

Political System: Under a new constitution approved by national referendum on February 2, 1987, the Philippine government is headed by a president, elected by popular vote to a single six-year term. The constitution also created a bicameral Congress, consisting of a 24-member Senate (popularly elected to six-year terms) and a 250-member House of Representatives (serving three-year terms). Two hundred House members are popularly elected, with the remainder appointed by the president from minority groups. In apparent reaction to the mostly dictatorial regime of former President Ferdinand E. Marcos (1965–1986), the new charter limits the power of the president to impose martial law; such declarations may now be overturned by a simple majority vote of Congress. The government faces political challenges on the right from former Marcos supporters and on the left from a persistent communist insurgency led by the so-called New People's Army. Philippine governments have also feuded with a Muslim-separatist movement in the south. A vast disparity in the distribution of wealth and land—a condition virtually unchanged in the nearly 10 years since Marcos's departure—feeds the undercurrent of domestic political unrest. Since the end of the Marcos regime, U.S. influence has gradually declined. The 1991 eruption of Mount Pinatubo so severely damaged Clark Air Force Base that the United States decided to abandon the base altogether. Negotiations to extend the U.S. lease on its Subic Bay naval facility ended in stalemate, and in September 1994 control over the base reverted to the Philippine government.

Economy

Financial Strength

(Historical data, relative to GDP)

Merchandise trade: –13.30%
Services: +1.49%
Income: –1.69%
Current account: –2.64%
Portfolio investment: +0.04%
Direct investment: +0.37%
Overall balance of payments: +0.56%
Budget: –1.72%
External debt: 57%
Investment/consumption ratio: 0.30

Figure 13.1.   Philippine Balance of Payments
Surplus/deficit of Philippine budget (black) and current account (gray), as percent of GDP.

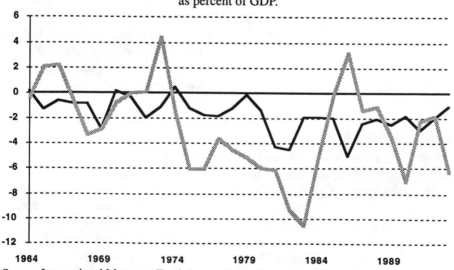

Source: International Monetary Fund, *International Financial Statistics Yearbook.*

Figure 13.2.   Philippine Currency
Pesos per U.S. dollar (inverted scale).

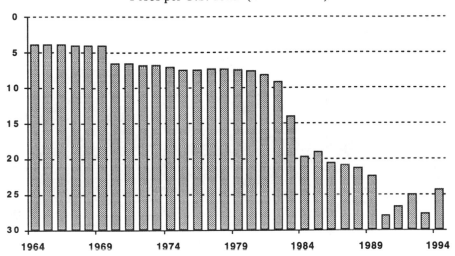

Source: International Monetary Fund, *International Financial Statistics Yearbook.*

Currency
(Historical data)

Money supply growth: 13%
Consumer price index: 12.04%
Monetary unit: Peso
Monetary unit relative to U.S. dollar: −85%

Economy
(Historical data)

GDP: $52 billion
GDP relative to U.S. GDP: 0.90%
GDP growth rate: 3.83%
GDP growth rate relative to U.S. GDP growth rate: 1.34x
Per capita GDP: $777
Per capita GDP relative to U.S. per capita GDP: 3%

Economic Summary

The Philippine economy has been the weak sister of the Asian group for most of
the past three decades. Average annual real gross domestic product (GDP)

Figure 13.3.   Philippine Economy

Annual percentage change in Philippine real GDP (bar graph, left scale). Growth in Philippine real GDP relative to U.S. real GDP, 1963 = 100 (line graph, right scale).

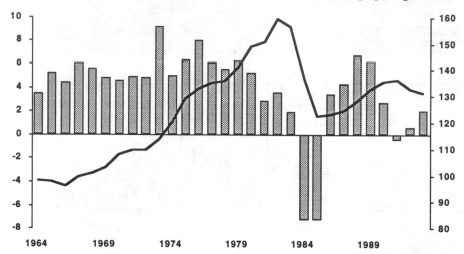

Source: International Monetary Fund, *International Financial Statistics Yearbook.*

growth of less than 4 percent since 1964 is less than half the rate of many Asian nations, and per capita GDP of $777 ranks the country among the poorest of the poor. The historical range of Philippine economic problems has included slow growth, high inflation, a generally weak currency, chronic budget deficits, large merchandise-trade shortfalls, a mostly negative current account, and mountains of foreign debt, much of it rung up under the regime of former President Ferdinand Marcos. A series of natural disasters, including the 1991 eruption of Mount Pinatubo, only exacerbated the underlying problems. Since 1964, Philippine inflation has averaged over 12 percent per year, nearly triple the U.S. rate. Along with spiraling prices has come the inevitable falling currency, with the Philippine peso depreciating by 85 percent against the U.S. dollar over the past 30 years. Not even a weak currency has done much to stimulate demand for Philippine exports; despite substantial growth over the past decade, exports still account for less than one-third of GDP, and merchandise-trade deficits have averaged a staggering 24 percent of GDP since 1980. Fortunately, the Philippines is relatively rich in natural resources, lowering its need to import energy. Fiscal policy has also contributed to the weak peso; since 1964, budget deficits have averaged 1.7 percent of GDP, although the shortfalls have trended lower since Marcos's departure in 1986.

The post-Marcos administrations of Corazon Aquino and Fidel V. Ramos have struggled to deal with years of economic mismanagement. Unfortunately, the new leaders found the Philippine economic cupboard nearly bare; in order to dampen inflation, stabilize the peso, and attract the kind of foreign investment needed for economic growth, interest rates were forced to stratospheric levels (Treasury bill yields averaged over 21 percent between 1989 and 1991), retarding economic growth through most of the first half of the 1990s. In keeping with global trends, however, privatization programs have begun, foreign-exchange controls have been lifted, and the nation's gargantuan foreign debt (almost 100 percent of GDP in 1986) has been restructured. There are also signs that confidence in the Philippine government is increasing: Since 1988, direct foreign investment in the Philippines has increased to an average of 1.32 percent of GDP per year, a nearly 10-fold increase over the meager 0.14 percent level of the Marcos years. In particular, public and private Japanese investment has firmed as opportunities elsewhere in southeast Asia and the United States (due to the weak dollar) have grown more limited. As the flow of direct and portfolio investment has increased, the Philippine peso has begun to rebound, reversing a long-term downtrend by appreciating by more than 10 percent against the dollar in 1994.

Philippine Stock Market

Exchange

Classification: Emerging
Capitalization: $30 billion
Capitalization relative to U.S. stock market: 0.48%
Number of issues: 170
Primary index: Philippine Stock Exchange Composite
Total return in local currency, 1988–1994: +1,435%
Total return in U.S. dollars, 1988–1994: +1,265%
Total return in U.S. dollars relative to U.S. stocks, 1988–1994: +1,131%

Volatility
(Historical)

Standard deviation: 38.45
Total monthly losses: 219%

Average monthly loss: 6.85%
Number of monthly losses: 32
Number of monthly losses greater than 5 percent: 14
Number of monthly losses greater than 10 percent: 7
Number of monthly losses greater than 15 percent: 3
Maximum monthly loss: 36.32%
Relative volatility ratio: 5.00

Price Cycles

Phase	From	To	Total return
Bull	January 1988	April 1989	+115%
Bear	May 1989	September 1990	–64%
Bull	October 1990	May 1991	+66%
Bear	June 1991	September 1991	–19%
Bull	October 1991	December 1993	+1,415%
Bear	January 1994	December 1994	–18%

Figure 13.4. Philippine Stocks

Return of Philippine stocks in local currency (black), U.S. dollars (gray), and S&P
500 (dotted); Dec. 1987 = 100 (logarithmic scale).

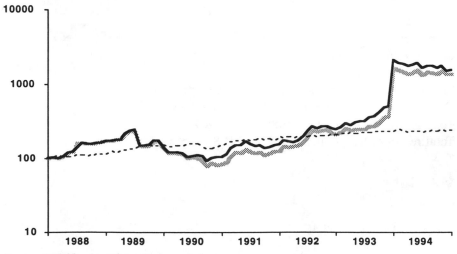

Source: Wilshire Associates Incorporated.

Correlations

Malaysia 0.42
Hong Kong 0.40
Thailand 0.37
Taiwan 0.33
Singapore 0.30
Indonesia 0.27
Australia 0.20
Sweden 0.19
Canada 0.16
France 0.15
Chile 0.14

New Zealand 0.14
Argentina 0.10
Germany 0.09
United Kingdom 0.09
Japan 0.07
Korea 0.06
Switzerland 0.06
United States 0.03
Mexico −0.01
Brazil −0.02

Country Funds

Name	Originated	Hedging	Structure	Discount/ Premium	Phone
First Philippine Fund	Nov. 1989	No	Closed end	−33 / +26	(800) 524-4458 (212) 765-0700

Source: Morningstar, Inc.

American Depositary Receipts

Name	Exchange	Symbol	Industry
Philippine Long Distance Telephone	NYSE	PHI	Telecommunication

Direct Listings

Name	Exchange	Symbol	Industry
Benguet	NYSE	BE	Mining

Stock Summary

Thanks to an explosive bull market from late 1991 through 1993, Philippine equities outperformed their U.S. counterparts by more than 10-fold over the 1988 to 1994 period. Even the inevitable correction that followed in 1994 was cushioned somewhat for American investors by newfound strength in the Philippine currency, which climbed against the dollar for one of the few times since the early 1960s.

Despite its overall winning ways, however, the Philippine market would have frazzled a few nerves along the way. Philippine equities have fully five times the downside volatility of U.S. stocks; on 14 separate occasions since 1988, investors would have lost 5 percent or more of their money in a single month, including a 36 percent bloodbath in July 1989. One of the three bear-market cycles over that period wiped out roughly two-thirds of the average Philippine stock's value. The extraordinary performance of the Philippine market relative to the U.S. market over the past seven years is entirely the result of the powerful uptrend that began in late 1991 as a combination of factors began to attract large foreign-portfolio investment to Manila. Those factors included an improving domestic political environment, a lifting of foreign-exchange restrictions, a drop in domestic interest rates, moderation in the rate of inflation, signs of a strong cyclical expansion, and continuing increases in the rate of foreign direct investment.

The Philippine equity market was restructured in mid-1993 to combine what had been two competing bourses—the Manila and Makati exchanges—into one unified market, known as the Philippine Stock Exchange. With the merger came a new index, the Philippine Stock Exchange Composite, which more accurately reflects aggregate market weightings. A number of privatizations in recent years, including Philippine Airlines and Petron (oil refining), has significantly expanded the menu for domestic and foreign investors. Americans considering buying into the Philippine stock market should take note of the low correlation (0.03) between Philippine and U.S. stocks, indicating Philippine equities offer Americans a substantial opportunity for real portfolio diversification. Specific plays on the Philippine bourse are more limited, but the only country fund available, First Philippine, has beaten the Morgan Stanley Capital International Index: Philippines over the five years of its existence. The fund has outperformed its market through a series of successful allocation plays during periods of overall price weakness, more than compensating for the fund's underperformance during Philippine bull markets. Two individual Philippine stocks are available on the NYSE or the NASDAQ, including Benguet, the long-time mining company based in Manila, and Philippine Long Distance Telephone, the country's largest provider of telecommunications services. Two other Philippine companies, Manila Electric and San Miguel (a food-and-beverage concern), are available as American depositary receipts on the over-the-counter market.

CHAPTER 14

Republic of Singapore

Overview

Singapore boasts one of the world's fastest-growing and most financially stable economies. Despite its tiny size, the nation occupies a strategically vital location in Southeast Asia and is perfectly positioned to capitalize on continued economic expansion in China and other less-developed Asian nations. Its equity market, while limiting opportunities for foreign investment, has nonetheless outperformed the American stock market, both in local currency and in U.S. dollars. The economic miracle of Singapore, however, has occurred alongside a nearly total lack of political freedom and Draconian crime-fighting measures. At the moment, the freedom-for-stability trade-off is accepted by the city-state's three million citizens as the necessary and worthwhile price of prosperity. Although prospective equity investors can take comfort in Singapore's nearly unprecedented financial strength, two cautionary alarms should be sounded: First, the government's tight grip on economic and political power may one day begin to slip, bringing with it instability and uncertainty. Second, and of more immediate concern, is the unmistakable resemblance of the Singapore government's economic micro-management to that of Japan, a practice that eventually strangled the Japanese economy in a mass of bureaucratic red tape. Only time will tell if the entire system of close government/business interaction is fundamentally flawed—and, thus, preordained to fail—or if the lessons of Japan (and to a lessor extent in Korea) only relate to the level of expertise that the planners bring to their respective tasks.

Geography

Area: 246 square miles
Size relative to United States: 0.0001%
Capital: Singapore
Population density per square mile: 11,755
Population density relative to United States: 159x

Demographics

Population: 3.22 million
Population relative to United States: 1.2%
Average annual rate of natural increase: 1.2%
Projected population by 2025: 3.9 million
Population change by 2025: +21%

Government

Type: Republic

Head of State: Goh Chok Tong, Prime Minister (1990)

Political System: The Singaporean legislative branch consists entirely of a unicameral Parliament, whose 81 members are elected by universal adult suffrage to five-year terms. Cabinet members are selected from the dominant political party in the legislature. Executive power rests with the prime minister, who heads the cabinet. Despite its status as a republic with a parliamentary form of government, Singapore is essentially a one-party nation, with the People's Action Party (PAP) dominating local politics since 1959. The PAP leader, former Prime Minister Lee Kuan Yew, is now considered the elder statesman of Singaporean politics. The government maintains strict control over information, speech, and nearly all other forms of citizen behavior. It imposes harsh penalties for such seemingly minor offenses as littering and failing to flush a public toilet.

Economy

Financial Strength
(Historical data, relative to GDP)

Merchandise trade: −71.37%
Services: +20.78%
Income: +0.68%
Current account: −6.67%
Portfolio investment: −0.32%
Direct investment: +6.16%
Overall balance of payments: +7.42%
Budget: +1.92%
External debt: 0%
Investment/consumption ratio: 0.59

Figure 14.1. Singaporean Balance of Payments
Surplus/deficit of Singapore budget (black) and current account (gray)
as percent of GDP.

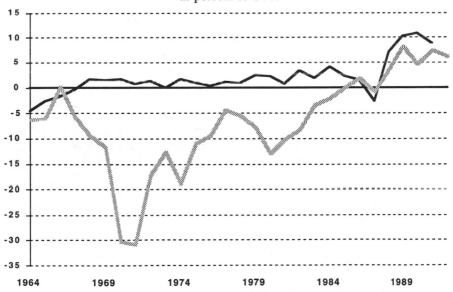

Source: International Monetary Fund, *International Financial Statistics Yearbook.*

Currency
(Historical data)

Money supply growth: 14.81%
Consumer price index: +3.75%
Monetary unit: Singapore dollar (S$)
Monetary unit against U.S. dollar: 190.68%

Economic Output
(Historical data)

GDP: $55 billion
GDP relative to U.S. GDP: 0.95%
GDP growth rate: 8.43%
GDP growth rate relative to U.S. GDP growth rate: 2.95x
Per capita GDP: $17,174
Per capita GDP relative to U.S. per capita GDP: 76%

Figure 14.2. Singaporean Currency
Singapore dollars per U.S. dollar (inverted scale).

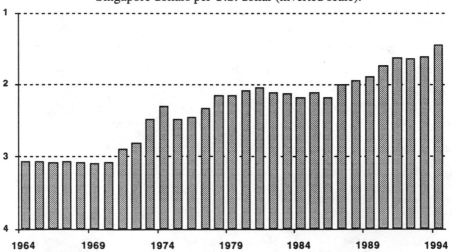

Source: International Monetary Fund, *International Financial Statistics Yearbook.*

Figure 14.3.   Singaporean Economy

Annual percentage change in Singapore real GDP (bar graph, left scale). Growth in Singapore real GDP relative to U.S. real GDP, 1963 = 100 (line graph, right scale).

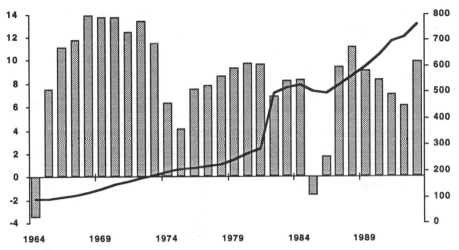

Source: International Monetary Fund, *International Financial Statistics Yearbook.*

Economic Summary

Singapore's 30-year annual growth rate of 8.43 percent makes it one of the fastest-growing economies in Southeast Asia and the world. Equally impressive as its growth, however, is the fact that the Singaporean economic engine generally runs clean, with no foreign debt and scant price instability. Between 1964 and 1993, consumer prices increased by an average of just 3.75 percent per year, more than 1.6 percent below the U.S. inflation rate despite two years of near hyperinflation in the mid-1970s.

Considered one of Asia's four "Little Tigers" (along with Hong Kong, Taiwan, and South Korea), Singapore is an odd combination of political authoritarianism and market economics. Added to the mix is a close government/business relationship resembling that found in Japan and South Korea, but with one vital difference: The word *bureaucratic* is rarely used in describing the Singapore government's economic planning. In fact, so coldly Darwinian is the government's approach to its economy that the country is sometimes known as Singapore Inc. The government sees its role as carefully orchestrating the development of local and multinational business investment through tax breaks and other incentives, such as providing a skilled workforce and a stable social climate in a strategically important setting. Over the past three decades, Singapore has gradually transformed its economy from a low-wage, low-cost manufacturer to one that has attracted tens of billions of dollars in high-tech multinational investment because of its highly skilled, English-speaking workforce. As of 1994, nearly three-quarters of the computer disk drives consumed worldwide were manufactured in Singapore.

Despite the current health of its economy, the Singapore government is already anticipating the next step in global and Asian economic evolution. The government is taking an active role in encouraging Singaporean businesses to relocate a substantial portion of their operations in neighboring countries, such as India, Indonesia, China, and Vietnam, both to access new markets and to capitalize on the vastly lower labor rates available in those countries. The large amount of international investment by cash-rich Singaporean business over the past decade should begin to pay handsome dividends in the coming years, both to insulate and diversify its local economy from cyclical downturns and to boost corporate profits. To offset the inevitable erosion of low-wage jobs to less mature Asian economies, Singapore is attempting to position itself as the financial and communications center of Asia.

The country already is the regional home of more than 100 banks and boasts the world's third-largest foreign-exchange market. Singapore was sharply criticized for inadequate securities-market regulation in the aftermath of the collapse of the British investment bank Barings PLC, whose employee Nicholas W. Leeson racked up over $1 billion of derivatives-related losses while trading on Singapore's International Monetary Exchange (SIMEX).

Despite the derivatives fiasco, however, Singapore remains in an enviable financial position. Massive capital inflows of direct investment, a strong fiscal policy, and a high savings rate (Singaporeans are required by law to channel a portion of their wages into a government-sponsored pension fund or other investment vehicle) have combined to make Singapore's balance sheet the model for emerging as well as developed economies. Over the past three decades, Singaporean investment has averaged 59 cents for every dollar consumed, more than double the world average. During the 1990s, that figure has increased to over 75 cents for every dollar consumed. As a result of Singapore's strong fiscal policy, the government has run budgetary surpluses in all but one year since 1971. Recent surpluses have averaged nearly 10 percent of GDP, compared with chronic U.S. annual shortfalls of more than 2 percent of GDP. Singapore is also a nation of savers, investing twice as much and consuming only half as much as the world as a whole. As of 1993, net Singaporean public and private investment reached more than 43 percent of GDP, compared with just 16.5 percent in the United States and just over 20 percent for the world as a whole. Singaporean consumption of 52 percent of GDP was also substantially below the world average of 80 percent. Singapore's healthy rates of internal investment and consumption coupled with its strong fiscal policy have more than offset a seriously weak merchandise-trade position, giving it one of the most favorable overall balance-of-payments-to-GDP ratios of any nation. For the 30 years ended 1993, Singapore averaged more than a 7 percent annual-balance-of-payments surplus, a figure that has increased to over 10 percent during the 1990s.

The strong overall balance-of-payments position has led to a steady appreciation in the Singapore currency against the U.S. dollar. The Singapore dollar has been a consistent ally of U.S. investors in Singapore, appreciating by roughly 90 percent against the U.S. dollar over the past three decades. Since 1985, Singapore government officials have allowed its currency to float freely in world exchange markets, but the Singapore Monetary Authority closely tracks the dollar's performance against a basket of trade-weighted currencies. Singapore's strong current account, especially compared with that of the United States, is likely to keep the currency a net long-term positive for American investors interested in buying Singaporean financial assets.

Singaporean Stock Market

Exchange

Classification: Developed
Capitalization: $136 billion
Capitalization relative to U.S. stock market: 2.18%
Number of issues: 251
Primary index: Straits Times Industrial
Total return in local currency, 1988–1994: +152%
Total return in U.S. dollars, 1988–1994: +242%
Total return in U.S. dollars relative to U.S. stocks, 1988–1994: +108%

Volatility
(Historical)

Standard deviation: 5.33
Total monthly losses: 109%

Average monthly loss: 3.65%
Number of monthly losses: 30
Number of monthly losses greater than 5 percent: 6
Number of monthly losses greater than 10 percent: 3
Number of monthly losses greater than 15 percent: 1
Maximum monthly loss: 16.45%
Relative volatility ratio: 1.63
Relative return per unit risk: 1.11

Price Cycles

Phase	From	To	Total return
Bull	January 1988	July 1990	+105.0%
Bear	August 1990	November 1991	−28.8%
Bull	December 1991	December 1994	+123.0%

Figure 14.4.   Singaporean Stocks

Return of Singaporean stocks in local currency (black), U.S. dollars (gray), and
S&P 500 (dotted); Dec. 1987 = 100.

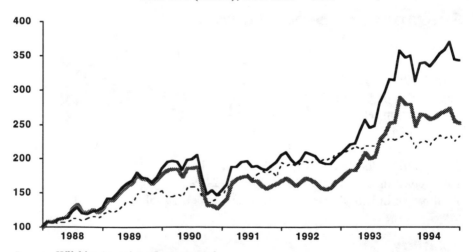

Source: Wilshire Associates Incorporated.

Correlations

Malaysia 0.75
Sweden 0.62
United Kingdom 0.59
Hong Kong 0.56
United States 0.55
Germany 0.46
Indonesia 0.44
Thailand 0.44
Japan 0.41
Canada 0.39
Australia 0.38

France 0.36
New Zealand 0.34
Philippines 0.30
Switzerland 0.29
Taiwan 0.29
Korea 0.24
Brazil 0.17
Chile 0.14
Mexico 0.14
Argentina –0.03

Country Funds

Name	Originated	Hedging	Discount/ Structure	Premium	Phones
Singapore Fund	July 1990	No	Closed end	–25 / +36	(800) 933-3440 (201) 915-3020

Source: Morningstar, Inc.

American Depositary Receipts

Name	Exchange	Symbol	Industry
China Yuchai International	NYSE	CYD	Manufacturing and sale diesel engines

Stock Summary

Compared to other Asian equity markets, the Singapore bourse has often been a scene of virtual tranquility. Singaporean stocks have been just 1.63 times as volatile as their American cousins, or barely half the rate of choppiness found on most Asian exchanges. Reflecting the relative lack of volatility, stock prices in Singapore have experienced just three bull/bear cycles over the past seven years, with the only bear market lasting just four months and resulting in "only" a 29 percent decline. (The timing and magnitude of the fall in Singaporean equities coincided nearly exactly with the 1990 bear market in the United States that began amid the Iraq-Kuwait crisis in the Persian Gulf.) Over the 1988 to 1994 period, Singaporean equities outperformed U.S. stocks by 108 percent, although 90 percent of the outperformance was the result of currency-related gains for U.S. investors. In local currency terms, Singaporean equities beat the U.S. market by just 18 percent over those seven years. Adjusted for volatility, Singapore is one of the few exchanges that has actually outperformed the U.S. stock market since 1988.

Despite its strong economy, investing in Singaporean equities can often be a frustrating experience for foreign investors. Many of the companies comprising the rapidly growing electronics sector, for example, are actually owned by foreign multinational corporations and are, therefore, off-limits for trading on the Singapore bourse. As of late 1994, less than 2 percent of the Singapore market's capitalization consisted of electronics stocks. Additionally, Singapore officials have placed ceilings of from 25 percent to 50 percent on the amount of any domestic company that may be owned by foreign investors. Once a given limit is reached, additional shares may only be acquired in foreign tranche trading, which often occurs at a premium to the locally available price. A substantial portion of the Singapore economy also remains in the hands of the government, which has moved only slowly to privatize its holdings. The last major privatization (Singapore Telecom, in 1993) was accomplished on terms that were clearly unfavorable to many foreign investors. As of early 1995, only one Singaporean American Depositary Receipt, China Yuchai International, was available to U.S. investors.

Recently, players in the Singapore market have become fearful of an asset-inflation bubble developing among the country's pricey real estate sector. With all-too-clear memories of similar debacles in Tokyo and Hong Kong, prices of many of the nation's commercial and residential real estate companies, which make up roughly 10 percent of the market's capitalization, were hammered in late 1994 and 1995. Singaporean stocks are also a bit pricey relative to the United States, with price/earnings ratios ranging from roughly 20 to 40 times earnings. The Singapore market correlates highly with a number of foreign bourses, with the strongest price correlations coming from nearby Malaysia at 0.75. Movements in Singaporean equities are also highly correlated to movements in the United States and Hong Kong, primarily because its large financial sector retains the same interest-rate sensitivity as that of the United States.

Only one country fund is available as a vehicle for targeted equity investment in Singapore. The Singapore Fund, however, may also invest in Malaysia and other Pacific Basin countries, a practice that distorts its record (for evaluation purposes) relative to the Morgan Stanley Capital International (MSCI) or Wilshire Singapore Indexes. Over the four full years since its inception, the Singapore Fund has underperformed the MSCI Index: Singapore by an average of roughly 6 percent per year. As of October 1995, Singapore Fund sold at a 2.7 percent premium to its net asset value.

CHAPTER 15

Republic of Korea (South Korea)

Overview

Investors in South Korean markets have more to worry about than the occasional political flare-ups with North Korea. A deeply entrenched economic and political bureaucracy—not unlike the interdependent government/business relationships found in Japan—is slowing needed reforms in South Korean capital and equity markets and threatening to make exports noncompetitive in the global marketplace. For most of the past three decades, South Korea has been among the shining stars of Asian economic growth, but a significant slowdown in economic growth in 1992 and 1993 underscored the deep institutional changes that must be made if the previous pace of growth is to resume. Recent evidence suggests that both the economy and the regulatory environment are improving, which augurs well for the long-term potential of equity investments in South Korea. The gradual opening of the South Korean stock market to overseas investors is a mixed blessing, however, as the benefits of increased foreign demand for stocks could be at least partially offset by sharply contracting discount/premium spreads for the closed-end country funds, the primary investment vehicle for Americans looking to buy Korean stocks.

Geography

Area: 38,031 square miles
Size relative to United States: 1%
Capital: Seoul
Population density per square mile: 1,170
Population density relative to United States: 16x

Demographics

Population: 44 million
Population relative to United States: 17%
Average annual rate of natural increase: 1.0%
Projected population by 2025: 53 million
Population change by 2025: +19%

Government

Type: Republic

Head of State: Kim Young Sam, President (1993)

Political System: Under a new constitution enacted in 1987, the South Korean president heads the executive branch of government and is elected by universal suffrage to a maximum of one five-year term. The legislative branch consists of the unicameral National Assembly, whose 299 members are popularly elected to a four-year term. Kim Young Sam, a former dissident, is the first civilian leader of Korea in 30 years. Since his inauguration in 1993, President Kim has attempted a broad program of economic reform but has run headlong into an entrenched bureaucracy intent on blocking his every move. In 1995, Mr. Kim's government announced the consolidation of roughly 10 percent of the federal bureaucracy, including the merging of the Finance Ministry and the Economic Planning Board into the Ministry of Finance and Economy. Mr. Kim has gradually toughened his rhetoric toward North Korea, especially as regards its alleged nuclear weapons program.

Economy

Financial Strength
(Historical data, relative to GDP)

Merchandise trade: −4.89%
Services: +10.14%
Income: −1.31%
Current account: −2.96%
Portfolio investment: +0.33%
Direct investment: +0.19%
Overall balance of payments: +1.14%
Budget: −1.02%
External debt: 12%
Investment/consumption ratio: 0.39

Figure 15.1.   South Korean Balance of Payments
Surplus/deficit of South Korean budget (black) and current account (gray)
as percent of GDP.

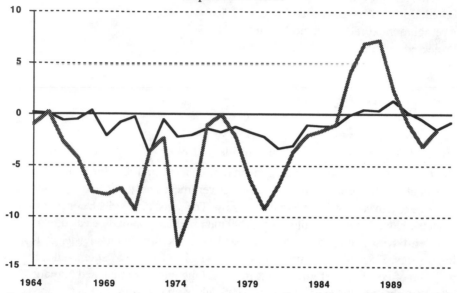

Source: International Monetary Fund, *International Financial Statistics Yearbook.*

Currency
(Historical data)

Money supply growth: 28.35%
Consumer price index: 11.08%
Monetary unit: Won
Monetary unit against U.S. dollar: –68%

Economic Output
(Historical data)

GDP: $328 billion
GDP relative to U.S. GDP: 5.64%
GDP growth rate: 8.74%
GDP growth rate relative to U.S. GDP growth rate: 3.06x
Per capita GDP: $7,352
Per capita GDP relative to U.S. per capita GDP: 32%

Figure 15.2.   South Korean Currency
Won per U.S. dollar (inverted scale).

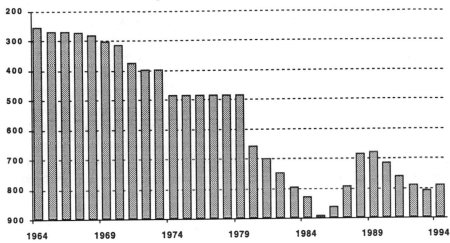

Source: International Monetary Fund, *International Financial Statistics Yearbook.*

Figure 15.3.   South Korean Economy
Annual percentage change in South Korean real GDP (bar graph, left scale).
Growth in South Korean real GDP relative to U.S. real GDP, 1963 = 100
(line graph, right scale).

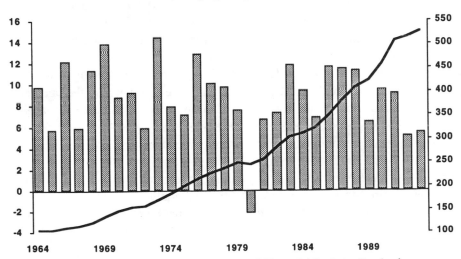

Source: International Monetary Fund, *International Financial Statistics Yearbook.*

Economic Summary

South Korea has been a high-growth, high-inflation economy for most of the past 30 years. Fueled by a cozy working relationship between government and business (similar to that of Japan) and by an accommodative monetary policy, South Korean gross domestic product (GDP) growth has often rivaled that of prosperous Asian neighbors China, Hong Kong, and Singapore. Over the past three decades, South Korean inflation-adjusted GDP has expanded by an average of 8.7 percent per year, triple the U.S. rate. Much of the growth has come from the export sector, with large South Korean industrial chaebols (conglomerates) selling such products as consumer electronics and automobiles abroad with phenomenal success. Between 1964 and 1993, for example, South Korean exports grew at a nearly 28 percent annual clip. Indeed, the South Korean economy has usually been so robust that the 1992 to 1993 average growth of 5.3 percent was considered "recessionary" by local standards.

Price stability, however, has often been a serious concern, with consumer inflation averaging more than 11 percent annually. South Korean inflation has significantly undermined its currency, with the won falling roughly two-thirds against the U.S. dollar since 1964. Fiscal policy has also been a mild negative, with budget deficits averaging 1 percent of GDP per year over the past 30 years. Although the budgetary deficits are not large (roughly one-third the size of U.S. shortfalls as a percent of GDP), South Korea has managed just four budget surpluses since 1969. Over the past decade, however, South Korea has run a tighter fiscal and monetary ship; since 1983, real growth in the money supply has been cut from over 20 percent per year to just 12 percent, causing a drop in consumer inflation to roughly a 5 percent annual rate. The lower inflation has helped stabilize the won, which traded in early 1995 at levels virtually unchanged from a decade earlier.

In the 1990s, however, clouds have formed on the once-glowing South Korean economic horizon. Export growth, the driving force behind the country's rapid industrialization, has slowed from a 31 percent annual pace from 1964 through 1988 to just 6.29 percent between 1989 and 1993. Most disturbingly, South Korea has begun to lag some of its Asian competitors in deregulating its businesses, opening its equity, capital, and import markets and welcoming foreign investment. Ironically, the major impediment to the kinds of structural changes required to keep the South Korean economy competitive in a global economy are the same tangled web of government/business relationships that helped nurture South Korean industry in the aftermath of the Korean war. A bureaucratic maze and ministerial-level infighting have often drowned domestic and foreign investment in a sea of red tape and and damaged the competitiveness of South Korean products in foreign markets. Like Japanese companies, the South Korean corporate culture has traditionally included the concept of lifetime employment, a principal that has helped foster a remarkably class-free society but that—coupled with other effects of the economic bureaucracy—has finally begun to hamper Korean productivity and competitiveness.

Despite the slow pace of reform, governmental and corporate efforts to transform South Korea into a market-driven economy seem significantly ahead of similar efforts in Japan, suggesting a possible return to the heady growth rates of the 1970s and 1980s. South Korean companies are gaining market share in Latin America and are making major inroads on traditional Japanese domination of the $20 billion global market in computer memory chips. Economic growth in 1994 also bounced back to nearly 8 percent, after its relative slump in the early 1990s.

Korean Stock Market

Exchange

Classification: Emerging
Capitalization: $191 billion
Capitalization relative to U.S. stock market: 3.06%
Number of issues: 699
Primary index: Korea Composite Stock Price Index
Total return in local currency, 1988–1994: +125%
Total return in U.S. dollars, 1988–1994: +100%
Total return in U.S. dollars relative to U.S. stocks, 1988–1994: –34%

Volatility
(Historical)

Standard deviation: 7.62
Total monthly losses: 210%
Average monthly loss: 5.01%
Number of monthly losses: 42
Number of monthly losses greater than 5 percent: 20
Number of monthly losses greater than 10 percent: 3

Number of monthly losses greater than 15 percent: 1
Maximum monthly loss: 19.63%
Relative volatility ratio: 3.13

Price Cycles

Phase	From	To	Total return
Bull	January 1988	November 1989	+91%
Bear	December 1989	August 1990	−39%
Bull	September 1990	November 1990	+16%
Bear	December 1990	June 1991	−15%
Bull	July 1991	September 1991	+19%
Bear	October 1991	September 1992	−34%
Bull	October 1992	December 1994	+119%

Figure 15.4.　South Korean Stocks

Return of South Korean stocks in local currency (black), U.S. dollars (gray),
and S&P 500 (dotted); Dec. 1987 = 100.

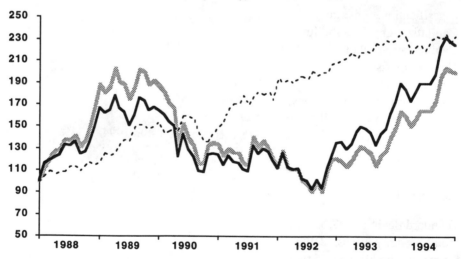

Source: Wilshire Associates Incorporated.

Correlations

Canada 0.37
Japan 0.35
United Kingdom 0.28
Sweden 0.25
Mexico 0.24
Singapore 0.24
Malaysia 0.21
United States 0.18
Hong Kong 0.16
Taiwan 0.15
Thailand 0.15

Australia 0.14
New Zealand 0.10
Switzerland 0.09
Brazil 0.08
Chile 0.08
Indonesia 0.07
Philippines 0.06
France 0.04
Germany 0.04
Argentina –0.10

Country Funds

Name	Originated	Hedging	Structure	Discount/ Premium	Phones
Fidelity Advisor Korea	October 1994	No	Closed end	+6 / +13	(800) 426-5523
Korea Equity	Nov. 1993	Possible	Closed end	–16 / +29	(800) 833-0018
Korea Fund	August 1984	No	Closed end	–6 / +157	(800) 349-4281 (212) 326-6200
Korean Investment	February 1992	No	Closed end	–16 / +34	(800) 247-4154 (800) 221-5672

Source: Morningstar, Inc.

American Depositary Receipts

Name	Exchange	Symbol	Industry
Korea Electric Power (Kepco)	NYSE	KEP	Utility
Pohang Iron & Steel (Posco)	NYSE	PKX	Steel producer

Direct Listings

None

Stock Summary

On balance, the Seoul bourse has been a bit of an underachiever over the past seven years, especially in light of the help it should be receiving from its often spectacular economy. From 1988 through 1994, the Wilshire Index: Korea climbed 125 percent in terms of the won and 100 percent in U.S. dollar terms, for a net dollar-denominated underperformance of the American market of 34 percent over those seven years. Volatility, at 3.13 times the U.S. market, is roughly in line with that of most other emerging equity indexes.

A significant portion of the Korean market's problems can be linked to its tight regulation. As in its dealings with the economy, the Korean government makes no secret of its attempts at price manipulation; specifically, the former Finance Ministry had occasionally advised local institutions to sell stocks in order to keep equity prices contained, lest an inflationary bubble emerge. Equally important are the continuing barriers to foreign ownership of Korean equities. Prior to 1992, foreigners were prohibited entirely from buying and selling Korean stocks. (The oldest of the four Korean closed-end mutual funds, the Korea Fund, owned local stocks only through a special arrangement with the Korean government.) The effective lockout of billions of dollars of potential buying demand has served to unnaturally restrain Korean equity prices. Among other fears, the South Korean government believes that increasing foreign portfolio investment would push the won higher, undermining South Korean exports, the backbone of its economy.

Over the past three years, however, a gradual liberalization of Korea's financial markets has taken place, with foreigners allowed to hold up to 10 percent of the capitalization of each Korean company from 1992 through December 1, 1994, when the ceiling was raised to 12 percent. While maximum levels of foreign-stock ownership are expected to be raised again in 1995 to 15 percent, the limits themselves and the uncertainty regarding their application create the potential for price swings unrelated to underlying economic fundamentals.

Given the apparent health of South Korea's economy and its prospects for continued above-average growth, the issue of foreign access to its capital markets remains the key variable in deciding whether to buy Korean stocks. The most recent bull market in Seoul began in October 1992, as local investors began discounting a return to at least trend-level economic growth and bidding up the prices of shares in anticipation of the inevitable wave of foreign buying. Each hint of hikes in the foreign-ownership ceiling has only increased the local speculation, creating the opportunity for domestic investors to buy low and sell high to cash-heavy foreigners committed to diving into Korea at virtually any price. Foreign money managers have already given ample evidence that they are willing to pay up, with prices for some blue-chip Korean equities selling to foreigners at a 30 percent to 50 percent premium over the prevailing Seoul Stock Exchange price through the Korean securities dealers network.

Because of the historical lack of access to Korean equities for most foreign investors, the four closed-end Korea funds have traditionally sold at large premiums to their net asset values (NAVs). The Korea Fund, for example, once traded at more than double its NAV, and the three newer entries each were treated to double-digit premiums in their first year of operations. As investors have come to realize that they will soon have more options, however, the premiums have all but disappeared. By April 1995, three of the four Korean closed-end equity funds were trading at discounts to NAV, with only Korea Fund hanging on to a slight 3.7 percent premium. Fluctuations in its discount/premium range aside, however, the long-term performance of the Korea Fund has been impressive, with the fund outperforming the Morgan Stanley Capital International Index: Korea each year since 1989. The fund's manager, John J. Lee, has managed the fund since December 1992.

American investors wanting to dabble in Korea without playing the discount/premium guessing game might consider the two South Korean American depositary receipts (ADRs) listed on the New York Stock Exchange in late 1994 as part of the Finance Ministry's attempt to increase foreign participation in its markets. Pohang Iron & Steel, known as Posco, is the world's second-largest steel producer, with projected 1995 net income of roughly 500 billion won ($650 million). The company is considered a model of industrial and managerial efficiency, with state-of-the art plants in Pohang and Kwangyang and a toehold in the otherwise highly restricted Japanese steel market. Posco's immediate future is uncertain, however, as the Korean government is considering selling its one-third stake in the company and opening the domestic steel market to competition. South Korea's other ADR, Korea Electric Power Company (Kepco), is the nation's monopoly provider of electricity. If the government continues its gradual liberalization of domestic quotas, several additional Korean blue-chips, including memory-chip maker Samsung Electronics and Hyundai Motor Services, may apply for ADR listing on the New York Stock Exchange.

CHAPTER 16

Taiwan (Republic of China)

Overview

Despite severe restrictions on foreign portfolio investment, Taiwan (Republic of China) represents an interesting play on the enormous economic ramifications of the opening of the Chinese market. The limitations themselves, while serving to contain prices over the past several years, may in time come to represent a long-term buying opportunity because the barriers serve to hold back the inevitable rush of global funds. Besides the likely continued loosening of restrictions on foreign ownership of Taiwanese securities, the government is planning a number of big-ticket privatizations that should add depth and diversity to what is presently a narrow equity market concentrated in the financial-services sector. Taiwan's economy has been among the most vibrant of any Asian nation, growing at an average rate of more than 8 percent over the past decade. The Taiwanese currency has also been a boon to American investors over the past several years, adding a substantial foreign-exchange kicker to the relatively modest gains of the Taiwan bourse itself.

Geography

Area: 13,895 square miles
Size relative to United States: 0.3%
Capital: Taipei
Population density per square mile: 1504
Population density relative to United States: 21x

Demographics

Population: 21.2 million
Population relative to United States: 8.1%
Average annual rate of natural increase: 0.92%
Projected population by 2025: 25.7 million
Population change by 2025: +21%

Government

Type: Multiparty Democratic Regime
Head of State: Lee Teng-hui, President (1988)
Political System: The Republic of China (also called Nationalist China) is governed by a constitution promulgated on January 1, 1947, while the nation still held control of the Chinese mainland. After the Communist revolution in 1949, Chinese nationalists, led by Generalissimo Chiang Kai-shck, retreated to the island of Taiwan, where they committed their political party to eventual re-unification (on their terms) with the mainland. Taiwan's political power is divided into five Yuans, or governing bodies, including the Legislative, Executive, Judicial, Control, and Examination. The Legislative Yuan is currently made up of 161 members, 125 of whom were directly elected in December 1992. Law-making power also rests with the National Assembly, whose 405 popularly elected members meet to appoint the president to a six year term and to amend the constitution, as recommended by the Legislative Yuan. The dominant political force in the Republic of China remains the Kuomintang party, which ruled the country under martial law until 1987 and emergency rule through April 1991, when it allowed free elections for the first time in decades. Results from the elections indicate continued widespread public support for the idea of a single, reunified China. The country's present leadership, however, led by President Lee Teng-hui and Premier Lien Chan, are both native Taiwanese, representing a generational shift away from the mainland exiles who ruled Taiwan for the previous four decades. The government has concluded agreements with China calling for a dialog between the two nations.

Economy

IMF data on currency, balance of payments, and economic output are not available.

Figure 16.1.   Taiwanese Stocks
Return of Taiwanese stocks in local currency (black), U.S. dollars (gray),
and S&P 500 (dotted); Dec. 1987 = 100.

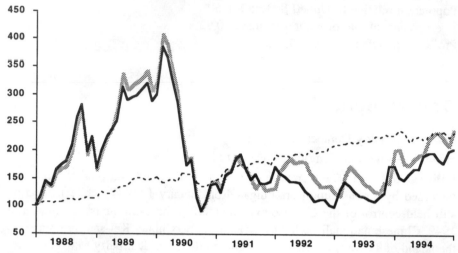

Source: Wilshire Associates Incorporated.

Taiwanese Stock Market

Exchange

Classification: Developed
Capitalization: $247 billion
Capitalization relative to U.S. stock market: 4.10%
Number of issues: 285
Primary index: TSE (Taiwan Stock Exchange) Weighted Index
Total return in local currency, 1990–1994: +90%
Total return in U.S. dollars, 1990–1994: +137%
Total return in U.S. dollars relative to U.S. stocks, 1990–1994: +3%

Volatility
(Historical)

Standard deviation: 13.85
Total monthly losses: 364%
Average monthly loss: 10.11%
Number of monthly losses: 36
Number of monthly losses greater than 5 percent: 26

Number of monthly losses greater than 10 percent: 14
Number of monthly losses greater than 15 percent: 6
Maximum monthly loss: −37.48%
Relative volatility ratio: 5.08

Price Cycles

Phase	From	To	Total return
Bull	January 1988	September 1988	+171%
Bear	October 1988	December 1988	−32%
Bull	January 1989	January 1990	+146%
Bear	February 1990	August 1990	−78%
Bull	September 1990	April 1991	+106%
Bear	May 1991	October 1991	−32%
Bull	November 1991	April 1992	+40%
Bear	May 1992	January 1993	−34%
Bull	February 1993	March 1993	+46%
Bear	April 1993	September 1993	−27%
Bull	October 1993	December 1994	+87%

Correlations

Thailand 0.37
Philippines 0.33
Singapore 0.29
Hong Kong 0.27
Malaysia 0.26
Indonesia 0.25
Germany 0.22
France 0.21
Canada 0.20
Mexico 0.18
Sweden 0.16

South Korea 0.15
Chile 0.14
United States 0.14
Japan 0.12
Australia 0.11
United Kingdom 0.11
New Zealand 0.07
Switzerland 0.05
Brazil 0.03
Argentina −0.07

Country Funds

Name	Originated	Hedging	Structure	Discount/ Premium	Phones
R.O.C. Taiwan	May 1989	No	Closed end	−27 / +29	(800) 343-9567 (212) 688-6840
Taiwan Equity	July 1994	No	Closed end	−16 / +8	(800) 933-3440
Taiwan Fund	Dec. 1986	No	Closed end	−15 / +172	(800) 426-5523

Source: Morningstar, Inc.

American Depositary Receipts

None

Direct Listings

None

Stock Summary

Taiwan's stock market is the third-largest in Asia but also the most restrictive of foreign investment. Prior to 1991, foreigners were banned altogether from buying Taiwanese securities. Even after regulations were loosened, the government's start-and-stop approach to financial-market liberalization has resulted in the lowest percentage of foreign participation of any Asian market, with total foreign ownership of Taiwanese securities limited to just 10 percent of the outstanding shares of any individual company and a market aggregate of $7.5 billion. Foreign individual investors remain prohibited from making direct purchases on the Taiwan bourse, and institutions must still be approved by Taiwan's Securities and Exchange Commission before being allowed to participate. The rationale for the restrictions is the same as that used in other emerging markets with similar, but less draconian, limitations on foreign portfolio investment: Because the Taiwanese economy is heavily dependent on exports, large positive net flows of investment funds could drive up the value of its currency, making Taiwan's products noncompetitive in global markets. Even with the restrictions in place, the Taiwanese dollar has risen by 60 percent against the U.S. dollar since the mid-1980s.

The Taiwan bourse gave investors a wild ride over the past seven years before ending virtually equal to the U.S. market in dollar terms. Over the 1988 to 1994 period, Taiwanese equities returned 90 percent in local currency and 137 percent in U.S. dollars, for a net outperformance of the Standard & Poor's 500 of a mere 3 percent. Earning that extra 3 percent would hardly have been worth the trouble, however, as Taiwanese stocks had more than five times the average downside volatility of their American counterparts. On 14 separate occasions, the Taiwan bourse fell by 10 percent or more in a single month, with the largest one-month fall of 37 percent in August 1990 occurring simultaneously with the onset of a bear market in the United States as Sadam Hussein's troops rumbled into Kuwait. No less than 11 price swings of 15 percent or more whipsawed equities over the past seven years, with the average bear market taking Taiwanese stocks lower by nearly 41 percent. The 78 percent bloodbath experienced between February and August of 1990 is among the largest bear-market declines of any market over the past decade. Making the decline worse was the fact that Taiwanese stocks had climbed too far too fast in the 24 months prior to the 1990 top; between January 1988 and January 1990, the average Taiwanese equity rose by more than 300 percent in U.S. dollars, then proceeded to fall by 60 percent until hitting bottom in September 1993. The huge speculations that pushed emerging-market prices higher throughout 1993 finally reached Taiwan's shores late in the year, as Taiwanese valuations relative to the overheated bourses of Hong Kong, Malaysia, and Thailand suddenly seemed more reasonable. The global bargain hunters also seized upon signs that the government might further ease restrictions on foreign investment, leading to a near doubling of the average Taiwanese equity by year-end 1994. A decline that began in late 1994 resumed in early 1995; as of May 1995, Taiwan's Weighted Stock Index, which comprises nearly all publicly traded companies on the Taiwan bourse, had declined by another 22 percent.

Although no American depositary receipts are available, Americans looking for a Taiwan play will find three closed-end country funds at their disposal. The oldest of the three, the Taiwan Fund, has outperformed the average Taiwanese stock over the 1988 to 1994 period, primarily because of the Fund's 219 percent return in 1989, a figure that beat the Wilshire Index: Taiwan by 126 percent. The Fund's aggregate losses over the period roughly approximate those of the overall Taiwanese market. The huge premiums to net asset value (NAV) that greeted the Fund when it came public in the late 1980s have largely disappeared; by May 1995, Taiwan Fund could be purchased for a 3 percent discount to NAV, a level near the bottom of its historical range. R.O.C. Taiwan Fund has a shorter track record but also has beaten the return of the broad market over the first five full years of its existence. R.O.C. Taiwan's aggregate losses of roughly 45 percent from 1990 to 1994 are significantly below those of the overall market for the identical period. As of October 1995, R.O.C. Taiwan was trading at an 11 percent premium to its NAV. Both Taiwan Fund and R.O.C. Taiwan have often attempted to time Taipei's notoriously mercurial market by moving heavily to cash when they perceived a decline to be imminent. The remaining Taiwanese closed-end fund, Taiwan Equity, began operations in July 1994.

CHAPTER 17

Kingdom of Thailand

Overview

Rapid and nearly uninterrupted growth has characterized the Thai economy for most of the past 30 years. Despite persistent political instability, the country has fostered a probusiness environment that has been translated into a reasonably strong national balance sheet, a relatively stable currency, and an equity market that has outperformed those of virtually all of its geographic neighbors since the late 1980s. Like many Asian nations, the root of Thailand's economic well-being resides in its high investment-to-consumption ratio, and the large amount of foreign capital that has been plowed into Thai infrastructure and manufacturing facilities. The country's stock market, while displaying the kind of volatility normally associated with a developing economy, has nonetheless tripled the return of U.S. stocks since 1988. Despite its spectacular past, however, it is probably unreasonable to expect Thailand to maintain the same level of economic growth over the coming decade. The country must deal with a serious merchandise-trade imbalance, along with a shortage of skilled workers likely to be needed in an increasingly high-tech economy. The Thai stock market, which is coming off several high-flying years in the early 1990s, could also be headed for at least a slowdown in its long-term rate of appreciation.

Geography

Area: 198,455 square miles
Size relative to United States: 5%
Capital: Bangkok

172

Population density per square mile: 299
Population density relative to United States: 4x

Demographics

Population: 60 million
Population relative to United States: 23%
Average annual rate of natural increase: 1.4%
Projected population by 2025: 83 million
Population change by 2025: +38%

Government

Type: Constitutional Monarchy
Head of State: Bhumibol Adulyadej, King (1946)
Political System: Instability has been the only constant during much of the postwar period in Thailand. Although Thailand has technically been a constitutional monarchy since 1932, spillover warfare and refugee problems from neighboring conflicts (principally in Vietnam and Cambodia), along with several coup attempts by military and antimilitary factions, have led to unrelenting domestic unrest and political turmoil, especially since U.S. influence in the country was diminished in the aftermath of the American withdrawal from Vietnam in 1975. After a military junta overthrew the democratically elected civilian regime and abolished the constitution in February 1991, a new constitution was promulgated later that year, establishing a National Assembly that consists of an elected House of Representatives and an appointed Senate. However, after the ensuing national election was dominated by military candidates, violent confrontations between prodemocracy civilians and the military led to the removal of the military's handpicked prime minister and the eventual appointment of Chuan Leekpai to the post in October 1992. Mr. Chuan's government lasted until May 1995, when a land-reform scandal led to the withdrawal of a key member of his ruling coalition. The Thai military, which in the past has used such parliamentary turmoil to reestablish its power, stayed on the sidelines in the early stages of the dispute. New elections were called for July 1995. The country's southern peninsula, which borders on Malaysia to the south, has experienced instability because of a Malaysian separatist movement.

Economy

Financial Strength
(Historical data, relative to GDP)

Merchandise trade: −3.99%
Services: 14.84%
Income: +1.02%
Current account: −3.51%
Portfolio investment: +0.38%
Direct investment: +0.91%
Overall balance of payments: +1.47%
Budget: −2.22%
External debt: 27%
Investment/consumption ratio: 0.33

Figure 17.1.   Thai Balance of Payments
Surplus/deficit of Thai budget (black) and current account (gray),
as percent of GDP.

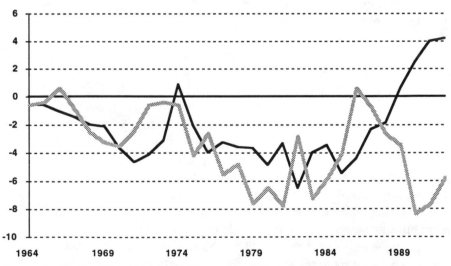

Source: International Monetary Fund, *International Financial Statistics Yearbook.*

Currency
(Historical data)

Money supply growth: 18.62%
Consumer price index: 5.65%
Monetary unit: Baht
Monetary unit against U.S. dollar: −18%

Economic Output
(Historical data)

GDP: $122 billion
GDP relative to U.S. GDP: 1.88%
GDP growth rate: 7.71%
GDP growth rate relative to U.S. GDP growth rate: 2.70x
Per capita GDP: $2,040
Per capita GDP relative to U.S. per capita GDP: 9%

Figure 17.2.   Thai Currency
Baht per U.S. dollar (inverted scale).

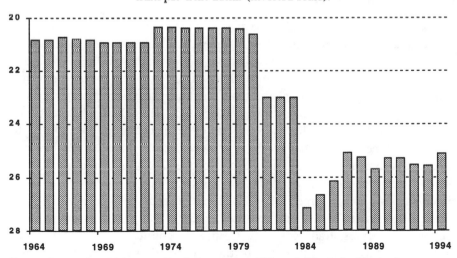

Source: International Monetary Fund, *International Financial Statistics Yearbook.*

Figure 17.3.　Thai Economy

Annual percentage change in Thai real GDP (bar graph, left scale). Growth in Thai
real GDP relative to U.S. real GDP, 1963 = 100 (line graph, right scale).

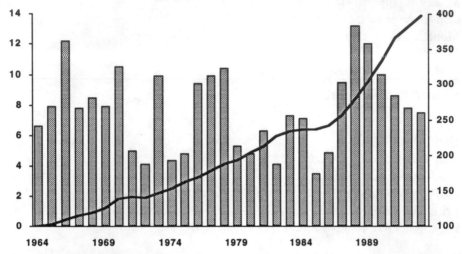

Source: International Monetary Fund, *International Financial Statistics Yearbook.*

Economic Summary

Thailand has been an economic superstar for most of the past 30 years, expanding at an average annual rate of 7.71 percent without a single recession and
with average annual inflation of just 5.65 percent. Over those 30 years, Thailand
has gradually transformed itself from a low-wage, commodities-based producer
into a mostly modern, industrial economy. Machinery and manufactures account
for three-quarters of Thai exports, with agricultural and fishing products (Thailand is one of the world's largest producers of rice) accounting for most of the
remainder. Since 1964, Thailand has averaged a 1.47 percent annual overall
balance-of-payments surplus, with the size of the surpluses increasing to more
than 4 percent per year since 1990. The basis for Thailand's relatively strong
financial position are large inflows of direct foreign investment, an above-
average investment-to-consumption ratio, and generally positive investment-
income and services-trade positions. Despite its political instability, the Thai
government has also contributed to the economy's health through a new
tightfistedness with the fiscal purse strings; since the late 1980s, Thailand has

averaged budget surpluses of nearly 3 percent of gross domestic product (GDP) per year, reversing its long-term trend of consistent fiscal red ink. The government has also dramatically lowered its foreign-debt burden; since the late 1980s, foreign IOUs as a percent of GDP have fallen from over 10 percent to just 3.46 percent. The Bank of Thailand has maintained a generally stable monetary policy, with nominal growth in the money supply averaging roughly 18 percent per year. Over the past 30 years, the value of Thailand's currency has drifted only marginally lower against the U.S. dollar, falling by 18 percent since 1964.

Despite its solid financial position, however, potential problems loom on the Thai economic horizon. The nation is no longer a low-wage producer; continuation of past growth rates will depend upon maintaining massive inflows of foreign investment, resolution of basic infrastructure problems, and the training of a highly skilled workforce. At the moment, Thailand has an insufficient amount of college graduates to produce the kind of highly skilled workforce required in an economy increasingly dependent upon the export of high-tech goods. Thailand also must solve its systemic merchandise-trade deficits before the flow of foreign capital dries up. Since 1964, Thai merchandise-trade shortfalls have averaged nearly 4 percent per year, with the size of the deficits increasing to over 7 percent annually since 1990 as its largest trading partner, Japan, has struggled to escape a prolonged recession. As services trade also turned sharply negative in the mid-1990s, the country's current-account deficit swelled to roughly 6.7 percent in 1994. In order to shore up its rupturing current account, Thai monetary officials may be forced to raise interest rates, a condition that would almost certainly lead to a slowdown in economic growth.

Thai Stock Market

Exchange

Classification: Emerging
Capitalization: $126 billion
Capitalization relative to U.S. stock market: 4.01%
Primary index: Thailand Stock Exchange (SET)
Number of issues: 389
Total return in local currency, 1988–1994: 286%
Total return in U.S. dollars, 1988–1994: 379%
Total return in U.S. dollars relative to U.S. stocks, 1988–1994: +245

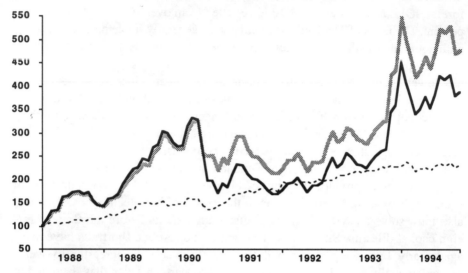

Figure 17.4.   Thai Stocks
Return of Thai stocks in local currency (black), U.S. dollars (gray),
and S&P 500 (dotted); Dec. 1987 = 100.

Source: Wilshire Associates Incorporated.

Volatility
(Historical)

Standard deviation: 8.50
Total monthly losses: 186%
Average monthly loss: 5.32%
Number of monthly losses: 35
Number of monthly losses greater than 5 percent: 18
Number of monthly losses greater than 10 percent: 4
Number of monthly losses greater than 15 percent: 1
Maximum monthly loss: 21.43%
Relative volatility ratio: 3.05

Price Cycles

Phase	From	To	Total return
Bull	January 1988	July 1990	+225%
Bear	August 1990	November 1990	–33%
Bull	December 1990	April 1991	+34%
Bear	May 1991	May 1992	–26%
Bull	June 1992	December 1993	+151%
Bear	January 1994	March 1994	–24%
Bull	April 1994	December 1994	+14%

Correlations

Malaysia 0.52
Singapore 0.44
Hong Kong 0.40
Canada 0.37
Philippines 0.37
Taiwan 0.37
United States 0.32
Indonesia 0.30
Switzerland 0.24
Australia 0.22
Chile 0.18

France 0.17
Sweden 0.16
Korea 0.15
New Zealand 0.15
Germany 0.14
United Kingdom 0.14
Mexico 0.12
Argentina 0.07
Japan 0.06
Brazil 0.02

Country Funds

Name	Originated	Hedging	Structure	Discount/ Premium	Phones
Thai Capital	May 1990	Possible	Closed end	–24 / +13	(800) 933-3440 (201) 915-3020
Thai Fund	February 1988	No	Closed end	–22 / +87	(212) 296-7200 (617) 557-8000

Source: Morningstar, Inc.

American Depositary Receipts

None

Direct Listings

None

Stock Summary

Reflecting its strong economy and generally stable currency, buy-and-hold investors in Thailand's emerging equity market would have been more than handsomely rewarded over the past several years. For the seven years ending December 31, 1994, Thai stocks would have returned a whopping 379 percent, nearly triple the performance of U.S. stocks over that same period. Investors would have required a strong stomach, however, since volatility in the Thai market was also roughly triple that for U.S. stocks. Thai equities fell by 5 percent or more in a single month on 18 separate occasions, with the largest single-month decline occurring in August 1990, coincident with the onset of the Persian Gulf crisis. Three bear-market cycles would have interrupted the long-term uptrend, with the average cyclical bear market taking Thai stocks lower by an average of 28 percent over seven months. The Thai equity market has relatively high correlations with neighboring Malaysia, Singapore, Hong Kong, Taiwan, and the Philippines. The U.S. correlation, at 0.32, is roughly average for an Asian emerging market.

U.S. investors looking for plays on the Thai economic growth machine will find relatively slim pickings, with no Thai listed American depositary receipts currently trading on either the NASDAQ or New York Stock Exchange. Two closed-end funds are available, however, and both have been in business long enough that proper performance evaluations are possible. The older of the funds, the Thai Fund, has beaten the Morgan Stanley Capital International (MSCI) Index: Thailand in five of the six full years of its existence, but often traded in the late 1980s at premiums of over 50 percent. As of October 1995, however, the fund's assets could be owned for just 88 cents on the dollar. The Thai Capital Fund, which also has outperformed the MSCI Index: Thailand over the first four full years of its existence, was trading at a 13 percent discount to net asset value as of October 1995, putting it toward the lower end of its historical discount/premium cycle.

Like other emerging markets, the Thailand Stock Exchange imposes limits on the percentage of domestic companies that may be owned by foreigners. As of early 1995, the limit was 49 percent for most stocks (lower for many financial-services concerns), occasionally resulting in substantial premiums for Thai equities purchased in foreign-tranche trading.

CHAPTER 18

Argentine Republic

Overview

Since taking office in 1989, Argentine President Carlos Menem has begun the long overdue remaking of his country's economy. Mr. Menem and his chief economic advisor, Domingo Cavillo, have linked growth in the Argentine money supply to hard-currency reserves while divesting large segments of the previously state-run economy. As a result, Argentina's hyperinflation has been arrested and its growth revitalized, with real gross domestic product (GDP) increasing by over 7 percent per year between 1991 and 1994.

Despite the remarkable progress, however, the country's past economic sins—plus some not of its own making—continue to haunt Argentina. Massive foreign debt rung up under previous administrations, complicated by fallout from Mexico's currency devaluation in December 1994, have at least temporarily undermined confidence in Argentina's financial system, stressing its commitment to a stable currency and forcing the country into an economic slowdown in 1995. Mr. Menem's reelection in May 1995, however, indicates that the Argentine population is prepared to accept near-term economic pain as a necessary consequence of preserving the prospect of long-term growth. The poor dollar-denominated record of the Argentine equity market is nearly entirely the result of the weak peso pre-June 1991. After that date, Argentine equities have performed reasonably well, especially given the deterioration of global market sentiment in the wake of the Mexican financial crisis. Like its political history, Argentine stocks will almost always be volatile but also deserve a careful look from investors with an especially long-term view.

Geography

Area: 1,072,067 square miles
Size relative to United States: 28%
Capital: Buenos Aires
Population density per square mile: 32
Population density relative to United States: 0.43x

Demographics

Population: 34 million
Population relative to United States: 13%
Average annual rate of natural increase: 1.3%
Projected population by 2025: 44 million
Population change by 2025: +29%

Government

Type: Federal Republic
Head of State: Carlos S. Menem, President (1989)
Political System: A constitution promulgated in 1853 is intended to rule Argentina, but in reality its terms have often been disregarded as civilian and military forces have alternated in controlling the country, sometimes by bloody means. The constitution places most of the nation's political clout in its executive branch, which is headed by a president popularly elected to a term of four years. (A constitutional amendment passed in 1993 provides that the president may seek reelection, but the term of office was reduced from the previous six years.) There is a bicameral Congress, consisting of a Chamber of Deputies and a Senate. Deputies are elected by universal adult suffrage to four-year terms, with half the members coming up for reelection every two years. The Argentine Senate consists of 48 members, chosen to nine-year terms by provincial legislatures. One-third of the Senate faces reelection every three years.

Because of the country's chronic economic woes, civil unrest has fed political instability, causing cycles of authoritarian control and suspension of constitutional law. The most recent such period began in March 1976 when a military coup removed Isabel de Peron (third wife of former president Juan Peron) and replaced her with a three-man junta that ruled the country until 1983, when civilian government was returned. Argentine politics is currently dominated by President Menem's Peronist Party (also known as the Justicialist Party) and the Radical Civic Union. In elections held in May 1995, Mr. Menem was returned to office for a four-year term with over 50 percent of the vote.

Economy

Financial Strength
(Historical data, relative to GDP)

Merchandise trade: +3.87%
Services: −0.63%
Income: −4.76%
Current account: −1.39%
Portfolio investment: 0.21%
Direct investment: +0.66%
Overall balance of payments: −3.02%
External debt: 24%
Budget: −4.45%
Investment/consumption ratio: 0.27

Figure 18.1.   Argentine Balance of Payments
Surplus/deficit of Argentine budget (black) and current account (gray),
as percent of GDP.

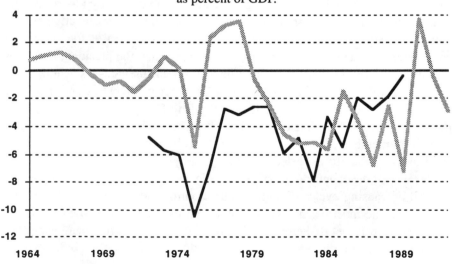

Source: International Monetary Fund, *International Financial Statistics Yearbook.*

Currency
(Historical data)

Money supply growth: 270%
Consumer price index: 321%
Monetary unit: Peso (also known as the Austral)
Monetary unit against U.S. dollar: −99.99%

Economic Output
(Historical data)

GDP: $228 billion
GDP relative to U.S. GDP: 3.92%
GDP growth rate: 2.28%
GDP growth rate relative to U.S. GDP growth rate: 0.80x
Per capita GDP: $6,730
Per capita GDP relative to U.S. per capita GDP: 30%

Economic Summary

For decades, the Argentine government's solution to its economic problems was
predictable: Goose the money supply. Over the past 30 years, the pile of Argen-

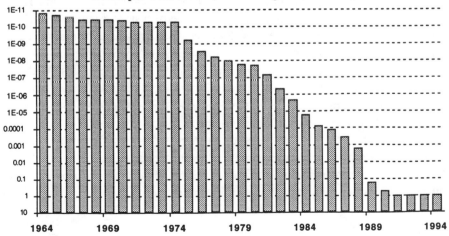

Figure 18.2.   Argentine Currency
Pesos per U.S. dollar (inverted logarithmic scale).

Source: International Monetary Fund, *International Financial Statistics Yearbook.*

Figure 18.3. Argentine Economy

Annual percentage change in Argentine real GDP (bar graph, left scale). Growth in
Argentine real GDP relative to U.S. real GDP, 1963 = 100 (line graph, right scale).

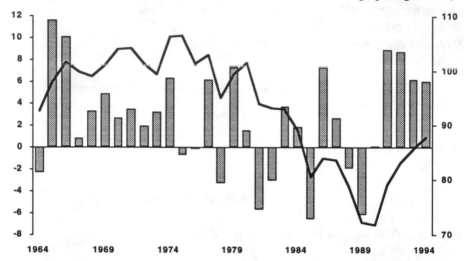

Source: International Monetary Fund, *International Financial Statistics Yearbook.*

tine pesos slushing about the country's financial institutions has grown at the
staggering rate of 270 percent per year. During that same period, the Argentine
currency lost 99.99 percent of its value against the U.S. dollar. Not surprisingly,
the proliferating pesos led to hyperinflation, with consumer prices rising at an
annual rate of more than 300 percent since 1964. Perhaps worst of all, inflating
the Argentine economy did not produce real growth; between 1964 and 1990,
inflation-adjusted GDP grew at a glacial-like pace of just 1.86 percent annually,
below the average for even the world's largest industrialized economies and
embarrassingly feeble for an economy with such a relatively small base.

    In the early 1990s, however, Argentina began to change its ways. With the
blessing of free-market President Carlos Menem, Economy Minister Domingo
Cavillo instituted a radical system of currency reform in which every Argentine
peso had to be backed by one dollar of hard-currency reserves. No sooner had
markets perceived the plan to be credible than its benefits began to become
obvious: Inflation fell sharply, economic growth accelerated to the Asia-like rate
of 8 percent per year and huge sums of foreign capital began to flow into the
country, much of it in the form of portfolio investment.

All was going well until December 1994, when financial-reform efforts in Mexico began to unravel, resulting in a 40 percent devaluation in the Mexican currency. Concerned that Argentina would eventually have to do the same, investors in Argentine stocks and bonds took their hefty profits and left the country, putting stress on foreign-exchange reserves and further encouraging currency speculators that an Argentine devaluation was inevitable. With hard-currency reserves dwindling and with no way to print new money under the convertibility system, the Argentine government had no choice but to deflate its economy, raising funds to plug its budget deficit through loans from international agencies and increased taxes on private business. The banking industry, long the weakest sector of the Argentine economy, experienced substantial formal and informal failures in 1995 as bond losses and the flight of capital exacerbated weak underlying fundamentals. The harsh remedies, including a sharp rise in interest rates to arrest capital flight, that are needed to maintain the peso's health threaten to produce a recession or at least a sharp slowdown in the rate of Argentine real economic growth in 1995.

The reaction to panics is often to paint markets with broad brushes; Argentina will go the way of Mexico, investors fear, because, like Mexico, it is an emerging market and in the same area of the world, no less. A careful look at the balance sheets of the two nations, however, reveals that Argentina is not Mexico. Whereas Mexico was running current-account deficits approaching double digits, the size of the corresponding Argentine shortfall is closer to just 2 percent of GDP. (Most of the current-account hemorrhaging in Argentina is the result of interest on its huge foreign debt, which has resulted in income imbalances averaging more than 4 percent of GDP.) Additionally, Argentina's hyperinflation was made unpalatable to its citizens because it failed to produce real growth; the country's determination to stay the course was made manifest through the reelection of President Menem in May 1995. Foreign direct investors (as opposed to those who buy Argentine securities) also have seemingly retained confidence in the Argentine long-term economic plan, pouring new money into Argentina at roughly the same pace, even as they scale back Mexican exposure. Terms of International Monetary Fund loans have mandated that Argentina begin to produce budget surpluses, historically the weakest area on the Argentine balance sheet. Argentina recently formed a free-trade zone with neighboring Brazil, creating the Mercosur Customs Union with 189 million people. Even before the agreement, Brazil was the leading buyer of Argentine goods, accounting for almost 12 percent of exports.

Figure 18.4.   Argentine Stocks

Return of Argentine stocks in local currency (black), U.S. dollars (gray), and S&P 500 (dotted); Dec. 1987 = 100 (logarithmic scale).

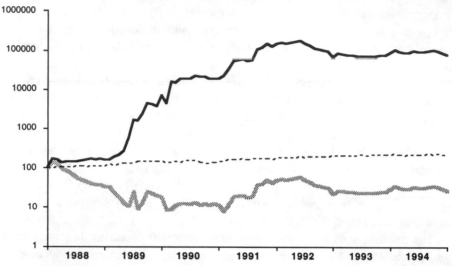

Source: Wilshire Associates Incorporated.

Argentine Stock Market

Exchange

Classification: Emerging
Primary location: Buenos Aires
Capitalization: $36 billion
Capitalization relative to U.S. stock market: 0.57%
Number of issues: 156
Primary index: Stock Exchange Value Index
Total return in local currency, 1988–1994: 79,358%
Total return in U.S. dollars, 1988–1994: –72%
Total return in U.S. dollars relative to U.S. stocks, 1988–1994: –206%

Volatility
(Historical)

Standard deviation: 27.19
Total monthly losses: 637%

Average monthly loss: 12.75%
Number of monthly losses: 50
Number of monthly losses greater than 5 percent: 41
Number of monthly losses greater than 10 percent: 25
Number of monthly losses greater than 15 percent: 13
Maximum monthly loss: 63.28%
Relative volatility ratio: 8.31

Price Cycles

Phase	From	To	Total return
Bull	January 1988	January 1988	+44%
Bear	February 1988	May 1989	–92%
Bull	June 1989	June 1989	+127%
Bear	July 1989	July 1989	–63%
Bull	August 1989	September 1989	+176%
Bear	October 1989	January 1990	–65%
Bull	February 1990	July 1990	+55%
Bear	August 1990	January 1991	–41%
Bull	February 1991	May 1992	+658%
Bear	June 1992	December 1992	–63%
Bull	January 1993	January 1994	+60%
Bear	February 1994	December 1994	–23%

Correlations

Philippines 0.10
Chile 0.07
Thailand 0.07
United States 0.06
Mexico 0.06
Canada 0.04
New Zealand 0.01
Australia –0.02
France –0.02
Sweden –0.02
Singapore –0.03

Germany –0.04
Switzerland –0.04
Hong Kong –0.06
Malaysia –0.06
Taiwan –0.07
Indonesia –0.08
United Kingdom –0.09
Korea –0.10
Japan –0.11
Brazil –0.21

Country Funds

Name	Originated	Hedging	Structure	Discount/ Premium	Phones
Argentina Fund	Oct. 1990	Possible	Closed end	−7 / +38	(800) 349-4281 (617) 330-5602

Source: Morningstar, Inc.

American Depositary Receipts

Name	Exchange	Symbol	Industry
Banco Frances del Rio de la Plata	NYSE	BFR	Banking
Banco de Galicia y Buenos Aires	NASDAQ	BGALY	Banking
Buenos Aires Embotelladora	NYSE	BAE	Bottler and distributor
Irsa Inversiones y Representaciones	NYSE	IRS	Real estate
MetroGas	NYSE	MGS	Gas distributor
Telecom Argentina	NYSE	TEO	Telecommunications
Telefonica de Argentina	NYSE	TAR	Telecommunications
Transportadora de Gas del Sur	NYSE	TGS	Gas transporter
YPF	NYSE	YPF	Oil and gas exploration

Direct Listings

None

Stock Summary

The history of the Argentine equity market can be divided into two periods—the preconvertibility period through May 1991 and the strong-peso period after that date. The absurd gap between Argentine stock prices when measured in pesos (up almost 80,000 percent) and when measured in dollars (down 72 percent) over the 1988 to 1994 period is an accurate reflection of precisely how weak the Argentine currency was before convertibility began in mid-1991. After the Argentine peso was pegged to the U.S. currency, peso- and dollar-denominated returns closely tracked each other (as one would expect), and the average Argentine stock actually showed a modest gain through year-end 1994, climbing about 35 percent in U.S. dollars, despite a substantial bear market in late 1994 as emerging markets worldwide were punished by investors fearing a replay of the Mexican devaluation.

Given the significant changes in economic policy in Argentina under the present administration, the shabby long-term record of the Argentine Bolsa should not necessarily be taken as a warning to entirely avoid Argentine equities in the future.

The government's privatizations offer foreign investors plenty of opportunity to buy into Argentina. With respect to American depositary receipts, several large-capitalization issues are on sale, including Banco de Galicia, Argentina's second largest bank, and YPF, the giant Argentine oil and gas concern that, thus far, represents the centerpiece of the government's privatization program. YPF, which put roughly $2.5 billion in government coffers when it was sold, has the highest capitalization on the Argentine bourse and is the world's 11th-largest publicly traded oil company. One country fund is available, the Argentina Fund, a closed-end version that has outperformed Argentine indexes over the first three full years of its existence. Internal demand for Argentine securities could increase as a result of the government's decision to privatize the country's pension system. Under the plan, which also reforms the social security system, Argentineans must contribute a portion of their wages and salaries to a private pension fund, which in turn may invest up to half its assets in domestic securities.

CHAPTER 19

Federative Republic of Brazil

Overview

Hold the presses! After suffering inflation of 50 billion percent since 1980, Brazil has belatedly joined the Fiscal Reformers Club of Latin America. Under the so-called Real Plan of new President Fernando Cardoso, the country created yet another currency (the real replaced the cruzeiro real, which replaced the cruzeiro, which replaced the cruzado novo, which replaced the cruzado, which replaced the cruzeiro, which replaced the cruzeiro novo, all since 1965) and vowed to stabilize its inflation rate, which had been running as high as 50 percent *per month* as of mid-1994. The plan, while still in its infant stages, has achieved notable results, with inflation dropping to roughly 1 percent per month by mid-1995, fueling a boom in consumption as real income stabilized.

Brazil seems determined to learn by the mistakes made by Mexico in its economic liberalization program and has the advantage of a healthy export sector that generates foreign exchange, thus taking some of the risk out of the huge flows of portfolio investment into the Brazilian equity market as privatization goes forward. Investors in the Sao Paulo Exchange, Brazil's principal equity market, have managed to make money even after currency translation, with the average Brazilian stock beating the Standard & Poor's 500 by sevenfold over the 1988 to 1994 period in dollar terms. Over the longer haul, however, Brazil will need to demonstrate that it can export without the benefit of a weak currency, maintain a strong current account without tariffs, remove the systemic causes of budgetary imbalances, and eliminate constitutional barriers to foreign investment. The return to 5 percent average growth rates in 1993 and 1994—levels reminis-

192

cent of the the boom days of the 1970s—indicates that the country is making progress on its road to a more fundamentally healthy economy.

Geography

Area: 3,286,470 square miles
Size relative to United States: 87%
Capital: Brasilia
Population density per square mile: 47
Population density relative to United States: 0.64x

Demographics

Population: 165 million
Population relative to United States: 63%
Average annual rate of natural increase: 1.7%
Projected population by 2025: 237 million
Population change by 2025: +44%

Government

Type: Federal Republic
Head of State: Fernando Henrique Cardoso, President (1995)
Political System: Brazil is governed under a constitution promulgated in 1988, three years after the end of military rule. The constitution vests executive power in the president, who is elected by universal adult suffrage to a term of five years and is not allowed to serve consecutive terms. A bicameral National Congress is made up of a Federal Senate, whose 81 members serve eight-year terms, and a Chamber of Deputies, with 503 members elected by proportional representation for a term of four years. The country is divided into 26 states and the Federal District of Brasilia.

Beginning with the overthrow of a democratically elected government in 1964, a series of military juntas led Brazil until 1985, when General Joao Baptista de Oliveira Figueiredo allowed for a return to democracy. The first popularly elected president under the new Brazilian constitution was Fernando Collor de Mello, who won 53 percent of the vote in 1989. After taking office in March 1990, Collor de Mello began a series of free-market reforms, but a sharp economic slump and political scandals quickly eroded his power. Collor de Mello was impeached in December 1992 and resigned shortly after the beginning of his trial, with Vice President Itamar Franco completing the remainder of Collor de Mello's term. In 1994, Fernando Cardoso, who had been Minister of the Economy under Mr. Franco and authored the New Real economic plan, was elected president. The Brazilian people recently rejected a proposal to return the country to a parliamentary and monarchal form of government.

Economy

Financial Strength
(Historical data, relative to GDP)

Merchandise trade: +2.65%
Services: −1.36%
Income: −3.72%
Current account: −2.53%
Portfolio investment: +0.24%
Direct investment: +0.92%
Overall balance of payments: −1.54%
Budget: −3.79%
External debt: 30%
Investment/consumption ratio: 0.30

Currency
(Historical data)

Money supply growth: 91%
Consumer price index: 343%
Monetary unit: Real
Monetary unit against U.S. dollar: −99.99%

Economic Output
(Historical data)

GDP: $409 billion
GDP relative to U.S. GDP: 7.7%

GDP growth rate: 5.51%
GDP growth rate relative to U.S. GDP growth rate: 1.96x
Per capita GDP: $2,479
Per capita GDP relative to U.S. per capita GDP: 11%

Economic Summary

Brazil comes to the task of reforming its economy several years later than regional rivals Argentina, Chile, and Mexico. It also finds itself with obstacles not
encountered by its Latin American brethren, principally constitutional roadblocks
to privatization and certain types of foreign investment. The list of past Brazilian
economic sins is headed by its massive budget deficits, which have averaged
almost 4 percent of gross domestic product (GDP) since 1964. During one particularly profligate period (1985–1989), fiscal red ink grew to more than 13 percent
of GDP per year, a five-year total rivaling the most egregious borrowings of any
Third-World nation. As a result of its need to fund its budgetary deficits, Brazilian governments have borrowed heavily, racking up external debt of $122 bil-
lion, or nearly one-third of GDP. (Much of the foreign debt was refinanced in

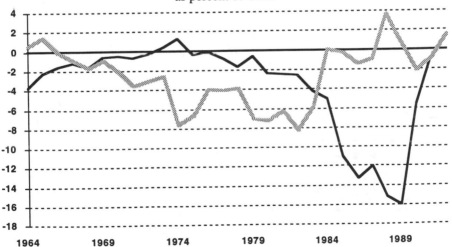

Figure 19.1. Brazilian Balance of Payments
Surplus/deficit of Brazilian budget (black) and current account (gray),
as percent of GDP.

Source: International Monetary Fund, *International Financial Statistics Yearbook.*

Figure 19.2.　Brazilian Currency
Real per U.S. dollar (inverted logarithmic scale).

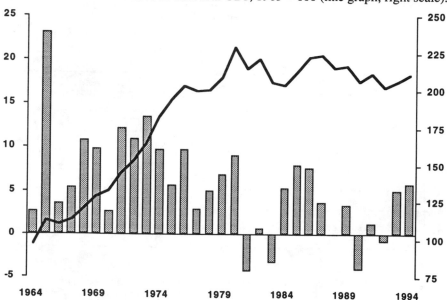

Source: International Monetary Fund, *International Financial Statistics Yearbook.*

Figure 19.3.　Brazilian Economy
Annual percentage change in Brazilian real GDP (bar graph, left scale). Growth in
Brazilian real GDP relative to U.S. real GDP, 1963 = 100 (line graph, right scale).

Sources: International Monetary Fund; *Wall Street Journal, New York Times.*

1992, giving the country fiscal breathing room.) What Brazil couldn't borrow it printed, with the money supply nearly doubling every year for 30 years.

The result of the borrow-and-print economic plan was chronic hyperinflation, with consumer prices increasing by an average of more than 300 percent per year since 1964. The budget deficits are the result of inadequate federal taxing authority, an overly generous social-security system, and a treasury-draining public pension plan. All three problems are addressed in a fiscal reform package submitted to the Brazilian Congress by President Cardoso since taking office in January 1995, but ultimate passage will face stiff opposition (even from within Cardoso's own ruling coalition) and could take years to accomplish.

Brazil's tardiness in cleaning up its economic act does carry some benefits, however, principally the ability to observe and learn from mistakes made by Mexico as that country embarked on its long journey toward economic reform. Fearing a repeat of currency imbalances resulting from an artificially strong Mexican peso, the Cardoso administration in March 1995 allowed the real to float 12 percent lower, temporarily reigniting inflation, but relieving export pressures that had pushed the traditionally healthy Brazilian merchandise-trade balance into the red in late 1994 and early 1995. Mr. Cardoso also reimposed tariffs on certain imports, again with the intention of addressing a flow-of-funds imbalance. The strongest card in Brazil's economic hand is its merchandise-trade account (aided by the weak currencies), which has averaged a surplus of 2.65 percent of GDP since 1964 and more than 8 percent per year since the late 1980s. Major merchandise exports include coffee, vegetables, beverages, tobacco, sugar, and mineral products. Roughly 20 percent of Brazilian exports are to the United States, with an increasing amount going to its new free-trading partner of Argentina.

Brazilian Stock Market

Exchange

Classification: Emerging
Capitalization: $185 billion
Capitalization relative to U.S. stock market: 2.9%
Number of issues: 549
Primary index: Bovespa
Total return in local currency, 1988–1994: 4,979,920,649%
Total return in U.S. dollars, 1988–1994: +986%
Total return in U.S. dollars relative to U.S. stocks, 1988–1994: +852%

Figure 19.4.   Brazilian Stocks

Return of Brazilian stocks in local currency (black), U.S. dollars (gray), and S&P 500 (dotted); Dec. 1987 = 100 (logarithmic scale).

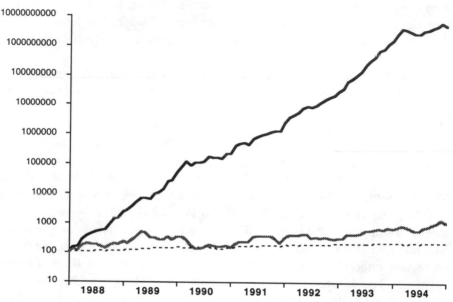

Sources: Wilshire Associates Incorporated; Federation Internationale des Bourses de Valeurs.

Volatility
(Historical)

Standard deviation: 18.44
Total monthly losses: 424%
Average monthly loss: 11.48%
Number of monthly losses: 37
Number of monthly losses greater than 5 percent: 26
Number of monthly losses greater than 10 percent: 20
Number of monthly losses greater than 15 percent: 11
Maximum monthly loss: 37.21%
Relative volatility ratio: 5.59

Price Cycles

Phase	From	To	Total return
Bull	January 1988	April 1988	+95%
Bear	May 1988	August 1988	−29%
Bull	September 1988	December 1988	+65%
Bear	January 1989	January 1989	−15%
Bull	February 1989	April 1989	+152%
Bear	May 1989	September 1989	−46%
Bull	October 1989	October 1989	+26%
Bear	November 1989	November 1989	−20%
Bull	December 1989	January 1990	+22%
Bear	February 1990	April 1990	−59%
Bull	May 1990	July 1990	+36%
Bear	August 1990	December 1990	−23%
Bull	January 1991	July 1991	+157%
Bear	August 1991	November 1991	−42%
Bull	December 1991	April 1992	+100%
Bear	May 1992	November 1992	35%
Bull	December 1992	February 1994	+194%
Bear	March 1994	May 1994	−30%
Bull	June 1994	November 1994	+133%
Bear	December 1994	December 1994	−22%

Correlations

Indonesia 0.26

Sweden 0.23

United States 0.19

Switzerland 0.18

Singapore 0.17

United Kingdom 0.17

Japan 0.16

New Zealand 0.14

Canada 0.13

Chile 0.11

Hong Kong 0.11

Malaysia 0.11

Mexico 0.10

Korea 0.08

Australia 0.07

France 0.05

Germany 0.03

Taiwan 0.03

Thailand 0.02

Philippines −0.02

Argentina −0.21

Country Funds

Name	Originated	Hedging	Structure	Discount/ Premium	Phones
Brazil Fund	April 1988	Possible	Closed end	−54 / +32	(800) 349-4281 (617) 330-5602
Brazilian Equity	April 1992	No	Closed end	−15 / +39	(212) 832-2626

Source: Morningstar, Inc.

American Depositary Receipts

Name	Exchange	Symbol	Industry
Aracruz Cellulose	NYSE	ARA	Eucalyptus pulp

Direct Listings

None

Stock Summary

American investors would not have been able to keep the nearly 5 billion percent return posted by Brazilian stocks in local currency terms over the 1988 to 1994 period, but few would have complained about the 986 percent that was left after conversion to dollars. Along with good times, however, came downside volatility of more than fivefold that of the U.S. market. No less than 10 declines of 15 percent or more occurred over those seven years, and Brazilian stocks lost more than 15 percent in a single month on 11 separate occasions. These shares are clearly of the buy-and-hold variety.

Only one exchange-traded American depositary receipt is available on Brazil, Aracruz Celulose, a supplier of pulp to the paper-products industry. The company relies heavily on exports for revenue, indicating that it is not a direct play on the Brazilian economy and could suffer if the Brazilian real holds its value over time. Two closed-end funds are available to capture a larger share of the Brazilian equity universe, and both have clearly benefited from being in the right country at the right time. The newer of the entries, Brazilian Equity, has returned 148 percent on net asset value (NAV) over the first two calendar years of its existence, an impressive return in nominal terms but still well short of both the Morgan Stanley Capital International (MSCI) and the Wilshire Brazil indexes. The other closed-end, the Brazil Fund, has seen its NAV climb almost 200 percent over the six full years it has been in business, putting its return considerably under both country indexes as well. In the only bloody year for the Brazilian market during that period, Brazil Fund lost 68 percent, just slightly more than the MSCI and Wilshire Brazil benchmarks. As of October 1995, the two Brazilian mutual funds sold at moderate disscounts to NAV.

Investors considering buying into Brazil should keep in mind that the issue of a fund's performance relative to a country benchmark becomes less important when the number of alternate investments are few and especially when no fund exists that mimics the return of the benchmark. To the extent that an investor wants Brazilian exposure, the portfolios and track records of both funds indicate you are likely to get dollar-denominated returns at least representative of what the overall Brazilian equity and currency market is producing.

CHAPTER 20

Canada

Overview

Governmental budget deficits and the mounting debt they create is the overriding story in Canada. As a result of 30 years of nearly nonstop fiscal red ink, total federal and provincial IOUs now total roughly $560 billion, or about equal to Canada's entire annual output of goods and services. Some 42 percent of the debt is external, putting downward pressure on the Canadian dollar and upward pressure on domestic interest rates, thus further slowing an economy that has only recently begun to recover from a deep recession in the early 1990s. Fortunately, Canada has a highly favorable merchandise-trade position due to its strong natural-resource and agricultural exports. The country's economic output, per capita income, and standard of living are similar to those of the United States. Political conditions in Canada, while generally stable, have periodically been frazzled by an ever-present separatist movement in the province of Quebec. Though Canadian voters have consistently rejected the idea of an independent Quebec, the issue is far from settled, and investors can be certain that it will return to the public agenda.

The government has only belatedly addressed its budget problems, and interim measures to stem the fiscal bleeding, even if successful, are modest in scope. Canada's stock market has the lowest amount of downside volatility of any developed or emerging market, though its has underperformed U.S. stocks since 1988. Because of the large amount of natural-resource companies in its economy, the Canadian equity market offers many outstanding commodities-based plays, including several dozen trading on the New York Stock Exchange. Like markets in other natural-resource economies, such as Australia, strong performance of Canadian equities relative to U.S. equities could be an early warning sign of global economic overheating and impending interest-rate hikes.

Geography

Area: 3,851,809 square miles
Size relative to United States: 102%
Capital: Ottawa
Population density per square mile: 7.5
Population density relative to United States: 0.10x

Demographics

Population: 28 million
Population relative to United States: 11%
Average annual rate of natural increase: 0.7%
Projected population by 2025: 33 million
Population change by 2025: +18%

Government

Type: Confederation with Parliamentary Democracy
Sovereign: Queen Elizabeth II (1952)
Head of State: Jean Chretien, Prime Minister (1993)
Politics: Canada is a fully independent member of the British Commonwealth of Nations. The Constitutional Act of 1982 vested legislative authority in the hands of a bicameral legislature and a sovereign (Queen Elizabeth II), whose interests are represented by a governor general acting only on behalf of the Canadian prime minister and Cabinet. The legislature is composed of a Senate, with 104 members appointed for life (or until age 75) by the governor general, and a House of Commons, with 295 members apportioned according to provincial population and elected for a term of up to five years. New elections must be called whenever the party in power is voted down or otherwise decides to put an issue to the public. The prime minister is elected by the majority party in the House of Commons.

Canada is essentially a two-party nation, with the Conservative and Liberal parties mirroring the Conservative and Labor parties in Britain and the Republican and Democratic parties in the United States. A national election in 1993 returned the Liberal Party to power after a 10-year absence, with the party winning 177 seats in the House of Commons. In the aftermath of the election, Jean Chretien was appointed prime minister, replacing Kim Campbell, the first female prime minister in Canadian history. The issue of independence for the Canadian province of Quebec (and, therefore, for the important financial center Montreal) remains an ongoing concern for investors in Canadian stocks. In 1994, the separatist Parti Quebecois won control of the Quebec legislature with 45 percent of the vote, and in October 1995 a referendum that would have created an independent Quebec nation was narrowly defeated.

Economy

Financial Strength
(Historical data, relative to GDP)

Merchandise trade:+2.02%
Services: −1.18%
Income: −2.42%
Current account: −1.49%
Portfolio investment: −0.10%
Direct investment: −0.19%
Overall balance of payments: −0.10%
External debt: 42%
Budget: −2.75%
Investment/consumption ratio: 0.29

Currency
(Historical data)

Money supply growth: 11%
Consumer price index: 5.76%
Monetary unit: Canadian dollar
Monetary unit against U.S. dollar: −18%

Economic Output
(Historical data)

GDP: $537 billion
GDP relative to U.S. GDP: 8.46%
GDP growth rate: 3.81%
GDP growth rate relative to U.S. GDP growth rate: 1.34x
Per capita GDP: $19,179
Per capita GDP relative to U.S. per capita GDP: 85%

Figure 20.1. Canadian Balance of Payments
Surplus/deficit of Canadian budget (black) and current account (gray),
as percent of GDP.

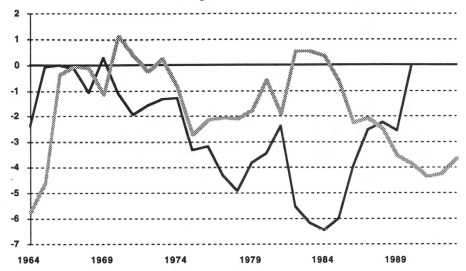

Source: International Monetary Fund, *International Financial Statistics Yearbook.*

Figure 20.2. Canadian Currency
Canadian dollars per U.S. dollar (inverted scale).

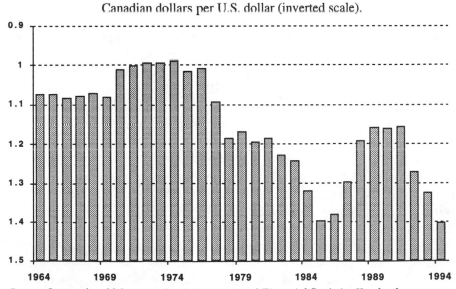

Source: International Monetary Fund, *International Financial Statistics Yearbook.*

Figure 20.3.   Canadian Economy

Annual percentage change in Canadian real GDP (bar graph, left scale). Growth in
Canadian real GDP relative to U.S. real GDP, 1963 = 100 (line graph, right scale).

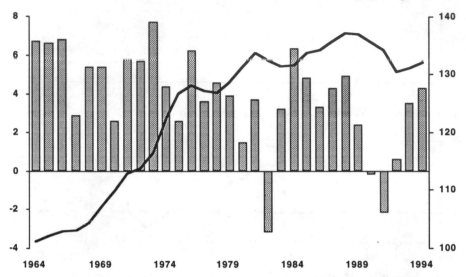

Source: International Monetary Fund, *International Financial Statistics Yearbook.*

Economic Summary

There is little wrong with the Canadian economy that a tighter fiscal policy
wouldn't cure. Canada is rich in natural resources and has successfully transformed itself from a largely agrarian economy to one in which industry accounts
for one-third of gross domestic product (GDP) and employs nearly one-quarter
of the country's population. Canada is the world's largest exporter of forestry
products, including paper, newsprint, wood pulp, lumber, and timber. Most of
the forest-products industry is centered in the provinces of British Columbia,
Ontario, and Quebec. The country also has abundant mineral reserves, such as
gold, platinum, nickel, copper, zinc, cobalt, lead, iron ore, petroleum, and natural
gas. Canada also exports large amounts of wheat, barley, oats, and other grains.
But while agriculture accounts for only 3 percent of GDP, it nonetheless is an
important source of foreign exchange.

Over the past three decades, Canada has averaged a 2 percent annual surplus
in merchandise trade, with only one down year. The positive balance of payments for goods, however, has usually been offset by deficits in services (aver-

aging 1.18 percent of GDP) and income, as the country has relied heavily upon foreigners to plug its growing budget deficit. Since 1964, income shortfalls on the balance of payments have amounted to 2.42 percent of GDP but have increased to an average of 3.38 percent since 1988. On the fiscal front, Canada's vast social-welfare system has contributed to budget deficits averaging 2.75 percent of GDP since 1964. As of fiscal 1992, more than 40 percent of government spending was allocated to health and other social-welfare programs. Included in the federal outlays is a medical insurance program that covers all Canadians against health-related expenses. The budget shortfalls, which are now larger than those in the United States as a percent of GDP, have forced Canadian monetary authorities and credit markets to keep interest rates high, which has the effect of slowing economic growth. Since 1964, Canada has averaged real annual GDP increases of 3.81 percent per year, but the pace has slowed to just 2.3 percent between 1989 and 1994. As a consequence of the accumulating debt, interest payments in Canada now eat up 37 cents of every tax dollar received by the federal government, compared with 15 cents on the budgetary buck in the United States.

As in the United States, however, there are nascent signs that the problem of a loose fiscal policy is being confronted. In early 1995, the Canadian government instituted a number of measures aimed at reducing its federal deficit to 3 percent of GDP by fiscal 1997. The plan requires a combination of spending cuts and tax increases, primarily directed at the corporate sector. Like all such deflationary measures, however, decreased spending coupled with increased taxes often results in still less tax revenues, which merely widens the budget gap. The country's investment-to-consumption ratio, at 0.29, is in line with the world average.

Canadian Stock Market

Exchange

Classification: Developed
Capitalization: $319 billion
Capitalization relative to U.S. stock market: 5.1%
Number of issues: 2,851
Primary index: TSE (Toronto Stock Exchange) Composite
Total return in local currency, 1988–1994: +122%
Total return in U.S. dollars, 1988–1994: +101%
Total return in U.S. dollars relative to U.S. stocks, 1988–1994: −33%

Figure 20.4.   Canadian Stocks

Return of Canadian stocks in local currency (black), U.S. dollars (gray),
and S&P 500 (dotted); Dec. 1987 = 100.

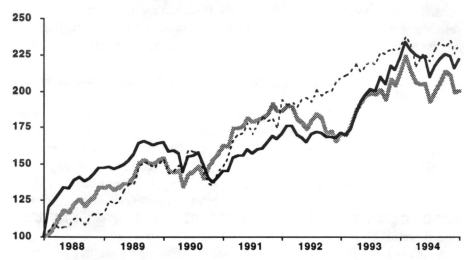

Source: Wilshire Associates Incorporated.

Volatility
(Historical)

Standard deviation: 3.42
Total monthly losses: 83.43%
Average monthly loss: 2.78%
Number of monthly losses: 30
Number of monthly losses greater than 5 percent: 6
Number of monthly losses greater than 10 percent: 0
Number of monthly losses greater than 15 percent: 0
Maximum monthly loss: 7.52%
Relative volatility ratio: 1.19

Price Cycles

Phase	From	To	Total return
Bull	January 1988	December 1994	+101%

Correlations

United States 0.47
Australia 0.45
Hong Kong 0.41
United Kingdom 0.41
Singapore 0.39
Korea 0.37
Thailand 0.37
Sweden 0.34
Japan 0.33
Malaysia 0.33
New Zealand 0.32

France 0.29
Indonesia 0.29
Germany 0.25
Mexico 0.22
Taiwan 0.20
Switzerland 0.19
Chile 0.17
Philippines 0.16
Brazil 0.13
Argentina 0.04

Country Funds

None

American Depositary Receipts

None

Direct Listings

Name	Exchange	Symbol	Industry
Abitibi-Price Inc.	NYSE	ABY	Newsprint, forest products
Agnico-Eagle Mines	NYSE	AEM	Mining
Alcan Aluminum Ltd.	NYSE	AL	Aluminum
Alias Research	NASDAQ	ADDDF	Technology
American Barrick Resources Corp.	NYSE	ABX	Gold mining
Arakis Energy	NASDAQ	AKSEF	Natural gas exploration and development
Bank of Montreal	NYSE	BMO	Banking
BCE Inc.	NYSE	BCE	Telecommunications
Big Rock Brewery	NASDAQ	BEERF	Beverages
Biochem Pharma	NASDAQ	BCHXF	Pharmaceuticals
Campbell Resources Inc.	NYSE	CCH	Coal, gas, and oil

(continued)

Name	Exchange	Symbol	Industry
Canadian Pacific Ltd.	NYSE	CP	Transportation
Cineplex Odeon Corp.	NYSE	CPX	Movie theatres
Domtar, Inc.	NYSE	DTC	Pulp, paper products
Glamis Gold Ltd.	NYSE	GLG	Mining
Horsham Corp.	NYSE	HSM	Oil and mining investments
Inco Ltd.	NYSE	N	Nickel and copper
International Colin Energy Corp.	NYSE	KCN	Oil and gas exploration
InterTan Inc.	NYSE	ITN	Retail electronics
Kinross Gold	NYSE	KGC	Gold producer
Laidlaw Inc. (Class A & B)	NYSE	LDW	Transportation and waste services
Magna International Inc.	NYSE	MGA	Automotive-part manufacturing
Mitel Corp.	NYSE	MLT	Telecommunications
Moore Corporation	NYSE	MCL	Business forms
Newbridge Networks	NYSE	NN	Digital networking products
Northern Telecom Ltd.	NYSE	NT	Telecommunications
Northgate Exploration Ltd.	NYSE	NGX	Exploration, mining
NOVA Corporation	NYSE	NVA	Gas pipelines, petrochemicals
Placer Dome Inc.	NYSE	PDG	Gold and silver mining
Potash Corp.	NYSE	POT	Mining
Premdor, Inc.	NYSE	PI	Door manufacturing
Ranger Oil Ltd.	NYSE	RGO	Oil and gas exploration, production
Seagram Company	NYSE	VO	Distilleries
TransCanada Pipeline	NYSE	TRP	Natural gas pipelines
TVX Gold	NYSE	TVX	Exploration and mining
United Dominion Industries Limited	NYSE	UDI	Industrial engineering
Westcoast Energy Inc.	NYSE	WE	Natural gas transmission

Stock Summary

It has been a smooth, if somewhat lackluster, ride for investors in Canadian equities since 1988, with stock prices doubling in U.S. dollar terms without a single retreat of 15 percent or more. Downside volatility has been almost exactly equal to the American market, as evidenced by the Canadian bourse's high overall correlation to U.S. stocks. Despite the steady climb, however, Canadian equities have hardly been the gold mine that many are in the literal sense, returning about one-third less than U.S. equities over the 1988 to 1994 period. The general weakness of the Canadian dollar—a by-product of the country's large budget deficits—played a role in the lower relative return, reducing the gain for American investors by about 10 percent. As of year-end 1994, Canadian equity markets were capitalized at an aggregate $579 billion, with more than 80 percent of the trading by value taking place on the Toronto Stock Exchange. The country's former financial hub, Montreal, accounts for 12 percent of dollar volume, with the remainder scattered among bourses in Vancouver, Alberta, and Winnipeg. More than half of the companies listed in Montreal trade in Toronto as well.

Reflecting the significant raw-materials component of the Canadian economy, one-third of the Toronto market's capitalization are natural-resource plays, a number of which are also directly listed on the NASDAQ or the New York Stock Exchange. Owning the type of commodities and metals companies that are available in substantial quantity on the Canadian exchange has several benefits. First, some Canadian corporations, such as Seagram (distilleries) and Alcan (aluminum products), derive a substantial portion of their earnings from exports, thus benefitting from the chronically weak Canadian dollar. Second, energy companies like Campbell Resources are paid in dollars, once again positioning themselves to gain if the Canadian currency falls. Finally, mining stocks, such as American Barrick, Placer Dome, and Northgate Exploration, can provide an important hedge against inflation, because the price of such commodities as gold and silver usually climbs when financial assets are under pressure from the side effects of inflation. And even without owning any Canadian stocks, watching the Toronto and Montreal markets might provide some important clues as to the direction of U.S. equities. Commodities companies tend to do best when the global economy is trending higher. Because it is virtually impossible for worldwide demand for raw materials to reach levels necessary to push prices (and therefore profits) north without the U.S. economy participating, the outperformance of natural-resource stocks could imply that the U.S. Federal Reserve would have to raise interest rates to short-circuit inflationary pressures, a development that almost always stops U.S. stocks dead in their tracks. The Australian market, which also has a high concentration of raw-materials companies (and which also has a high correlation to the Toronto bourse), also could serve a similar dual purpose.

CHAPTER 21

Republic of Chile

Overview

Chile survived the political chaos of the 1970s to emerge as the financial heavy-weight of Latin America in the 1990s. The performance of Chilean stocks over the past several years reflects the relative strength of the nation's balance sheet, which can claim regular budget and merchandise-trade surpluses. The government has taken a strongly probusiness stance while attempting to manage the amount of foreign portfolio investment flowing into the Santiago market, thus avoiding a replay of the capital flight that menaced the Mexican Bolsa in 1994. Unlike Mexico, Chile's currency has stabilized and rebounded in recent years after free-falling for most of the past quarter century. The country continues to have problems with inflation, however, and is also somewhat vulnerable to a drop in commodities prices, particularly copper, which represents more than one-third of exports.

Seventeen Chilean American depositary receipts (ADRs) trade on American exchanges, though taken together they are not necessarily indicative of the broad market. One closed-end country fund, the Chile Fund, has returned more than 400 percent since inception in 1989. American investors who have experienced only good times in Chile should reasonably expect somewhat slower going in the years ahead, but the country's stable politics and strong finances argue that Chile is the safest and possibly best long-term play in Latin America.

Geography

Area: 38,031 square miles
Size relative to United States: 1%
Capital: Santiago
Population density per square mile: 48
Population density relative to United States: 0.65x

Demographics

Population: 14 million
Population relative to United States: 5%
Average annual rate of natural increase: 1.7%
Projected population by 2025: 19 million
Population change by 2025: +36%

Government

Type: Republic

Head of State: Eduardo Frei Ruiz-Tagle, President (1994)

Political System: Chile is governed under a constitution passed by plebiscite in 1980. The current document replaced a 1925 charter that was abolished in the wake of a military coup and subsequent suspension of constitutional law in 1973. The 1980 constitution vests executive power in the president, who is elected to an eight-year term. (A 1989 amendment to the constitution stipulated that the winner of the 1989 presidential election would serve a term of only four years and not be eligible for immediate reelection.) Chile has a bicameral legislature known as the National Congress, consisting of a 47-member Senate and a 120-member Chamber of Deputies. Thirty-nine of the Senators are directly elected and serve eight-year terms. All Deputies are popularly elected to four-year terms.

During most of the twentieth century, Chilean politics has swung wildly between left- and right-wing extremes. In 1970, Dr. Salvador Allende Gossens became the first Marxist-Leninist to be freely elected to the presidency of a noncommunist nation and immediately moved to nationalize Chilean and American industry and expropriate land from the country's economic elite. In 1973, amid civil unrest and mass demonstrations against the government, Chile lurched sharply to the right as Allende was overthrown by a military junta led by Army Chief of Staff Augusto Pinochet Ugarte. A staunch anticommunist, Mr. Pinochet vowed to "exterminate Marxism" and proceeded to suspend constitutional law and abolish political parties. Over the following 16 years, however, the Pinochet government would gradually move the country away from economic statism and reinstitute political freedoms. Mr. Pinochet was prohibited under terms of a 1988 plebiscite from running again for the presidency in 1989 and was succeeded in office by Patricio Aylwin in 1990, who served a four-year term. Chile's current president, Eduardo Frei, is considered a left-centrist politically. Mr. Frei was elected in December 1993 with 58 percent of the vote as his Christian Democratic Party gained pluralities in both chambers of the legislature. Barring an-

other political upheaval, Mr. Frei, whose father was also president of Chile during the 1960s, will serve as president until March 2002.

Economy

Financial Strength
(Historical data, relative to GDP)

Merchandise trade: +2.64%
Services: –2.24%
Income: –4.39%
Current account: –4.87%
Portfolio investment: +0.54%
Direct investment: +0.24%
Overall balance of payments: –3.12%
Budget: –1.22%
External debt: 53%
Investment/consumption ratio: 0.22

Figure 21.1.   Chilean Balance of Payments
Surplus/deficit of Chilean budget (black) and current account (gray),
as percent of GDP.

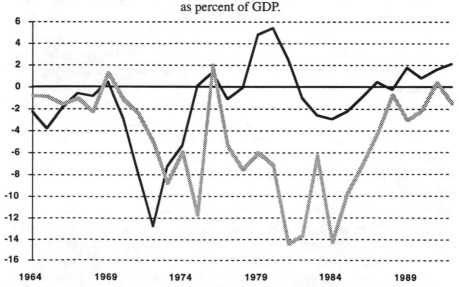

Source: International Monetary Fund, *International Financial Statistics Yearbook.*

Currency
(Historical data)

Money supply growth: 90%
Consumer price index: 73%
Monetary unit: Peso
Monetary unit against U.S. dollar: –99.99%

Economic Output
(Historical data)

GDP: $41 billion
GDP relative to U.S. GDP: 0.64%
GDP growth rate: 3.65%
GDP growth rate relative to U.S. GDP growth rate: 1.28x
Per capita GDP: $2,929
Per capita GDP relative to U.S. per capita GDP: 13%

Figure 21.2.   Chilean Currency
Pesos per U.S. dollar (inverted logarithmic scale).

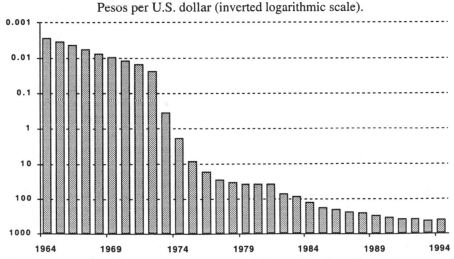

Source: International Monetary Fund, *International Financial Statistics Yearbook.*

Figure 21.3. Chilean Economy

Annual percentage change in Chilean real GDP (bar graph, left scale). Growth in
Chilean real GDP relative to U.S. real GDP, 1963 = 100 (line graph, right scale).

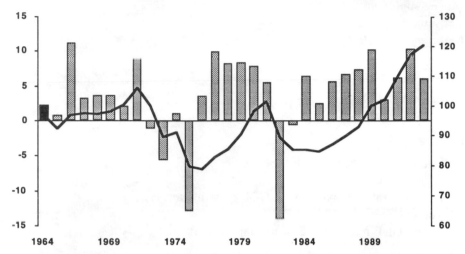

Source: International Monetary Fund, *International Financial Statistics Yearbook.*

Economic Summary

Chile is the economic superstar of Latin America, having gotten its financial house
in good working order in the aftermath of nearly two decades of political chaos.
After racking up double-digit deficits in its budget and current account for nearly
15 years, the probusiness policies of former President Augusto Pinochet finally
began to show results by the late 1980s, and the country now finds itself in stron-
ger financial shape than any nation in the region. Since 1987, Chile has averaged
a budget surplus of more than 1 percent of GDP per year and reduced the size
of its current-account deficit to just 1.87 percent of GDP, a lower figure than that
of the United States. Most of the Chilean current-account shortfalls are the result
of interest on its external debt, which amounts to more than half of GDP. Since
1987, Chile's investment-to-consumption ratio also nearly doubled to 0.33 from
just 0.18 for the previous two decades. In addition to its healthy fiscal policy,
Chile's financial strength is derived from consistent merchandise-trade surpluses,
which have averaged 2.64 percent per year since 1964.

Unlike Mexico, which attracted most of its foreign capital in the form of highly
fickle (and not always productivity-enhancing) portfolio investment, Chile has

acquired foreign reserves by selling *things*, primarily copper (Chile is the largest copper producer) and other minerals, such as gold, silver, and iron ore. In addition to minerals and forest products, the country also exports large quantities of fruit, vegetables, fishmeal, and wine. One-third of Chilean exports go to the United States and Japan. Chile's dependence on copper sales—currently running at 38 percent of exports—can be a double-edged sword: When the price of the commodity declines, revenues can be seriously affected, leading to trade and budget deficits and weakness in the currency.

The government manages the float of the Chilean peso, which has lost 99.99 percent of its value against the dollar since 1964, although it has held up reasonably well since the mid-1980s. As of May 1995, the peso was trading at nearly the same level relative to the dollar as in 1991 and at somewhat above its 1992 to 1994 range. Given the long-term weakness in the currency, however, inflation has been a continuing problem, averaging 74 percent per year since 1964 (mostly because of hyperinflation in the mid-1970s), though the rate has fallen to an average of 14 percent between 1992 and 1994.

President Frei has vowed to continue the probusiness policies instituted by Mr. Pinochet and continued under his immediate successor, Patricio Aylwin. The U.S. Congress is considering legislation that would expand the North American Free Trade Agreement (NAFTA) to include Chile and eventually to other South American nations, but the move faces considerable political hurdles in both countries, given the Mexican economic collapse less than one year after NAFTA went into effect. Chilean tariffs are already among the lowest in the region, and American goods currently represent 20 percent of all Chilean imports, double the amount of Japan, the second-largest seller to the Chilean market.

Chilean Stock Market

Exchange

Classification: Emerging
Capitalization: $68 billion
Capitalization relative to U.S. stock market: 1.1%
Number of issues: 281
Primary index: General (IGPA)
Total return in local currency, 1988–1994: +2,345%
Total return in U.S. dollars, 1988–1994: +1,317%
Total return in U.S. dollars relative to U.S. stocks: 1988–1994: +1,183

Figure 21.4   Chilean Stocks

Return of Chilean stocks in local currency (black), U.S. dollars (gray), and S&P 500 (dotted); Dec. 1987 = 100 (logarithmic scale).

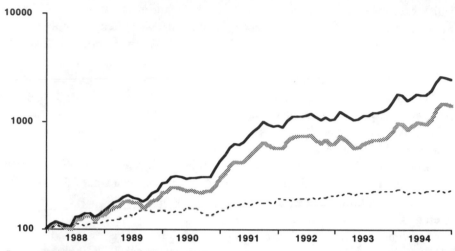

Source: Wilshire Associates Incorporated.

Volatility
(Historical)

Standard deviation: 7.64
Total monthly losses: 134%
Average monthly loss: 5.38%
Number of monthly losses: 25
Number of monthly losses greater than 5 percent: 12
Number of monthly losses greater than 10 percent: 3
Number of monthly losses greater than 15 percent: 0
Maximum monthly loss: 11.82%
Relative volatility ratio: 2.26

Price Cycles

Phase	From	To	Total return
Bull	January 1988	July 1992	+656%
Bear	August 1992	November 1992	−17%
Bull	December 1992	January 1993	+19%
Bear	February 1993	April 1993	−23%
Bull	May 1993	December 1994	+147%

Correlations

Hong Kong 0.22
United States 0.20
Thailand 0.18
Canada 0.17
Indonesia 0.15
Philippines 0.14
Singapore 0.14
Taiwan 0.14
Brazil 0.11
Malaysia 0.09
Korea 0.08

Argentina 0.07
Mexico 0.07
Sweden 0.05
France 0.02
Switzerland 0.00
United Kingdom 0.00
Australia −0.10
Germany −0.10
Japan −0.20
New Zealand −0.20

Country Funds

Name	Originated	Hedging	Structure	Discount/ Premium	Phone
Chile Fund	Sept. 1989	Possible	Closed end	−26 / + 28	(212) 832-2626

American Depositary Receipts

Name	Exchange	Symbol	Industry
Administradora de Fondos de Pensiones Provida	NYSE	PVD	Pension fund administration
Banco O'Higgins	NYSE	OHG	Banking
Banco Osorno y La Union	NYSE	BOU	Banking
Chilgener	NYSE	CHR	Electric generating
Compania Cervecerias Unidas	NASDAQ	CCUUY	Beverages
Compania de Telefonos de Chile	NYSE	CTC	Telecommunications
Cristalerias de Chile	NYSE	CGW	Glass manufacturing
Embotelladora Andina	NYSE	AKO	Coca-Cola production and distribution
Empresas Telex-Chile	NYSE	TL	Telecommunication
ENDESA	NYSE	EOC	Electric generating
Enersis	NYSE	ENI	Electric holding company
Laboratorio Chile	NYSE	LBC	Pharmaceutical
Madeco	NYSE	MAD	Telecom and industrial
MASISA-Maderas y Siteticos	NYSE	MYS	Wood products

(continued)

Name	Exchange	Symbol	Industry
SQM-Sociedad Quimica y Minera de Chile	NYSE	SQM	Chemical
Telefonos de Chile	NYSE	CTC	Telecommunications
Vina Concha y Tora	NYSE	VCO	Wine producer/exporter

Direct Listings

None

Stock Summary

The spectacular performance of the Chilean equity market reflects its connection to the star economy and financial system of Latin America. Over the 1988 to 1994 period, Chilean stocks climbed roughly 1,300 percent in dollar terms, or 10 times the gain of the American Standard & Poor's 500-Stock Index. The financial windfall to U.S. investors would have been still larger if not for a downward float in the Chilean peso. There were the usual bumps along the way, of course, with two bear markets averaging 20 percent over three months interrupting the climb. Chilean stocks have averaged slightly more than double the downside volatility of U.S. equities and carry generally low correlations to other global equity markets.

Chile's main stock exchange is located in the capital city of Santiago and is actually one of the smaller bourses in the region. Capitalized at $68.2 billion at year-end 1994, the Santiago Bolsa is just one-third the size of the Brazilian market and barely half the value of the Mexican exchange. Besides reflecting a smaller overall economy, the Chilean market also carries a lower capitalization because of restrictions on foreign investment in and repatriation from the Santiago market. The foreign restrictions are designed to avoid the capital flight that contributed to the Mexican financial meltdown in December 1994. A healthy, domestic, private-pension system functions to give the support for Chilean equities that nations with smaller or less-well-accessed savings pools must rely on foreigners to provide. (Chilean citizens are required to make regular contributions to the country's pension system.) But while creating stability and reasonable valuations through modest restrictions on foreign portfolio investment may be sound policy, it does have the effect of limiting the ways in which Americans can play Chile. The number of American depositary receipts (ADRs) on the Chilean market has grown from zero in 1992 to 17 by 1995; but, in the aggregate, the offerings do not represent a substantial share of the overall Santiago market, creating the likelihood of considerable divergence (be it good or bad) between returns on ADRs and the broad market. Still, several large-cap stocks are available, including Telefonos de Chile, the country's largest provider of phone service, and ENDESA, Chile's largest utility.

Investors looking to capture a broader representation of the Chilean market might look at the Chile Fund, a closed-end offering that has climbed an average of 42 percent per year over the first five years of its existence. The fund has virtually matched the Morgan Stanley and Wilshire Chile indexes, indicating that portfolio-management skill, not just location, are behind the fund's success. Despite its rousing returns, Chile Fund has often been on the bargain counter, trading at more than a 20 percent discount to its net asset value (NAV) even for much of its run-up year of 1991, when the Fund and the broad Chilean market climbed roughly 90 percent in dollar terms. (Closed-end funds will sometimes retain their discounts even when sentiment is highly positive if the underlying market is going up faster than new money can flow in.) As of October 1995, Chile Fund was trading at a 15 percent discount to its NAV.

CHAPTER 22

United Mexican States

Overview

Just when it began to look like Mexico was going to make the jump from Third World pretender to First World competitor, it all fell apart. Political unrest, a widening trade deficit, and an imbalance in foreign investment exposed a fundamental lack of global competitiveness, which ultimately forced the Mexican government to abandon its long-term plan to gradually build an export-based economy.

Under former President Carlos Salinas de Gortari, the Mexican government in the 1980s began an ambitious privatization program that resulted in the sale of more than 80 percent of its 1,100 businesses, raising $21 billion. The government also succeeded in bringing its notoriously bloated federal budget into balance and even steadied the free-falling peso for a time in the early 1990s. And as the Mexican currency steadied, inflation declined, and privatization rolled on, foreign investors flocked into the Mexican Bolsa, pushing prices to classic bull-market extremes.

On the trade front, however, Mexico was not selling its goods abroad, and the North American Free Trade Agreement only fueled import consumption, leading to a hemorrhaging of its balance-of-payments accounts and eventual currency devaluation. The financial collapse exposed the inability of Mexican companies to compete abroad without the benefits of a low currency. For Mexico to eventually compete successfully, it will have to attract the more stable type of foreign investment that improves its inadequate infrastructure and its shortage of high-tech industries. Making progress more difficult will be the continuing undercurrent of social unrest, particularly in the southern state of Chiapas, where ethnic Indian uprisings had begun even before the onset of the 1994–1995 financial crisis. A population that has grown at an average rate of 2.2 percent per year and that is expected to increase by another 50 percent by 2025 will make the task of growing the Mexican economy even more difficult.

Geography

Area: 761,600 square miles
Size relative to United States: 20%
Capital: Mexico City
Population density per square mile: 120
Population density relative to United States: 1.63x

Demographics

Population: 95 million
Population relative to United States: 37%
Average annual rate of natural increase: 2.2%
Projected population by 2025: 141 million
Population change by 2025: +48%

Government

Type: Federal Republic
Head of State: Ernesto Zedillo, President (1994)
Political System: Mexico is comprised of 31 states and a Federal District around the capital of Mexico City. Under a constitution promulgated in 1917, executive power is vested in a president, who is directly elected by universal adult suffrage for a single term of six years. The legislature consists of a bicameral Congress, including a Senate, with 64 members (two from each state and the Federal District) elected to six-year terms, and a Chamber of Deputies, whose 500 members are apportioned by population and serve for three years. Political power in Mexico is concentrated in the Institutional Revolutionary Party (PRI), which has won

every presidential election since the current constitution went into effect. The Mexican ethos tolerates an authoritarian element in its democracy, and the Mexican political system creates a strong, one-term, civilian president whose ability to hand out favors perpetuates party power.

Violence has increasingly become a part of the Mexican political scene, however, as rebel groups have demonstrated against the vast disparity between the country's rich and poor, and political assassination has rocked the electoral process. In March 1994, while campaigning for president in Tijuana, PRI candidate Luis Donaldo Colosio was shot and killed. He was replaced on the PRI ticket by free-market devotee Ernesto Zedillo, who was elected with 50 percent of the vote in the August 1994 election. Economic policy is guided by Guillermo Ortiz, a Stanford-educated economist who took over as Finance Minister in the wake of the peso devaluation. Prior to the financial meltdown, political sentiment seemed to be growing for addressing social ills.

Economy

Financial Strength
(Historical data, relative to GDP)

Merchandise trade: −0.14%
Services: +0.96%
Income: −3.64%
Current account: −2.83%
Portfolio investment: +0.26%
Direct investment: +0.96%
Overall balance of payments: −0.47%
Budget: −5.30%
External debt: 20%
Investment/consumption ratio: 0.28

Currency

(Historical data)

Money supply growth: 41%
Consumer price index: 30%
Monetary unit: Peso
Monetary unit against U.S. dollar: −99%

Figure 22.1.   Mexican Balance of Payments
Surplus/deficit of Mexican budget (black) and current account (gray),
as percent of GDP.

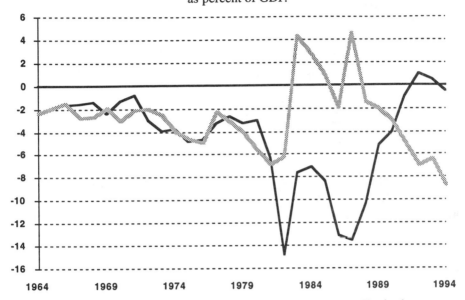

Source: International Monetary Fund, *International Financial Statistics Yearbook.*

Figure 22.2.   Mexican Currency
Pesos per U.S. dollar (inverted logarithmic scale).

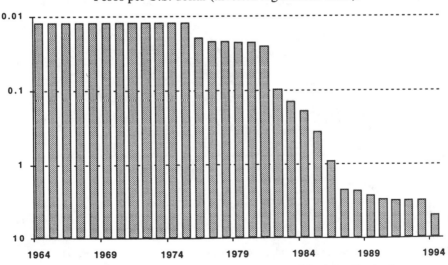

Source: International Monetary Fund, *International Financial Statistics Yearbook.*

Economic Output

(Historical data)

GDP: $331 billion
GDP relative to U.S. GDP: 5.3%
GDP growth rate: 4.69%
GDP growth rate relative to U.S. GDP growth rate: 1.67x
Per capita GDP: $3,489
Per capita GDP relative to U.S. per capita GDP: 10.2%

Economic Summary

The roots of Mexico's economic difficulties are found in its decayed infrastructure and lagging productivity, both of which result in a shortage of competitive
products in domestic and foreign markets. The strong-peso policy of former
President Carlos Salinas de Gortari, which was intended to reassure foreign investors that financial commitments in Mexico would be safe, had the additional
and unintended consequence of discouraging Mexican business from developing
export markets while making higher-quality foreign goods still more attractive

Figure 22.3.   Mexican Economy
Annual percentage change in Mexican real GDP (bar graph, left scale). Growth in
Mexican real GDP relative to U.S. real GDP, 1963 = 100 (line graph, right scale).

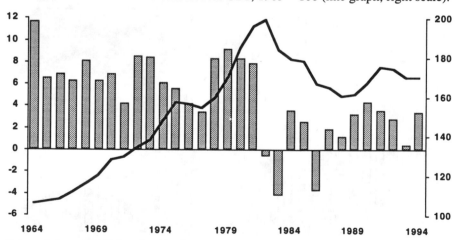

Source: International Monetary Fund, *International Financial Statistics Yearbook.*

to a Mexican consumer suddenly holding a reliable currency. As the peso stabilized in the early 1990s after decades of weakness, Mexican exports became progressively less competitive and merchandise-trade deficits grew to more than 6 percent of gross domestic product (GDP) by 1992. At the same time, the relatively stable peso was succeeding in sucking in foreign investment, but much of the money was destined for the Mexican stock or bond market rather than for the kinds of long-term projects that ultimately would improve the country's transportation system and private productive capacity.

While direct investment in Mexico did increase dramatically between 1988 and 1994, investments in Mexican financial assets increased even more. In 1991 and 1992, for example, foreign portfolio investment was more than double the amount channeled to more stable direct investment. After the North American Free Trade Agreement went into effect in January 1994, the balance of payments quickly worsened, and Mexico's deficit on its current account soared to roughly 8 percent of GDP. Suddenly, investors holding Mexican stocks—a major source of the foreign exchange Mexico needed to finance its trade imbalance—were looking at increasingly turbulent domestic, political, and social situations and dwindling hard-currency reserves. The decision was easy: Sell. Faced with foreign portfolio investors calling in their chips, the Mexican government had little choice but to devalue its currency by 30 percent in December 1994. Over the ensuing months, the peso would float lower by another 20 percent in world currency markets. Since 1964, Mexican old and new pesos have gone from an adjusted value of 80 U.S. dollars to a mere 17 cents.

In the wake of the implosion in its economy, Mexico received a $52 billion bailout from the United States and international agencies. The remedies required to solve the basic Mexican economic problem—its inability to get significant net foreign exchange except through portfolio investment—were draconian enough to make a recession likely in 1995 and, perhaps, 1996. The peso devaluation sent inflation back to the double-digit figures of the late 1980s, while the high domestic interest rates required to curb capital flight (48 percent on short-term government debt as of May 1995) would inevitably lead to an economic slowdown. Early evidence, however, suggests that the devalued peso has at least put a band-aid on Mexico's current-account hemorrhaging. In February 1995, for example, the country reported a trade surplus of $452 million, the first time its trade account was in the black since November 1990. A modest rebound in foreign-currency reserves by mid-1995 was also signaling a possible return to Mexico by foreign investors.

Over the long term, Mexico's ability to compete in global consumer markets will depend on the upgrading of its infrastructure and capital equipment to include, ideally, a significant high-technology component. As of the mid-1990s, Mexico derives most of whatever export advantages it has from energy products and cheap labor.

Mexican Stock Market

Exchange

Classification: Emerging
Capitalization: $130 billion
Capitalization relative to U.S. stock market: 2.1%
Number of issues: 206
Primary index: Price and Quotations Index (IPC)
Total return in local currency, 1988–1994: +1,663%
Total return in U.S. dollars, 1988–1994: +708%
Total return in U.S. dollars relative to U.S. stocks, 1988–1994: +574%

Figure 22.4   Mexican Stocks
Return of Mexican stocks in local currency (black), U.S. dollars (gray), and S&P 500 (dotted); Dec. 1987 = 100 (logarithmic scale).

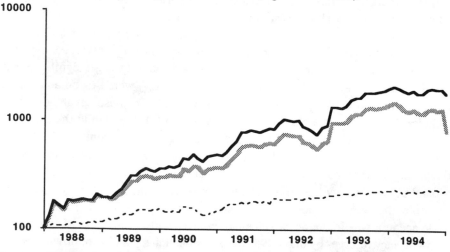

Sources: Wilshire Associates Incorporated; Federation Internationale des Bourses de Valeur.

Volatility

(Historical)

Standard deviation: 10.41
Total monthly losses: 168%
Average monthly loss: 5.27%
Number of monthly losses: 32
Number of monthly losses greater than 5 percent: 10
Number of monthly losses greater than 10 percent: 3
Number of monthly losses greater than 15 percent: 1
Maximum monthly loss: 36.32%
Relative volatility ratio: 2.31

Price Cycles

Phase	From	To	Total return
Bull	January 1988	February 1988	+73%
Bear	March 1988	April 1988	−15%
Bull	May 1988	February 1992	+414%
Bear	March 1992	September 1992	−29%
Bull	October 1992	January 1994	+172%
Bear	February 1994	December 1994	−45%

Correlations

Korea 0.24
Canada 0.22
United States 0.20
Taiwan 0.18
Singapore 0.14
Indonesia 0.13
Thailand 0.12
Australia 0.11
Brazil 0.10
Malaysia 0.09
Sweden 0.09

Hong Kong 0.08
Japan 0.08
Chile 0.07
France 0.07
United Kingdom 0.07
Argentina 0.06
Switzerland 0.02
New Zealand 0.02
Philippines −0.01
Germany −0.03

Country Funds

Name	Originated	Hedging	Structure	Discount/ Premium	Phones
Emerging Mexico	Oct. 1990	Possible	Closed end	−20 / + 26	(212) 713-2000
Mexico Equity & Income	Aug.1990	No	Closed end	−21 / + 27	(800) 421-4777 (212) 667-5000
Mexico Fund	June 1981	No	Closed end	−46 / + 134	(800) 224-4134 (212) 936-5100

Source: Morningstar, Inc.

American Depositary Receipts

Name	Exchange	Symbol	Industry
Banca Quadrum	NASDAQ	QDRMY	Banking
Banpais	NYSE	BPS	Banking
Bufete Industrial	NYSE	GBI	Engineering, construction
Coca-Cola Femsa S.A.	NYSE	KOF	Bottling
Consorcio G Grupo Dina	NYSE	DIN	Truck and bus manufacturing
Desc	NYSE	DES	Diversified services
Empress ICA Sociedad Controladora	NYSE	ICA	Construction
Empress La Moderna	NYSE	ELM	Cigarettes producer
Grupo Casa Autry	NYSE	ATY	Distributor
Grupo Elektra	NYSE	EKT	Electronics retailer
Grupo Embotellador de Mexico	NYSE	GEM	Bottling
Grupo Financiero Serfin	NYSE	SFN	Financial services
Grupo Industrial Durango	NYSE	GID	Forest products
Grupo Industrial Maseca	NYSE	MSK	Corn flour producer
Grupo Iusacell	NYSE	CEL	Telecommunications
Grupo Mexicao de Desarrollo	NYSE	GMD	Construction
Grupo Radio Centro	NYSE	RC	Radio broadcasting
Grupo Televisa	NYSE	TV	Media
Grupo Tribasa	NYSE	GTR	Construction
Internacional de Ceramica	NYSE	ICM	Ceramic tile manufacturing and distribution
Servicios Financieros Quadrum	NASDAQ	QDRMY	Financial services
Telefonos de Mexico S.A.	NYSE	TMX	Telecommunications
Transportacion Maritima Mexicana	NYSE	TMM	Shipping
Vitro, Sociedad Anonima	NYSE	VTO	Glassware manufacturing

Direct Listings

None

Stock Summary

For all the front-page news about Mexico's embarrassing financial crisis, long-term investors in the Bolsa are crying all the way to the bank. Despite a drop of nearly 50 percent in dollar terms during 1994, holders of the average Mexican stock would still have earned more than five times the U.S. market's return over the 1988 to 1994 period, as Mexican equities went almost straight up amid the euphoria generated by the government's economic liberalization and budget austerity. When the Mexican market finally crashed—first because of Chiapas, then because of political uncertainty, and finally because of the fallout of the developing devaluation—it brought down with it most other emerging markets, especially those in neighboring Latin American economies.

Investors wanting a piece of the Mexican action will find plenty of ways to get it, with three closed-end funds and 24 NYSE- or NASDAQ-traded American depository receipts (ADRs). One of the funds, Mexico Equity & Income, theoretically should be somewhat less volatile than the Bolsa because its portfolio holds at least 20 percent cash and bonds. Both Emerging Mexico and Mexico Fund are straight equity plays; and, while both have racked up extraordinary returns, they have nonetheless underperformed the Morgan Stanley Capital International Index: Mexico over their respective lifetimes. On the ADR front, the best-known Mexican stock, Telefonos de Mexico, is considered a proxy for the Mexican market, with its capitalization equal to roughly one-third the overall value of the Bolsa. Telmex is presently the country's monopoly provider of telecommunications services, but deregulation will bring competition beginning in 1997. Other Mexican ADRs cut across a wide range of industries, but the largest bank of the group, Banpais, has incurred the wrath of regulators because of a sloppy balance sheet and has stopped trading on the NYSE. As long as the peso remains under pressure, the most stable group on the Bolsa is likely to be those stocks that derive the highest percentage of revenue from exports. A weak peso, of course, will help the earnings of export-driven companies by increasing foreign competitiveness and creating gains from currency repatriation.

CHAPTER 23

French Republic

Overview

The growing dichotomy between France's budget deficit and its trade surplus underscores the country's widening social gap, a condition that led to the election of conservative candidate Jacques Chirac in the 1995 presidential election. While segments of France are recovering nicely from a deep and prolonged recession, unemployment has been rising, partly because of the previous French government's commitment to maintain a strong franc policy in preparation for a single European currency in 1999, as mandated by the Maastricht Treaty. The large French budget deficits are the result of a vast social-welfare system that is common to many European nations. President Chirac will have to reconcile the need to reduce the budget deficit (under terms of Maastricht, federal red ink may not exceed 3 percent of gross domestic product) with the harsh reality of the country's chronically high unemployment.

Despite the strong franc, French exports have been booming in recent years, and the current account is now in the black. Over the past three decades, French economic growth has averaged slightly more than 3 percent per year, but its economy has underperformed that of the United States since 1982. The French equity market has also been disappointing, returning just 63 percent in dollar terms over the 1988 to 1994 period, a 71 percent underperformance of the U.S. market. Despite its problems, France has the world's sixth-largest economy and per capita gross domestic product (GDP) of more than $24,000, nearly equal to the United States.

Geography

Area: 212,918 square miles
Size relative to United States: 5.62%
Capital: Paris
Population density per square mile: 272
Population density relative to United States: 3.69x

Demographics

Population: 57 million
Population relative to United States: 22%
Average annual rate of natural increase: 0.4%
Projected population by 2025: 62 million
Population change by 2025: +8.77%

Government

Type: Republic

Head of State: Jacques Chirac, President (1995)

Political System: Under a constitution promulgated in 1958 and amended in 1962 and 1992, legislative power is vested in a bicameral Parliament consisting of a Senate and a National Assembly. The 321 members comprising the Senate are elected to nine-year terms by an electoral college made up of National Assembly members and other departmental and local officials. The National Assembly consists of 577 members chosen by universal adult suffrage to a term of five years, subject to dissolution. Executive power is vested in a president, who is elected to a seven-year term by popular vote. The prime minister is appointed by the president.

French politics are dominated by the conservative Gaullist Party and the Socialists, whose leader, Francois Mitterrand, held the presidency from 1981 until 1995. Upon assuming office, Mr. Mitterand launched an aggressive program of industrial nationalizations, which he later modified and began to reverse. Much of Mr. Mitterand's term in office was spent in an awkward power-sharing arrangement with a conservative government and Parliament. In May 1995, Gaullist candidate Jacques Chirac was elected to the presidency on his third try, defeating Socialist Lionel Jospin by a 53 percent to 47 percent margin. Mr. Chirac is a strong advocate of free markets but made seemingly contradictory statements in his campaign about the need to reduce unemployment—thus implying an expansionist monetary policy—and a commitment to the Maastricht Treaty, which implicitly limits the ability of governments to inflate themselves out of economic trouble.

Economy

Financial Strength
(Historical data, relative to GDP)

Merchandise trade: −0.75%
Services: +1.16%
Income: −0.06%
Current account: −0.23%
Portfolio investment: +0.61%
Direct investment: −0.18%
Overall balance of payments: +0.03%
Budget: −1.68%
External debt: 22%
Investment/consumption ratio: 0.30

Currency
(Historical data)

Money supply growth: 14.84%
Consumer price index: 6.52%
Monetary unit: Franc
Monetary unit against U.S. dollar: −17%

Economic Output
(Historical data)

GDP: $1.37 trillion
GDP relative to U.S. GDP: 18%
GDP growth rate: 3.18%
GDP growth rate relative to U.S. GDP growth rate: 1.11x
Per capita GDP: $24,175
Per capita GDP relative to U.S. per capita GDP: 93%

Figure 23.1.   French Balance of Payments
Surplus/deficit of French budget (black) and current account (gray),
as percent of GDP.

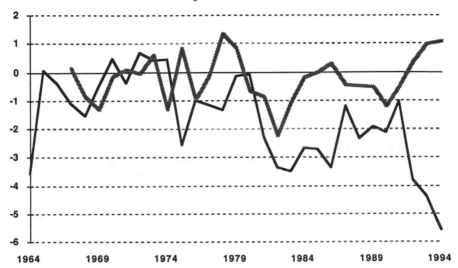

Sources: International Monetary Fund; *Europa World Yearbook*; French government;
European Monetary Institute.

Figure 23.2   French Currency
Francs per U.S. dollar (inverted scale).

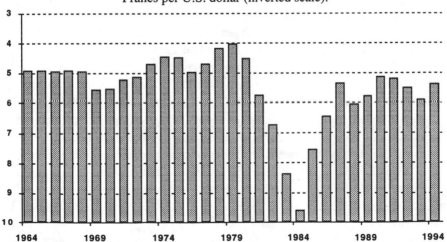

Source: International Monetary Fund, *International Financial Statistics Yearbook.*

Figure 23.3. French Economy

Annual percentage change in French real GDP (bar graph, left scale). Growth in French real GDP relative to U.S. real GDP, 1963 = 100 (line graph, right scale).

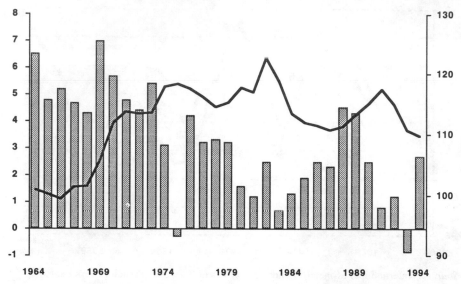

Sources: International Monetary Fund; French Government.

Economic Summary

With a gross domestic product (GDP) of $1.37 trillion, France has Europe's second-largest economy and the sixth-largest in the world. Since the mid-1960s, real growth has averaged 3.18 percent per year, slightly above the U.S. rate. After several years of above-trend growth in the late 1980s, however, France joined much of Europe in experiencing a lingering recession in the early 1990s, with virtually no increase in output between 1991 and 1993. An economic recovery finally took hold in 1994, with French GDP growing by 2.7 percent.

Since 1983, a series of French governments have remained committed to the so-called "franc fort" policy, that is, maintaining rough equilibrium between the franc and deutsche mark under the exchange-rate mechanism of the European Monetary System. This results in a strong currency but occasionally sedates the economy due to the artificially high interest rates required to maintain parity. Even as the French economy recovered, unemployment grew to more than 12 percent in 1995.

Major elements of the French economy were nationalized beginning in the late 1930s, and the country controls its business sector to a degree that is virtually unmatched in Europe. Despite an increasing momentum to its privatization efforts, the French government remains the major shareholder in nearly 2,000 companies, including some of the more spectacularly unprofitable enterprises in Europe, most notably banking giant Credit Lyonnais and Air France, the national air carrier. Over the past year, the government has sold more than $17 billion of state-run businesses, including oil behemoth Société Nationale Elf Aquitaine;but the process is complicated by a lack of large pools of private capital capable of soaking up the new shares and imposing free-market managerial discipline. The process of privatization is being pushed along by the European Union, which is pressuring France to open its markets and divest state-run operations.

The French economy is well diversified, with a growing and profitable service sector now representing an important source of foreign exchange while contributing 43 percent of GDP. Over the past three decades, services trade has averaged a surplus of more than 1 percent of GDP, offsetting modest annual shortfalls in merchandise trade. Industry, primarily machinery and transportation equipment, provides about one-third of French GDP and employs about one-quarter of the workforce. France is self-sufficient in agricultural products and is a net exporter of such items as wheat, dairy products, and wine. Its largest trading markets include Germany, Italy, Belgium, Luxembourg, and the United Kingdom, which together account for almost half of all French exports. Less than 7 percent of French exports are to the United States.

In addition to dealing with the issues of privatization, relaxation of tariffs, and eventual incorporation into a unified European market, the new French government of President Jacques Chirac will have to contend with a budget deficit that had reached more than 5 percent of GDP by 1994. Historically, budget deficits in France have been of modest though significant proportions, averaging 1.68 percent of GDP since 1964. Recently, however, fiscal red ink has increased dramatically, averaging 2.88 percent of GDP since 1981. The French current account is in far better shape, aided by a dramatic improvement in merchandise trade since 1992. Over the past three decades, the deficit on the current account of the balance of payments has averaged a manageable 0.23 percent.

French Stock Market

Exchange

Classification: Developed
Capitalization: $452 billion
Capitalization relative to U.S. stock market: 7.26%

Number of issues: 922
Primary index: CAC-40
Total return in local currency, 1988–1994: +63%
Total return in U.S. dollars, 1988–1994: +63%
Total return in U.S. dollars relative to U.S. stocks, 1988–1994: –71%

Volatility
(Historical)

Standard deviation: 5.37
Total monthly losses: 136%
Average monthly loss: 3.51%
Number of monthly losses: 39
Number of monthly losses greater than 5 percent: 8
Number of monthly losses greater than 10 percent: 3
Number of monthly losses greater than 15 percent: 1
Maximum monthly loss: 15.29%
Relative volatility ratio: 1.80

Figure 23.4.   French Stocks
Return of French stocks in local currency (black), U.S. dollars (gray),
and S&P 500 (dotted); Dec. 1987 = 100.

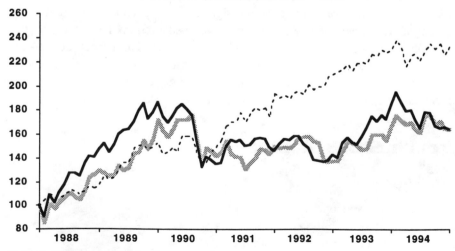

Source: Wilshire Associates Incorporated.

Price Cycles

Phase	From	To	Total return
Bear	January 1988	January 1988	−15%
Bull	February 1988	July 1990	+107%
Bear	August 1990	June 1991	−26%
Bull	July 1991	July 1992	+22%
Bear	August 1992	November 1992	−15%
Bull	December 1992	December 1994	+19%

Correlations

Germany 0.80
United Kingdom 0.54
United States 0.45
Japan 0.41
Sweden 0.41
Switzerland 0.37
Singapore 0.36
Australia 0.33
Hong Kong 0.31
Canada 0.29
Malaysia 0.22

Taiwan 0.21
New Zealand 0.17
Thailand 0.17
Philippines 0.15
Indonesia 0.10
Mexico 0.07
Brazil 0.05
Korea 0.04
Argentina −0.02
Chile −0.02

Country Funds

Name	Originated	Hedging	Structure	Discount/ Premium	Phones
France Growth	May 1990	Possible	Closed end	−27 / +14	(212) 713-2421 (212) 713-2848

Source: Morningstar, Inc.

American Depositary Receipts

Name	Exchange	Symbol	Industry
Alcatel Alsthom	NYSE	ALA	Telecommunication equipment
Business Objects	NASDAQ	BOBJY	Computer software
LVMH Moet Hennessy Louis Vuitton	NASDAQ	LVMHY	Consumer products
Rhone-Poulenc	NYSE	RPU	Diversified chemicals
Societe Nationale Elf Aquitaine	NYSE	ELF	Petroleum
Thomson-CSF	NASDAQ	TCSFY	Electronic equipment
Total	NYSE	TOT	Petroleum

Direct Listings

Name	Exchange	Symbol	Industry
SGS-Thomson Microelectronics	NYSE	STM	Semiconductors

Stock Summary

Given the underperformance of the French economy over the past decade, it should come as no surprise that French equities have produced miserly returns as well. Over the 1988 to 1994 period, the Wilshire Index: France earned just 63 percent in franc and dollar terms, for a net underperformance of the U.S. market of 71 percent. As of mid-1995, the Paris bourse was trading at roughly the same level as July 1990. French equities have a downside volatility ratio of 1.80, about equal to the United Kingdom and slightly less than Germany. Paris stocks carry an extremely high correlation with German stocks (0.80) and an above-average correlation with U.S. stocks, suggesting that the French market offers only modest portfolio diversification for American investors. The onset of the 1990 bear market in France, for example, exactly coincided with a similar decline in the United States.

Eight French stocks and one closed-end country fund are traded as American depositary receipts (ADRs) or are directly listed on the New York and NASDAQ exchanges. The ADR menu includes several of France's largest corporations, including Société Nationale Elf Aquitaine, the newly privatized oil giant, and chemical-producer Rhone-Poulenc. ADR shares of Alcatel Alsthom, a multinational producer of telecommunications equipment and France's second-largest company by market capitalization, lost almost 40 percent of its value in 1994 amid falling earnings. Several other French companies—most notably L'Oreal—trade over the counter. The single closed-end fund available, France Growth, produced a hard-earned 21.5 percent return over the first four full years of its existence, for a slight outperformance of the Wilshire Index: France. France Growth tends to trade at substantial discounts to its net asset value (NAV) and, as of October 1995, still sold 19 percent below its NAV as French stocks treaded water over the first nine months of 1995. The government's deregulation of the telecommunications industry—a step mandated by the European Union—will result in the privatization of France Telecom.

CHAPTER 24

Federal Republic of Germany

Overview

Germany is a textbook example of the fact that a strong currency does not a stock market make. Despite the repatriation advantages to foreign investors of an appreciating mark, the unfortunate economic side effects of a strong currency—loss of market share at home and loss of competitiveness abroad resulting in tepid profits growth—have weighed down heavily on the Frankfurt bourse since the U.S. dollar peaked against the mark in the mid-1980s. Even as its equity market founders and its economy grows only slowly, the German central bank, or Bundesbank—arguably the most powerful single economic institution in Europe and perhaps in the world—has held ever tighter to the monetary purse strings, keeping interest rates relatively high and money growth low, all in the name of fighting an inflation that remains mild by most standards.

Fundamental to understanding the unshakable German commitment to its currency is its painful history of hyperinflation in the Weimar Republic of the 1920s, a condition that sowed the seeds for the emergence of Hitler's Nazi Party. Several other factors, however, have also contributed to the relative under-performance of the German economy and equity market over the past decade. While German engineering excellence is virtually unmatched and the quality of its export manufactures unquestioned, the country has a generally unproductive service sector, with high wages and poor customer service impairing profitability and leading to chronic deficits in its services-trade account. The costs of financing the reunification with former East Germany have also been higher than expected, dampening growth and forcing the Bundesbank to keep rates artificially high to soak up inflationary pressures. On balance, however, a strong currency is a pleasant problem to have, and recent efforts to change the German corporate culture by heightening sensitivity to shareholder interests are showing encouraging results.

Geography

Area: 137,838
Size relative to United States: 3.64%
Capital: Bonn (until the year 2000, when most administrative functions will move to Berlin)
Population density per square mile: 589
Population density relative to United States: 7.99x

Demographics

Population: 81 million
Population relative to United States USA: 31%
Average annual rate of natural increase: –0.1%
Projected population by 2025: 79 million
Population increase by 2025: –2%

Government

Type: Federal Republic
Head of State: Helmut Kohl, Chancellor (1982)
Political System: Germany operates under a constitution promulgated in 1949 that established a parliamentary democracy form of government. Following the collapse of the Communist government in the former German Democratic Republic in 1990, East Germans voted to rejoin the Federal Republic after having been divided since 1945. Legislative power is vested in a bicameral parliament (there is no official name for the body as a whole) consisting of the Federal Council (Bundesrat), whose members are appointed by the German states, and the Federal Diet (Bundestag), whose 662 members are elected to four-year terms by universal adult suffrage. The country's executive leader is the chancellor (equiva-

lent to the post of prime minister), who is elected to a four-year term by Federal Diet members. The office of president is a largely ceremonial position.

Germany has several political parties, but power has been concentrated in the Christian Democrats, led by Chancellor Helmut Kohl, and the Social Democrats, who have been out of power since 1982 when the Free Democratic Party bolted their ruling coalition, forcing the ouster of Chancellor Helmut Schmidt. The former Communist party in Germany is represented by the Party of Democratic Socialism.

In the most recent elections, held in October 1994, Chancellor Kohl was returned to office as his conservative coalition won a narrow 10-seat majority in the Federal Diet. The razor-slim margin of victory created concerns among investors about the ability of Chancellor Kohl's government to deal effectively with the country's mounting budget deficit.

Economy

Financial Strength
(Historical data, relative to GDP)

Merchandise trade: +3.54
Services: −1.01%
Income: +0.23%
Current account: +1.18%
Portfolio investment: +0.54%
Direct investment: −0.30%
Overall balance of payments: +0.38%
Budget: −1.18%
External debt: N/A
Investment/consumption ratio: 0.31

Currency
(Historical data)

Money supply growth: 8.45%
Consumer price index: 3.55%
Monetary unit: Deutsche mark
Monetary unit against U.S. dollar: +130%

Figure 24.1.   German Balance of Payments
Surplus/deficit of German budget (black) and current account (gray),
as percent of GDP.

Source: International Monetary Fund, *International Financial Statistics Yearbook.*

Figure 24.2.   German Currency
Marks per U.S. dollar (inverted scale).

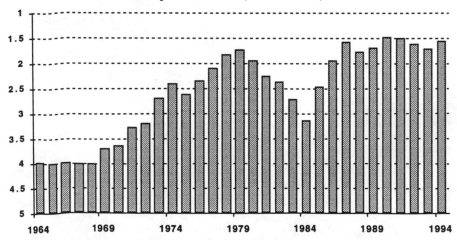

Source: International Monetary Fund, *International Financial Statistics Yearbook.*

Economic Output

(Historical data)

GDP: $1.64 trillion
GDP relative to U.S. GDP: 28%
GDP growth rate: 2.82%
GDP growth rate relative to U.S. GDP growth rate: 0.99x
Per capita GDP: $20,379
Per capita GDP relative to U.S. per capita GDP: 90%

Economic Summary

Germany has an export-based economy, centered primarily around big-ticket industrial manufactures and finished goods. Over the past three decades, the German merchandise trade account has averaged a 3.65 percent surplus, more than enough to offset a chronically weak position in services trade. The size and consistency of the merchandise surpluses are especially impressive in the context of the strong German currency, which has appreciated by 130 percent against

Figure 24.3.   German Economy

Annual percentage change in German real GDP (bar graph, left scale). Growth in German real GDP relative to U.S. real GDP, 1963 = 100 (line graph, right scale).

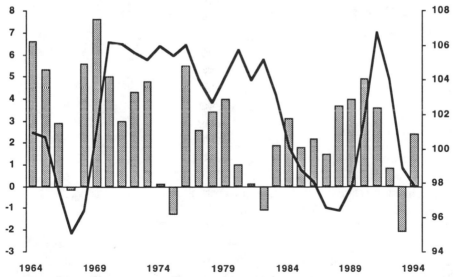

Source: International Monetary Fund, *International Financial Statistics Yearbook.*

the U.S. dollar since 1964 and was still climbing to new all-time highs, despite central bank interventions, as of May 1995. The economic strains caused by the strong mark are beginning to show, however; the German current account has slipped into deficit for each of the past four fiscal years, even as the size of its budget shortfall has ballooned to almost 3 percent of GDP. Taken together, the current-account and budget problems raise the specter of the evil "twin deficits" that so haunts the U.S. economy.

Real German economic growth since the mid-1960s has averaged 2.82 percent annually, almost exactly matching the U.S. pace. The mild but prolonged recession that first hit the American economy in 1990 finally reached Europe two years later, with Germany showing negative growth over 1992 and 1993 before finally emerging from recession in 1994. Despite its relatively slow growth in recent years, the German economy remains the engine that pulls Europe, both because of its large export market and because a number of European countries— notably France, Austria, Switzerland, Belgium, and the Netherlands—tie their currencies to the mark. (The United Kingdom withdrew from the European Monetary Union's exchange-rate mechanism in 1992.) As the German recovery gained steam in early 1995, there was evidence of growing price pressures at the wholesale level, placing Bundesbank President Hans Tietmeyer in the unenviable position of choosing between damaging the economy through higher inflation or damaging the economy through a higher mark. Fortunately for the German economy, Japanese investors looking for safe havens for their ever-growing stack of yen have recently taken a liking to German bonds, or Bunds, pushing down on the long end of the German yield curve and helping to reliquify the German economy.

German Stock Market

Exchange

Classification: Developed
Capitalization: $499 billion
Capitalization relative to U.S. stock market: 8.01%
Number of issues: 1,467
Primary index: DAX
Total return in local currency, 1988–1994: +93%
Total return in U.S. dollars, 1988–1994: +95%
Total return in U.S. dollars relative to U.S. stocks, 1988–1994: −39%

Figure 24.4. German Stocks
Return of German stocks in local currency (black), U.S. dollars (gray),
and S&P 500 (dotted); Dec. 1987 = 100.

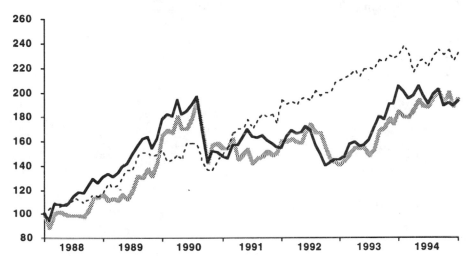

Source: Wilshire Associates Incorporated.

Volatility
(Historical)

Standard deviation: 5.45
Total monthly losses: 134%
Average monthly loss: 3.73%
Number of monthly losses: 36
Number of monthly losses greater than 5 percent: 10
Number of monthly losses greater than 10 percent: 4
Number of monthly losses greater than 15 percent: 1
Maximum monthly loss: 15.44%
Relative volatility ratio: 1.96

Price Cycles

Phase	From	To	Total return
Bull	January 1988	June 1990	+78%
Bear	July 1990	August 1990	−20%
Bull	September 1990	June 1992	+22%
Bear	July 1992	December 1992	−16%
Bull	January 1993	December 1994	+39%

Correlations

France 0.80	Switzerland 0.24
United Kingdom 0.56	Taiwan 0.22
Singapore 0.46	New Zealand 0.18
Sweden 0.42	Thailand 0.14
Japan 0.37	Philippines 0.09
United States 0.33	Korea 0.04
Indonesia 0.31	Brazil 0.03
Hong Kong 0.29	Mexico −0.03
Malaysia 0.29	Argentina −0.04
Australia 0.26	Chile −0.06
Canada 0.25	

Country Funds

Name	Originated	Hedging	Structure	Discount/ Premium	Phones
Emerging Germany	April 1990	No	Closed end	−23 / -4	(800) 356-6122 (212) 363-5100
Central European Equity Fund	March 1990	Possible	Closed end	−25 / +15	(800) 437-6269 (212) 474-7000
Germany Fund	July 1986	Possible	Closed end	−18 / +58	(800) 437-6269 (212) 474-7000
New Germany	January 1990	Possible	Closed end	−23 / +64	(800) 437-6269 (212) 437-6269

Sources: Morningstar, Inc.; Barron's.

American Depositary Receipts

Name	Exchange	Symbol	Industry
Daimler-Benz Corporation	NYSE	DAI	Holding company

Direct Listings

None

Stock Summary

The equity market in Germany is notable for its lack of size, especially relative to its economy. With German gross domestic product (GDP) pushing $2 trillion and the market's capitalization a mere $500 million, German stocks represent just one-quarter of the value of the underlying economy, among the lowest share of the economic pie for any nation. In an attempt to attract more institutional and global investors, the German stock exchange—now concentrated in Frankfurt but divided among several regional bourses—will be unified under a central electronic-trading system over the next few years. In theory, the plan should create greater liquidity and better trade executions, thus encouraging midsized German firms to go public and institutional investors to take larger positions. In early 1995, a miniboom in the initial public offering (IPO) market helped expand the breadth of the German exchange, albeit modestly; and the largest IPO yet, newly privatized Deutsche Telekom, will come public in 1995 with an expected value of $40 billion. (Despite its presence in an economy noted for manufacturing excellence, customers of Deutsche Telekom relate horror stories about service gaffes usually associated with Third World phone companies.) German initial and secondary public offerings raised just $18.5 billion in 1994, less than 6 percent of the global total, despite having the world's third-largest economy. Other factors contributing to the unpopularity of the German equity market are the country's underdeveloped service sector, an unreliable accounting system, lack of transparency (Wall Street jargon for the ability to hide investor identities), and a cultural ethos that abhors the kinds of risks usually associated with stock ownership.

Over the 1988 to 1994 period, the average German share price roughly doubled in both local currency and dollar terms, representing a 39 percent underperformance of the American stock market. Frankfurt equities had a relative downside volatility ratio of about twice that of U.S. equities, but bull/bear cycles were considerably more extended than those often found on Asian and Latin American bourses and, thus, more closely resembled the American market. The overriding economic reasons behind the German market's relatively pedestrian long-term performance are the low productivity of the country's service industry, high wages in some manufacturing sectors, and the fierce determination of the Bundesbank to defend the mark, even at the price of corporate earnings. The monetary remedy used to accomplish that end—high interest rates—has the effect of slowing the economy, increasing unemployment, making imports more competitive, and crunching the profit margins of Germany's large manufacturing exporters.

A shortage of exchange-listed American depositary receipts (ADRs) makes the four closed-end country funds the best way for most American investors to play Germany. Three of the entries came onto the scene amid the euphoria of the end to Communist rule in East Germany in 1990. Of the new funds, Central European Equity Fund (formerly Future Germany) has performed best, roughly matching the Morgan Stanley Capital International (MSCI) Index: Germany and outperforming Wilshire Index: Germany by a small annual margin. The old-timer of the group, Germany Fund, has also nearly equaled the return of MSCI Germany since 1987. Historical data on the premium side of the discount/premium cycle is misleading because global investors briefly clamored for a way to get in on the promise of a newly united Germany after the Berlin Wall came down in late 1989, pushing premiums to 50 percent or more. After sentiment fell back, all four funds have mostly traded at significant discounts to net asset value, with the magnitude of the discounts reaching nearly 20 percent for all four funds as of October 1995. Investors looking to buy individual German stocks could be disappointed by the lack of exchange-traded ADRs. There are no NASDAQ listings; and only Daimler-Benz, the giant auto maker, trades on the NYSE, although several other German large multinationals, including BASF (chemicals), Bayer (pharmaceuticals), Deutsche Bank (banking), Siemens (electronics), and Volkswagen (autos) trade over the counter. Daimler is in the process of slashing worker payrolls and nonperforming businesses in an effort to regain competitiveness in the cutthroat global car market made still more difficult by the strong mark. After reporting a loss for the first time in its postwar history in 1993, Daimler returned to the black in 1994 with net income of $766 million.

CHAPTER 25

Kingdom of Sweden

Overview

After suffering through the deepest recession of all the recession-ridden European economies, Sweden changed political leadership in late 1994—the new Socialist Government vowed to cut the country's 14 percent unemployment rate and reduce taxes, while still moving toward the lower budget deficits mandated as part of the country's recent commitment to the European Union. Given the magnitude of Sweden's budgetary red ink—estimates put the fiscal 1995 shortfall at about 11 percent of gross domestic product (GDP)—that task will not be an easy one.

Sweden has one of the developed world's slowest-growing economies over the past 30 years, with real GDP increasing at barely 2 percent per year. Total output relative to the United States since 1964 has fallen by 20 percent. The country has a large social-welfare system, however, that has provided for both rich and poor; and the country's standard of living remains high, with per capita GDP of nearly 90 percent of the U.S. rate. The Swedish stock market has fairly reflected the country's economic woes, but the American depositary receipts (ADRs) available on U.S. exchanges tend to be cyclical multinational plays that minimize exposure to the Swedish economy and benefit from the country's weak currency. The biggest challenge for the new Socialist Government will be to foster policies that lower the federal deficit and promote faster economic growth, while maintaining most of the social-support programs still favored by the electorate.

Geography

Area: 173,800 square miles
Size relative to United States: 4.59%

251

Capital: Stockholm
Population density per square mile: 51
Population density relative to United States: 0.69x

Demographics

Population: 8.7 million
Population relative to United States: 3%
Average annual rate of natural increase: 0.3%
Projected population by 2025: 9.3 million
Population change by 2025: +6.90%

Government

Type: Constitutional Monarchy
Sovereign: King Carl XVI Gustaf (1973)
Head of State: Ingvar Carlsson, Prime Minister (1994)
Political System: Under a 1975 constitution, Sweden is governed by a unicameral parliament (Riksdag) composed of 349 members elected by universal adult suffrage to three-year terms according to proportional representation. Executive power is vested in the prime minister, who is nominated by the speaker of the parliament and confirmed by a vote of the entire legislative body. A hereditary monarch is the symbolic head of the country but has little practical power. The major political organizations in Sweden are the Social Democratic Party (Socialists), which has held power for all but six years since 1932, and the Moderate Party, formerly known as the Conservative Party. The Social Democrats have a large union and public-sector constituency and are pledged to the goal of maintaining full employment. The Moderate Party supports somewhat more free-market economic policies.

Between 1991 and 1994, Sweden was ruled by a center-right coalition led by Moderate Party leader Carl Bildt. National elections in September 1994 returned the Social Democrats to power, although the party won just 45 percent of the vote, requiring the formation of a coalition government. Social Democratic Party leader Ingvar Carlsson was installed as prime minister. Swedish voters approved a referendum in November 1994 allowing the country to join the European Union (EU), effective January 1, 1995. The move has significant implications for economic policy in Sweden because of the EU's insistence on budget austerity.

Economy

Financial Strength

(Historical data, relative to GDP)

Merchandise trade: +1.74%
Services: −0.65%
Income: −1.08%
Current account: −0.63%
Portfolio investment: +0.25%
Direct investment: −0.95%
Overall balance of payments: −0.85%
Budget: −1.95%
External debt: 19%
Investment/consumption ratio: 0.27

Figure 25.1.   Swedish Balance of Payments
Surplus/deficit of Swedish budget (black) and current account (gray),
as percent of GDP.

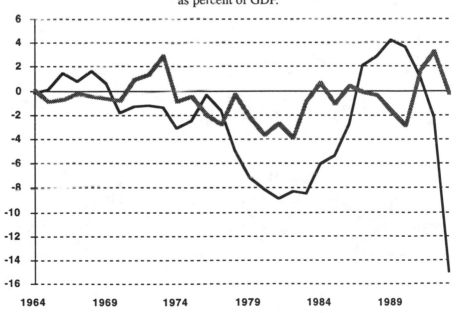

Sources: International Monetary Fund; Europa World Yearbook.

Currency
(Historical data)

Money supply growth: 8.71%
Consumer price index: 7.03%
Monetary unit: Krona
Monetary unit against U.S. dollar: −38%

Economic Output
(Historical data)

GDP: $175 billion
GDP relative to U.S. GDP: 2.75%
GDP growth rate: 2.06%
GDP growth rate relative to U.S. GDP growth rate: 0.72x
Per capita GDP: $20,058
Per capita GDP relative to U.S. per capita GDP: 88%

Figure 25.2. Swedish Currency
Krona per U.S. dollar (inverted scale).

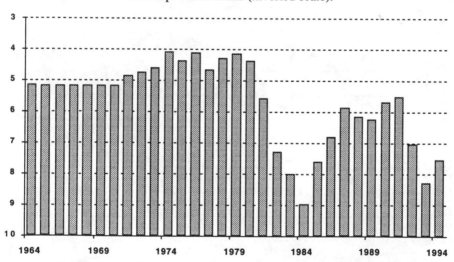

Source: International Monetary Fund, *International Financial Statistics Yearbook.*

Figure 25.3.   Swedish Economy

Annual percentage change in Swedish real GDP (bar graph, left scale). Growth in Swedish real GDP relative to U.S. real GDP, 1963 = 100 (line graph, right scale).

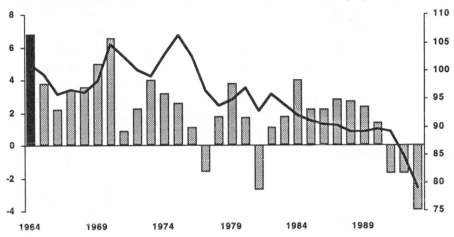

Source: International Monetary Fund, *International Financial Statistics Yearbook.*

Economic Summary

After showing dramatic improvement in the late 1980s, Sweden is again experiencing a hemorrhaging of its federal budget, with the size of the annual deficits reaching more than 10 percent of GDP by the mid-1990s, the highest for any developed nation. The fiscal red ink has also led to a sharp rise in external debt, which now stands at $34 billion, or roughly 19 percent of GDP. Sweden is noted for its heavy government spending on social-welfare programs, which presently account for about one-quarter of the entire federal budget. Sweden's vote to join the European Union will require that the country drastically reduce the size of its deficits in coming years. If the political leadership resorts to tax hikes, however, it could have the effect of slowing the already somnolent Swedish economy, which finally emerged from a three-year recession in 1994. The sharp slowdown, in which GDP declined by an average of 2.5 percent between 1991 and 1993, forced the cancellation of the Bildt government's plan to privatize a number of state-run industries. Over the past 30 years, Swedish real GDP has grown by an average of just 2.06 percent annually, for a net underperformance of the U.S. economy of 20 percent since 1964.

Sweden is rich in iron ore and forest resources and has an export-driven economy, with automobiles, machinery, steel, and paper products contributing to a consistently positive merchandise-trade account. Over the past three decades, Sweden has averaged a 1.74 percent surplus in merchandise trade, offsetting weakness in service trade and investment income. About two-thirds of Swedish exports are to Europe, with the largest shares going to Germany, Norway, Denmark, and the United Kingdom. The United States accounts for less than 10 percent of Swedish exports. The country's current account has averaged a tolerable 0.63 percent deficit since 1964 and even showed large surpluses in 1992 and 1993 as a weak krona led to an export boom. Exports are helped by a generally weak currency, with the Swedish krona losing about one-third of its value against the U.S. dollar since 1964.

Swedish Stock Market

Exchange

Classification: Developed
Capitalization: $131 billion
Capitalization relative to U.S. stock market: 2.10%
Number of issues: 229
Primary index: Affarsvarlden General
Total return in local currency, 1988–1994: +36%
Total return in U.S. dollars, 1988–1994: +5%
Total return in US dollars relative to U.S. stocks, 1988–1994: –129%

Volatility
(Historical)

Standard deviation: 6.57
Total monthly losses: 197%
Average monthly loss: 4.69%
Number of monthly losses: 42
Number of monthly losses greater than 5 percent: 14
Number of monthly losses greater than 10 percent: 6
Number of monthly losses greater than 15 percent: 1
Maximum monthly loss: 19.38%
Relative volatility ratio: 2.61

Figure 25.4.   Swedish Stocks

Return of Swedish stocks in local currency (black), U.S. dollars (gray),
and S&P 500 (dotted); Dec. 1987 = 100.

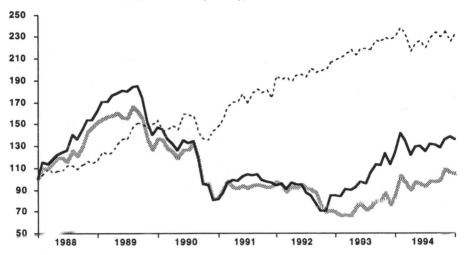

Source: Wilshire Associates Incorporated.

Price Cycles

Phase	From	To	Total return
Bull	January 1988	June 1989	+66%
Bear	July 1989	November 1990	−50%
Bull	December 1990	December 1991	+18%
Bear	January 1992	March 1993	−32%
Bull	April 1993	December 1994	+58%

Correlations

Singapore 0.62

United Kingdom 0.56

Japan 0.53

Australia 0.49

New Zealand 0.46

Germany 0.42

France 0.41

Hong Kong 0.39

United States 0.38

Canada 0.34

Indonesia 0.30

Korea 0.25

Malaysia 0.24

Brazil 0.23

Philippines 0.19

Switzerland 0.16

Taiwan 0.16

Thailand 0.16

Mexico 0.09

Chile 0.05

Argentina −0.02

Country Funds

None

American Depositary Receipts

Name	Exchange	Symbol	Industry
Asea	NASDAQ	ASEAY	Holding company
Electrolux	NASDAQ	ELUXY	Household appliances
Ericsson Telephone	NASDAQ	ERICY	Telecommunications
Gambro	NASDAQ	GAMBY	Medical technology
Pharmacia	NASDAQ	PHARY	Pharmaceuticals
SKF	NASDAQ	SKFRY	Ball bearings manufacturer
Volvo	NASDAQ	VOLVY	Automobiles

Direct Listings

None

Stock Summary

Swedish stocks barely broke even in dollar terms between 1988 and 1994, underperforming the U.S. market by 129 percent over the period. The Stockholm market, capitalized at $131 billion, has the highest downside risk of any European bourse and suffered through two bear markets averaging 41 percent. Swedish stocks have been trending higher over the past two years, however, amid signs of a domestic recovery and growing strength in Sweden's primary export markets in Europe. From April 1993 through year-end 1994, Swedish equities advanced nearly 60 percent in dollar terms. Through May 1995, the Stockholm market's Affarsvarlden General index had tacked on another 10 percent. Swedish stocks carry a moderate correlation (0.38) to the U.S. equity market.

While American investors might not want to own a broad share of the Stockholm market, the Swedish ADRs available on U.S. exchanges tend to be mid- to large-cap multinationals that benefit from a weak krona and have only limited exposure to the chronically sluggish Swedish economy. In fact, from 1988 through February 1995, *Morningstar American Depositary Receipts* index of Swedish ADRs returned 124 percent, putting it close to the American market's total return. Among the notable Swedish offerings are Volvo, which does virtually all its auto and truck business outside the country, Pharmacia, a pharmaceutical and biotechnology firm, and SKF, a leading manufacturer of ball bearings. There are no country funds currently available on the Swedish market.

CHAPTER 26

Swiss Confederation

Overview

Switzerland is the world's richest nation, with per capita gross domestic product (GDP) of $34,000, almost one-third more than the United States. The country's economic success is based on political stability, a strong and reliable currency, a credible banking system, and unsurpassed excellence in precision engineering. Given its wealth, Switzerland need not concern itself with trying to achieve Asia-like growth rates. In fact, over the past three decades, Swiss real GDP has increased at the relatively pedestrian pace of just 2.3 percent annually, below the rate of the United States and many other large, industrialized democracies. Despite the consistently modest growth, the rate of unemployment remains the lowest of any European nation, and almost one-quarter of Swiss workers are foreigners. Even during the recession year of 1993, Swiss unemployment was just 5 percent.

As the country tries to shake off the effects of the recession, however, Swiss officials find themselves hemmed in by the strong-mark policy of the German Bundesbank, which forces the Swiss central bank to keep interest rates high in order to defend its currency, an absolute prerequisite to the country's long-term economic health. Swiss stocks have nearly doubled in price over the 1988 to 1994 period, with only one bear cycle and less downside volatility than any other European market. In coming years, Switzerland will need to address its position within the European community in an era of increasing free trade.

Geography

Area: 15,941 square miles
Size relative to United States: 0.42%
Capital: Bern

Population density per square mile: 439
Population density relative to United States: 5.96x

Demographics

Population: 6.88 million
Population relative to United States: 3.0%
Average annual rate of natural increase: 3.7%
Projected population by 2025: 7.15 million
Population increase by 2025: +3.9%

Government

Type: Federal Republic
Head of State: Adolf Ogi, President (1993)
Political System: The Swiss Confederation is composed of 23 states, or cantons. The country's constitution, passed in 1848 and extensively amended in 1874, is modeled after that of the United States and vests legislative power in a bicameral Federal Assembly composed of the Council of States and the National Council. The Council of States is made up of 46 members (two from each of the cantons) who are elected to four-year terms by the people through procedures specified in each of the cantonal constitutions. The National Council has 200 members who are directly elected by the voters for a term of four years according to proportional representation.

Executive authority is held by the Federal Council, or Bundesrat, whose seven members are elected to four-year terms by the Federal Assembly. Each year the Federal Assembly elects a president and a vice president of the Confederation from among the seven members of the Federal Council. Both the president and vice president serve one-year terms. Whereas national policy is set by the Federal Assembly and Federal Council, considerable political power in Switzerland remains in the cantons, which hold all power not specifically assigned to the federal government by the constitution. The dominant political organizations in Switzerland are the Free Democratic Party, the Christian Democratic People's Party, and the Social Democratic Party.

Switzerland has a long tradition of armed neutrality, a position consistently supported by the electorate. High on the list of issues currently confronting the political leadership is the degree of Swiss integration into the world and European economic communities. In 1992, Swiss voters approved a referendum allowing the country to join the World Bank and International Monetary Fund.

Economy

Financial Strength
(Historical data, relative to GDP)

Merchandise trade: −3.77%
Services: +2.93%
Income: +4.02%
Current account: +1.90%
Portfolio investment: −4.25%
Direct investment: −1.33%
Overall balance of payments: +1.64%
Budget: −0.38%
External debt: N/A
Investment/consumption ratio: 0.37

Figure 26.1.   Swiss Balance of Payments
Surplus/deficit of Swiss budget (black) and current account (gray),
as percent of GDP.

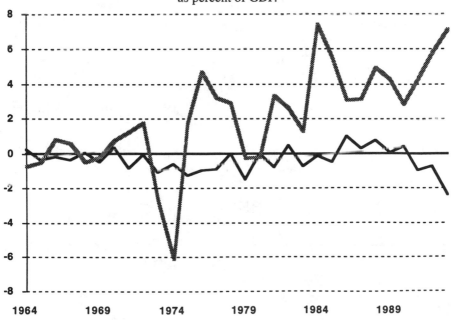

Source: International Monetary Fund, *International Financial Statistics Yearbook.*

Currency
(Historical data)

Money supply growth: 7.14%
Consumer price index: 3.95%
Monetary unit: Franc
Monetary unit against U.S. dollar: +191%

Economic Output
(Historical data)

GDP: $234 billion
GDP relative to U.S. GDP: 3.47%
GDP growth rate: 2.13%
GDP growth rate relative to U.S. GDP growth rate: 0.75x
Per capita GDP: $34,012
Per capita GDP relative to U.S. per capita GDP: 1.31x

Figure 26.2.   Swiss Currency
Francs per U.S. dollar (inverted scale).

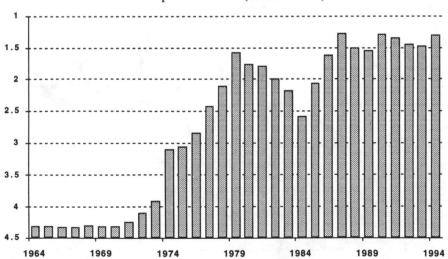

Source: International Monetary Fund, *International Financial Statistics Yearbook.*

Figure 26.3.   Swiss Economy

Annual percentage change in Swiss real GDP (bar graph, left scale). Growth in
Swiss real GDP relative to U.S. real GDP, 1963 = 100 (line graph, right scale).

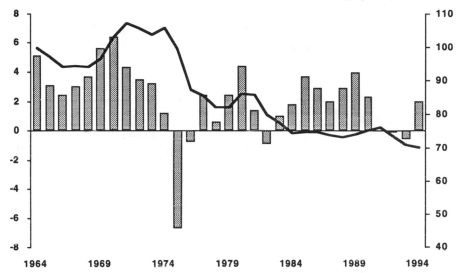

Source: International Monetary Fund, *International Financial Statistics Yearbook.*

Economic Summary

Despite limited natural resources, Switzerland has averaged a 1.9 percent annual
surplus in its current account since 1964, including more than 6 percent average
surpluses in 1992 and 1993. The lack of natural resources contributes to chronic
deficits in the Swiss merchandise-trade account, but these deficits are more than
offset by positive flows in services and income. The service sector is dominated
by the country's large Zurich-based financial services industry, primarily insurance and banking.

Funds are drawn into the Swiss banking system from all regions of the globe
because of the country's commitment to secrecy, high capital standards, and the
safety of the franc, which reassures depositors of maintaining or even gaining
value upon repatriation. Swiss banks manage more than one-third of the world's
$4.75 trillion pot of private offshore money management. Earnings from those
portfolios—which are frequently invested outside of Switzerland—flow back into
the country, producing consistent surpluses in investment income.

The bulk of Swiss exports are to neighboring European countries, with Germany, France, Belgium, Italy, and the United Kingdom accounting for almost half of foreign sales. Exports to the United States amount to less than 10 percent of the Swiss total.

Switzerland's positive balance on its current account feeds and reinforces the Swiss franc, which is regarded as one of the world's most stable currencies. Since 1964, the franc has nearly doubled its value against the U.S. dollar, despite a mild downturn between 1990 and 1994. Swiss budgets have generally been austere, although the country did run a deficit in 1993 of nearly 2 percent of GDP as a recession cut tax revenue and social-services spending increased amid the downturn. Fiscal red ink has historically not been a problem in Switzerland, however, with budget deficits averaging a relatively tiny 0.38 percent of GDP since 1964.

Swiss Stock Market

Exchange
Classification: Developed
Capitalization: $284 billion
Capitalization relative to U.S. stock market: 4.56%
Number of issues: 458
Primary index: Swiss Performance Index (SPI)
Total return in local currency, 1988–1994: +118%
Total return in U.S. dollars, 1988–1994: +87%
Total return in US dollars relative to U.S. stocks, 1988–1994: –47%

Volatility
(Historical)

Standard deviation: 5.17
Total monthly losses: 99.04%
Average monthly loss: 3.10%
Number of monthly losses: 32
Number of monthly losses greater than 5 percent: 3
Number of monthly losses greater than 10 percent: 1
Number of monthly losses greater than 15 percent: 1
Maximum monthly loss: 18.38%
Relative volatility ratio: 1.40

Figure 26.4. Swiss Stocks
Return of Swiss stocks in local currency (black), U.S. dollars (gray),
and S&P 500 (dotted); Dec. 1987 = 100.

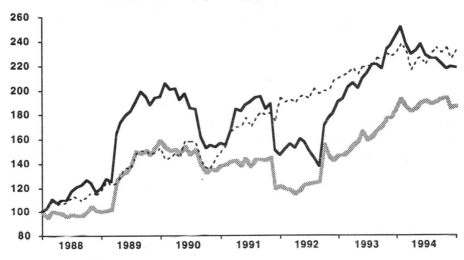

Source: Wilshire Associates Incorporated.

Price Cycles

Phase	From	To	Total return
Bull	January 1988	October 1991	+45%
Bear	November 1991	March 1992	−21%
Bull	April 1992	December 1994	+64%

Correlations

United States 0.41   Sweden 0.16
UK 0.34   Hong Kong 0.15
France 0.37   New Zealand 0.15
Singapore 0.29   Indonesia 0.12
Japan 0.26   Philippines 0.06
Malaysia 0.26   Taiwan 0.05
Germany 0.24   Korea 0.04
Thailand 0.24   Mexico 0.02
Canada 0.19   Chile 0.00
Brazil 0.18   Argentina −0.04
Australia 0.16

Country Funds

Name	Originated	Hedging	Structure	Discount/ Premium	Phone
Swiss Helvetia	August 1987	No	Closed end	−23 / +16	(212) 332-7930

Source: Morningstar, Inc.

American Depositary Receipts

Name	Exchange	Symbol	Industry
Adia	NASDAQ	ADIAJ	Temporary personnel

Direct Listings

None

Stock Summary

Investors may not have gotten rich in Swiss stocks over the past decade, but neither have they needed to tranquilize themselves to tolerate the ride. Swiss equities have the lowest downside risk relative to American stocks of any European market and are second only to Canada in that category among global bourses. The Wilshire Index: Switzerland returned 87 percent in U.S. dollars from 1988 to 1994, for a net underperformance of U.S. equities of 47 percent. Typical of the more sedate European bourses, only two trend reversals broke the relative tranquility of the Swiss exchange, with the single bear market taking the average stock lower by a relatively mild 21 percent. At a reading of 0.41, American stocks have the highest correlation of any market to Swiss equities, in part because rises in U.S. interest rates tend to torpedo both markets. Zurich stocks are linked to U.S. rate moves because higher rates in the United States could dampen demand for Swiss exports and force Swiss rates higher to protect the value of the franc, thus slowing the domestic economy as well.

In June 1995, Switzerland's equity market, which had been scattered across a number of regional exchanges, was electronically linked, creating the Swiss Stock Exchange. The newly centralized bourse is headquartered in Zurich, the country's financial center. Other reforms, passed by the Federal Assembly in March 1995 and scheduled to go into effect April 1, 1996, are designed to create greater liquidity and openness (transparency) in the Swiss market, which many foreign investors believe has often unfairly limited minority shareholder rights. The new electronic trading system also may allow for greater investor access to the numerous small-cap issues trading on the Swiss market. At present, most of the value of the Swiss exchange is concentrated in a few large multinationals, making Zurich stocks especially sensitive to appreciation in the franc because of a strong domestic currency's negative impact on exports. As of year-end 1994, 11 companies (out of 458 trading on the Swiss exchange) accounted for 69 percent of the market's aggregate value.

Only one Swiss American depositary receipt (ADR) is listed on an American exchange, although seven others trade over the counter. The listed issue, Adia, provides temporary-personnel services to companies throughout Europe and North America. Other well-known Swiss companies available as ADRs on the U.S. over-the-counter market include Nestlé, the food-producing giant, and CS Holding, which owns the investment bank CS First Boston and Credit Suisse, the country's largest commercial bank. Along with Swiss Bank, which also trades over the counter, Credit Suisse recently suffered the indignity of seeing its vaunted AAA credit rating lowered to AA+ by Standard & Poor's, reflecting the impact of bond-trading losses and some derivatives exposure. Investors looking for a more diversified play on the Swiss economy might consider the Swiss Helvetia Fund, a closed-end offering that began operations in August 1987. Over the 1988 to 1994 period, Swiss Helvetia's net asset value grew by 93.6 percent, for a slight outperformance of the Wilshire Index: Switzerland. The fund's assets, which usually trade at a moderate discount to actual value, were available as of October 1995 for 87 cents on the dollar.

CHAPTER 27

United Kingdom

Overview

England was the birthplace of the Industrial Revolution, which began in the late eighteenth century; and, by the time of the American Civil War, the United Kingdom had become the undisputed global economic leader in output and trade. However, the rise of competing economies in the United States, Europe, and Asia, along with the loss of its colonies (which had supplied abundant natural resources), led to the gradual economic decline of the United Kingdom (U.K.) in the twentieth century.

Since the 1960s, the United Kingdom has been an economic underachiever, with aggregate gross domestic product (GDP) falling almost 20 percent relative to the United States amid bouts of high unemployment and unacceptable inflation. The governments of Margaret Thatcher and John Major have attempted to put the country on more solid economic footing, placing a priority on reducing inflation and on privatizing a number of steel and utility companies that had been nationalized in the 1940s. The main economic problem currently confronting the United Kingdom is a large budget deficit, the treatment of which threatens to put a further drag on the slow but steady recovery from the recession of 1990.

Because of its continuing problems with relatively slow economic growth and high unemployment, the U.K. equity market has hardly been a source of riches for American investors, returning less than half that of the U.S. market since 1988. Despite its long-term decline, the United Kingdom remains a world-class financial hub and a potent economic force, with a $1 trillion economy and per capita GDP of more than $17,000. Because of a high correlation to the U.S. market, U.K. equities are not a particularly good way for American investors to achieve portfolio diversification.

Geography

Area: 94,247 square miles
Size relative to United States: 2%
Capital: London
Population density per square mile: 619
Population density relative to United States: 8.40x

Demographics

Population: 58 million
Population relative to United States: 22%
Average annual rate of natural increase: +0.2%
Projected population by 2025: 62 million
Population change by 2025: +6.90%

Government

Type: Constitutional Monarchy
Sovereign: Queen Elizabeth II (1952)
Head of State: John Major, Prime Minister (1990)
Political System: Legislative power in the United Kingdom is vested in a bi-cameral Parliament, which consists of the House of Lords and the House of Commons. The 830 seats in the upper house, or House of Lords, are passed along to the country's elite through a hereditary system; the 650 members of the House of Commons are popularly elected. Elections are to be held every five years, or sooner if the ruling government chooses to have one or is voted down in the House of Commons. The country's executive authority resides in the Cabinet, headed by the prime minister. The majority party in the House of Commons selects the prime minister, who is then formally appointed to the post by the sovereign. All Cabinet members must be members of Parliament. Most of the lawmaking responsibility in the Parliament rests with the House of Commons; the House of Lords, for example, may not stall appropriations legislation but may delay other bills for up to one year. The two major political parties in the United Kingdom include the Conservative Party (Tories), which is generally viewed as probusiness, and the Labor Party, which has tended to favor more extensive regulation of the

private sector and higher taxes on the upper class. Post-World War II British politics have been dominated by the Conservative Party, which has controlled Parliament for 33 of the 50 years since 1945. Conservative Party Prime Ministers Margaret Thatcher and John Major have held office since 1979. The December 1994 defeat of fiscal legislation proposed by Mr. Major threatened to bring down his government before the next scheduled elections in 1997

Economy

Financial Strength
(Historical, as percent of GDP)

Merchandise trade: −1.72%
Services: +1.01%
Income: +0.90%
Current account: −0.48%
Portfolio investment: −0.86%
Direct investment: −1.08%
Overall balance of payments: −0.62%
Budget: −2.64%
External debt: 1.5%
Investment/consumption ratio: 0.23

Currency
(Historical data)

Money supply growth: 15.29%
Consumer price index: 8.20%
Monetary unit: Pound Sterling
Monetary unit against U.S. dollar: −47%

Economic Output
(Historical data)

GDP: $1.03 trillion
GDP relative to U.S. GDP: 15%
GDP growth rate: 2.28%
Per capita GDP: $17,689
Per capita GDP relative to U.S. per capita GDP: 68%

Figure 27.1.   United Kingdom Balance of Payments
Surplus/deficit of U.K. budget (black) and current account (gray),
as percent of GDP.

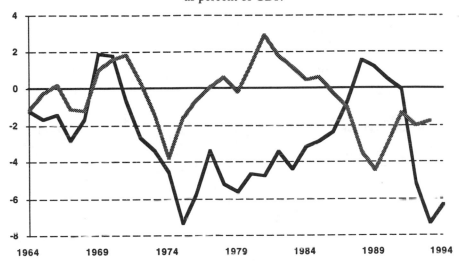

Sources: International Monetary Fund; European Monetary Institute.

Figure 27.2.   United Kingdom Currency
Pounds per U.S. dollar (inverted scale).

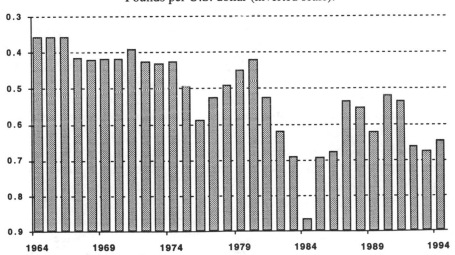

Source: International Monetary Fund, *International Financial Statistics Yearbook.*

Figure 27.3. United Kingdom Economy

Annual percentage change in U.K. real GDP (bar graph, left scale). Growth in U.K. real GDP relative to U.S. real GDP, 1963 = 100 (line graph, right scale).

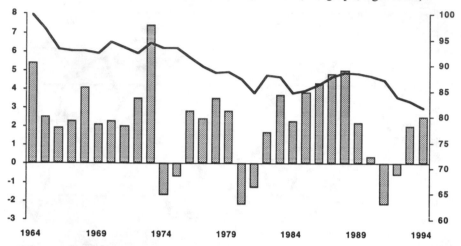

Sources: International Monetary Fund; *Europa World Yearbook.*

Economic Summary

The United Kingdom has rebounded modestly from the deep recession of 1990 to 1992, led by a growing export sector, the strength of which has partially offset continued weak domestic consumer spending. Britain's withdrawal from the European exchange-rate mechanism in 1992 resulted in a 15 percent devaluation of the pound sterling, making U.K. goods more competitive in its main export markets of Germany, France, the Netherlands, Italy, and the United States. The United Kingdom routinely runs relatively large deficits in merchandise trade, but its current account is usually rescued by a vibrant services sector, primarily in banking, brokerage, and insurance. As of fiscal 1992, service-related industries accounted for two-thirds of GDP and employed over 70 percent of the workforce. The British virtually invented the concept of foreign investing, and the large annual outflows of portfolio investment tend to put downward pressure on the currency, a condition that is partially offset by income received through the investments themselves. Over the past two fiscal years, budget deficits have again become a problem, with fiscal red ink exceeding 6 percent of GDP in 1993 and 1994. Inflation, however, has been reduced to under 3 percent since 1992, well below the United Kingdom's long-term trendline of 8 percent. Since 1979, the Conservative Party governments of Margaret Thatcher and John Major have privatized several large state-run businesses, reducing the government's share of industry by nearly two-thirds. Reports in 1995 of huge profits and salaries at several of the utilities privatized in 1990 created fears of a backlash that could bring about severe regulatory changes in the industry.

United Kingdom Stock Market

Exchange

Classification: Developed
Capitalization: $1.16 trillion
Capitalization relative to U.S. stock market: 18.6%
Number of issues: 2,209
Primary index: Financial Times 100 (FT-SE 100)
Total return in local currency, 1988–1994: 90%
Total return in U.S. dollars, 1988–1994: 58%
Total return in US dollars relative to U.S. stocks, 1988–1994: −76%

Figure 27.4.   United Kingdom Stocks
Return of U.K. stocks in local currency (black), U.S. dollars (gray), and S&P 500 (dotted); Dec. 1987 = 100.

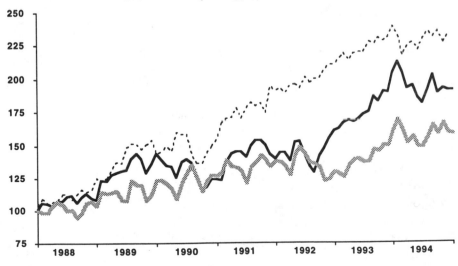

Source: Wilshire Associates Incorporated.

Volatility
(Historical)

Standard deviation: 5.12
Total monthly losses: 145.11
Average monthly loss: 3.30%
Number of monthly losses: 44
Number of monthly losses greater than 5 percent: 10
Number of monthly losses greater than 10 percent: 1
Number of monthly losses greater than 15 percent: 0
Maximum monthly loss: 10%
Relative volatility ratio: 1.81

Price Cycles

Phase	From	To	Total return
Bull	January 1988	July 1990	+34.7%
Bear	August 1990	September 1990	−15.2%
Bull	October 1990	September 1991	+24.2%
Bear	October 1991	October 1992	−15.0%
Bull	November 1992	December 1994	+29.6%

Correlations

Singapore 0.59
Germany 0.56
Sweden 0.56
United States 0.55
France 0.54
Australia 0.51
Japan 0.50
Hong Kong 0.46
Canada 0.41
New Zealand 0.37
Switzerland 0.34

Malaysia 0.30
Korea 0.28
Indonesia 0.22
Brazil 0.17
Thailand 0.14
Taiwan 0.11
Philippines 0.09
Mexico 0.07
Chile 0.00
Argentina −0.09

Country Funds

Name	Originated	Hedging	Structure	Discount/ Premium	Phones
United Kingdom Fund	August 1987	No	Closed end	−26 / +5	(800) 524-4458 (212) 272-2105

Source: Morningstar, Inc.

American Depositary Receipts

Name	Exchange	Symbol	Industry
Attwoods	NYSE	A	Waste management
Automated Security	NYSE	ASI	Security systems
Barclays	NYSE	BCS	Banking
Bass	NYSE	BAS	Brewing, hotels
Bell Cablemedia	NASDAQ	BCMPY	Telecommunications, cable TV
BET	NYSE	BEP	Industrial services
Bowater	NASDAQ	BWTRY	Packaging
British Airways	NYSE	BAB	Airline
British Gas	NYSE	BRG	Energy
British Petroleum	NYSE	BP	Energy
British Sky Broadcasting Group	NYSE	BSY	Satellite and cable TV
British Steel	NYSE	BST	Steel
British Telecommunications	NYSE	BTY	Telecommunications
Burmah Castrol	NASDAQ	BURMY	Chemicals
Cable and Wireless plc	NYSE	CWP	Telecommunications
Cadbury Schweppes	NASDAQ	CADBY	Beverages
Carlton Communications	NASDAQ	CCTVY	Broadcasting
Cordiant (formerly Saatchi & Saatchi)	NYSE	CDA	Advertising
Danka Business Systems	NASDAQ	DANKY	Business equipment
English China Clays (ECC)	NYSE	ENC	Paper, ceramics
Enterprise Oil	NYSE	ETP	Petroleum
Fisons	NASDAQ	FISNY	Pharmaceuticals
Glaxo Holdings	NYSE	GLX	Pharmaceuticals
Govett & Company	NASDAQ	GOVTY	Investment management
Grand Metropolitan	NYSE	GRM	Food, beverages
Hanson plc	NYSE	HAN	Diverse industrial company
Huntingdon International Holdings	NYSE	HTD	Biological research, engineering, and chemicals
Imperial Chemical Industries	NYSE	ICI	Chemicals

(continued)

Name	Exchange	Symbol	Industry
Lasmo	NYSE	LSO	Oil and gas exploration, productioin
London & Overseas Freighters	NASDAQ	LOFSY	Marine transportation
London International Group	NASDAQ	LONDY	Contraceptive products
Micro Focus Group	NASDAQ	MIFGY	Software
National Power	NYSE	NP	Utility
NatWest Group	NYSE	NW	Banking
NORWEB	NASDAQ	NORWY	Electric utility
PowerGen	NYSE	PWG	Utility
Rank Organisation	NASDAQ	RANKY	Leisure
Reed International	NASDAQ	RUK	Publishing
Reuters	NASDAQ	RTRSY	Financial media
Royal Bank of Scotland Group	NYSE	RBS	Banking
RTZ	NYSE	RTZ	Mining
Shell Transport and Trading	NYSE	SC	Petroleum
SmithKline Beecham	NYSE	SBE	Pharmaceuticals
TeleWest Communications	NASDAQ	TWSTY	Cable television
Tiphook	NYSE	TPH	Transport
Tomkins	NYSE	TKS	Industrial management
Unilever	NYSE	UL	Food, commodities
United Newspapers	NASDAQ	UNEWY	Publishing
Vodafonc Group	NYSE	VOD	Telecommunications
Waste Management	NYSE	WME	Environmental service
Wellcome	NYSE	WEL	Pharmaceuticals
Willis Corroon	NYSE	WCG	Insurance
WPP Group	NASDAQ	WPPGY	Advertising, marketing
Zeneca Group	NYSE	ZEN	Pharmaceuticals

Direct Listings

None

Stock Summary

The London Stock Exchange is the world's third-largest equity market, behind only the New York and Tokyo bourses. Capitalized at $1.16 trillion at year-end 1994, London stocks account for 13.3 percent of the aggregate value of all non-U.S. equity markets and also represent roughly 110 percent of the value of the U.K. economy's entire annual GDP. The continuing preeminence of the U.K. stock market reflects the nation's historical economic importance and the country's long free-market tradition. U.K. equities are also a favorite foreign holding of U.S. investors; in 1993, for example, net purchases of U.K. stocks by Americans totaled $11.2 billion, more than in any other country and representing about 16 percent of all net foreign purchases by U.S. investors. Partly as a result of American interest in U.K. stocks and because U.K. interest rates tend to track those in the United States, the London market (along with Singapore, at 0.55) has the highest correlation to American equities of the 21 bourses profiled in this book. London equities also carry high correlations with neighboring Germany, France, and Sweden.

The London exchange is popular among individual and institutional investors, not only for its size and number of available securities but also for its high degree of liquidity and reporting requirements. But whereas the U.K. market may be large, familiar, and user-friendly, the average of its stocks has not been particularly profitable over the long haul, especially for U.S. investors who have the additional concern of dealing with the U.K.'s occasionally vulnerable currency. Over the 1988 to 1994 period, the Wilshire Index: United Kingdom climbed only 90 percent in pounds and a mere 58 percent in dollars, or 76 percent less than the Standard & Poor's 500. Two bear markets of 15 percent each stalled the market's infrequent and relatively modest advances. The London bourse carries a downside volatility ratio of 1.81 times that of U.S. equities.

Not surprisingly, given its liquidity and attraction to U.S. investors, the U.K. market presents plenty of opportunities for U.S. investors to buy into the British economy. One country fund is available to individual investors, the United Kingdom Fund, a closed-end offering that historically has traded at a wide discount to its net asset value (NAV). United Kingdom Fund has underperformed the Morgan Stanley Capital International's Index: United Kingdom by a modest amount since 1988, although the fund's NAV has managed to end in the black in each of the first seven full years of its existence. As of October 1995, United Kingdom Fund was selling at more than a 15 percent discount to its NAV, despite a double-digit rebound in British equities over the first nine months of the year. The poor sentiment reflected in the deep discount may be an indication of investor concerns about a possible return to power of the Labor Party, widely perceived to be less probusiness than the Conservative Party.

American investors will find plenty of individual U.K. stocks available, with no less than 127 American depositary receipts (ADRs) listed on U.S. markets, including those trading over the counter. The list includes many of the best-known and largest of British corporations, including Barclays (banking), British Petroleum (energy), Glaxo (drugs), Reuters (business news services), and SmithKline Beecham (pharmaceuticals). United Kingdom ADRs have an aggregate market value of nearly two-thirds that of the entire London exchange. The five corporate behemoths noted represent by themselves nearly one-fifth the combined capitalization of all U.K. ADRs trading in the United States.

World Equity Market Correlations

World Equity Market Correlations

	Malaysia	Korea	Thailand	Philippines	Indonesia	Mexico	Brazil	Chile	Argentina	Hong Kong
Malaysia	1	0.21	0.52	0.42	0.3	0.09	0.11	0.09	−0.06	0.55
Korea	0.21	1	0.15	0.06	0.07	0.24	0.08	0.08	−0.1	0.16
Thailand	0.52	0.15	1	0.37	0.43	0.12	0.02	0.18	0.07	0.4
Philippines	0.42	0.06	0.37	1	0.27	−0.01	−0.02	0.14	0.1	0.4
Indonesia	0.3	0.07	0.3	0.27	1	0.13	0.26	0.15	−0.08	0.48
Mexico	0.09	0.24	0.12	0.01	0.13	1	0.1	0.07	0.06	0.08
Brazil	0.11	0.08	0.02	−0.02	0.26	0.1	1	0.11	−0.21	0.11
Chile	0.09	0.08	0.18	0.14	0.15	0.07	0.11	1	0.07	0.22
Argentina	−0.06	−0.1	0.07	0.1	−0.08	0.06	−0.21	0.07	1	−0.06
Hong Kong	0.55	0.16	0.4	0.4	0.48	0.08	0.11	0.22	−0.06	1
Singapore	0.75	0.24	0.44	0.3	0.44	0.14	0.17	0.14	−0.03	0.56
Japan	0.24	0.35	0.06	0.07	−0.04	0.08	0.16	−0.2	−0.11	0.17
France	0.22	0.04	0.17	0.15	0.1	0.07	0.05	0.02	−0.02	0.31
Germany	0.29	0.04	0.14	0.09	0.31	−0.03	0.03	−0.1	−0.04	0.29
Switzerland	0.26	0.09	0.24	0.06	0.12	0.02	0.18	0	−0.04	0.15
United Kingdom	0.3	0.28	0.14	0.09	0.22	0.07	0.17	0	−0.09	0.46
Sweden	0.24	0.25	0.16	0.19	0.3	0.09	0.23	0.05	−0.02	0.39
New Zealand	0.24	0.1	0.15	0.14	0.29	0.02	0.14	−0.2	0.01	0.27
Canada	0.33	0.37	0.37	0.16	0.29	0.22	0.13	0.17	0.04	0.41
Australia	0.22	0.14	0.22	0.2	0.33	0.11	0.07	−0.1	−0.02	0.42
Taiwan	0.26	0.15	0.37	0.33	0.25	0.18	0.03	0.14	−0.07	0.27
United States	0.37	0.18	0.32	0.03	0.22	0.2	0.19	0.2	0.06	0.38

Singapore	Japan	France	Germany	Switzerland	United Kingdom	Sweden	New Zealand	Canada	Australia	Taiwan	United States
0.75	0.24	0.22	0.29	0.26	0.3	0.24	0.24	0.33	0.22	0.26	**0.37**
0.24	0.35	0.04	0.04	0.09	0.28	0.25	0.1	0.37	0.14	0.15	**0.18**
0.44	0.06	0.17	0.14	0.24	0.14	0.16	0.15	0.37	0.22	0.37	**0.32**
0.3	0.07	0.15	0.09	0.06	0.09	0.19	0.14	0.16	0.2	0.33	**0.03**
0.44	0	0.1	0.31	0.12	0.22	0.3	0.29	0.29	0.33	0.25	**0.22**
0.14	0.08	0.07	−0.03	0.02	0.07	0.09	0.02	0.22	0.11	0.18	**0.2**
0.17	0.16	0.05	0.03	0.18	0.17	0.23	0.14	0.13	0.07	0.03	**0.19**
0.14	−0.2	−0.02	−0.06	0	0	0.05	−0.15	0.17	−0.05	0.14	**0.2**
−0.03	−0.1	−0.02	−0.04	−0.04	−0.09	−0.02	0.01	0.04	−0.02	−0.07	**0.06**
0.56	0.17	0.31	0.29	0.15	0.46	0.39	0.27	0.41	0.42	0.27	**0.38**
1	0.41	0.36	0.46	0.29	0.59	0.62	0.34	0.39	0.38	0.29	**0.55**
0.41	1	0.41	0.37	0.26	0.5	0.53	0.26	0.33	0.25	0.12	**0.25**
0.36	0.41	1	0.8	0.37	0.54	0.41	0.17	0.29	0.33	0.21	**0.45**
0.46	0.37	0.8	1	0.24	0.56	0.42	0.18	0.25	0.26	0.22	**0.33**
0.29	0.26	0.37	0.24	1	0.34	0.16	0.15	0.19	0.16	0.05	**0.41**
0.59	0.5	0.54	0.56	0.34	1	0.56	0.37	0.41	0.51	0.11	**0.55**
0.62	0.53	0.41	0.42	0.16	0.56	1	0.46	0.34	0.49	0.16	**0.38**
0.34	0.26	0.17	0.18	0.15	0.37	0.46	1	0.32	0.61	0.07	**0.25**
0.39	0.33	0.29	0.25	0.19	0.41	0.34	0.32	1	0.45	0.2	**0.47**
0.38	0.25	0.33	0.26	0.16	0.51	0.49	0.61	0.45	1	0.11	**0.31**
0.29	0.12	0.21	0.22	0.05	0.11	0.16	0.07	0.2	0.11	1	**0.14**
0.55	0.25	0.45	0.33	0.41	0.55	0.38	0.25	0.47	0.31	0.14	**1**

Index